D1572239

THE SIMPLE MECHANICS OF MAKING MORE AND WORKING LESS

WORK THE SYSTEM

—FOURTH EDITION—

SAM CARPENTER

Epilogue by JOSH FONGER

 (Continued on the Disclaimer page—an extension of the copyright page—on page 283.)

Published by Greenleaf Book Group Press
Austin, Texas
www.gbgpress.com

Distributed by Greenleaf Book Group

For bookstore or wholesale ordering information, contact Greenleaf Book Group at PO Box 91869, Austin, TX 78709, 512.891.6100.

For corporate or event bulk purchases and foreign rights, contact North Sister Publishing, 141 NW Greenwood Ave, Suite 200, Bend, OR 97703, info@workthesystem.com, 800.664.7448

Design and composition by Greenleaf Book Group and Kim Lance
Cover design by Greenleaf Book Group and Kim Lance

Publisher's Cataloging-in-Publication

Carpenter, Sam.
Work the System: The Simple Mechanics of Making More and Working Less /
Sam Carpenter—4th ed.
p.; cm.
First ed. published: Bend, Oregon: North Sister Publishing, 2008.
Includes bibliographical references and index.
Ebook ISBN: 978-1-62634-770-0
1. Business Management. 2. Business & Economics/Personal Success.
3. Success in Business. I. Title.
HD58.9 .C377 2009
658.4/02
ISBN: 978-1-62634-769-4

Printed in the United States of America on acid-free paper

21 22 23 24 25 26   11 10 9 8 7 6 5 4 3 2

First Edition: April 2008
Second Edition: April 2009
Third Edition: June 2014
Fourth Edition: 2nd Printing, February 2022
2008943859

ALSO BY SAM CARPENTER

The Systems Mindset: Managing the Machinery of Your Life

To Dad

"Just get on with it," he would say.

Ockham's Razor:
One should choose the simplest explanation,
the one requiring the fewest assumptions and principles.

—William of Ockham, fourteenth-century English philosopher

CONTENTS

FOREWORD

If I had eight hours to cut down a tree, I'd spend six sharpening my axe.

—Abraham Lincoln

I say this without hyperbole: *Work the System* is one of the most useful business books you'll ever read. I should know—I read business books for a living, and teach creative people from all over the world how to build businesses that are profitable, enjoyable, and sustainable.

Here are the top three questions I'm asked every single day:

- "Starting a business seems so complicated. Where do I begin?"
- "I'm working a lot, but not making much money. How can I improve my profitability?"
- "I'm constantly stressed and anxious. How can I run my business without going crazy?"

The answer to these questions is always the same: learn how to work the system.

Fundamentally, every business is a system: a collection of processes that, together, reliably produce an intended result. The more you focus on improving your business systems, the better results you'll produce. It's as simple as that.

When most people hear the word "system," however, their eyes glaze over. Most of us are trained to think that standard operating procedures, checklists, documentation, and the like are boring and bureaucratic.

Nothing could be further from the truth. Here's what happens when you begin improving your systems:

You make more money, but do less work.

You have more focus and energy to do your best work.

You make far fewer errors.

You fix the mistakes you make quickly and permanently. You feel more calm, collected, and under control.

Solid business systems are largely a product of calm, rational, straightforward thinking. It's a skill that can be learned quickly, and a method that can be applied to improve every aspect of your life.

I use the ideas in *Work the System* every day when building my own business, and I've recommended this book to my readers and clients since the publication of the first edition.

I'm glad this book has found its way into your hands. *Work the System* will help you make better decisions, get more done, and have more fun along the way.

—Josh Kaufman, author of *The Personal MBA* and *The First 20 Hours*

PREFACE TO THE FOURTH EDITION

Dysfunction Is Gold

(February 2022)

This book is different.

Its main thrust goes beyond providing new information. The root purpose of *Work the System* is to guide you to a more precise view of reality's simple mechanics so you can gain better command of your life and therefore be better able to get what you want out of it.

There will be a mechanical adjustment in the way you see your world, and when this profound mental shift occurs, systems methodology will make irrefutable sense and your work and life will never be the same. I like to call this mini-awakening "getting it," and in Part One I describe exactly what that is and how to achieve it.

The nutshell premise? Your life is a collection of individual systems. *Fix those systems, one at a time, and you will fix your life.*

To whom is this book intended? It's written especially for anyone who operates a business, from the founder of a brand-new mom-and-pop start-up to the seasoned CEO of a multinational. At either extreme and in between, the tenets apply uniformly because life's fundamental formula works the same way all the time, everywhere.

Here's an insight that Mike, the owner of a $50 million overseas enterprise, and one of our first consulting clients, gave me: "Sam! I now see that *dysfunction is gold!*" Mike "gets it," and is exactly correct. If you are enduring the typical organizational inefficiency and then suddenly see that inefficiency, and then confidently plow ahead step by step to eliminate it, you will create additional significant bottom-line profits. Is there lots of dysfunction in your organization? Then there is lots of gold to be extracted.

This increased cash flow will be in addition to the new growth you will experience.

The current internal dysfunction in your business is the gold that has been there all along. *You just need to get busy excavating.*

I changed my life after a moment of insight, moving from a nightmarish existence to a life of peace and prosperity. In my primary business, I now work less than one hour a month. Yes, we are financially secure now, with more than my wife, Diana, and I need, which enables us to invest and share. I've had the same small business for thirty-six years, and this is the story of how I transformed it from a chaotic ordeal into a gold mine, pulling my staff upward with me while delivering the highest quality of service available in my industry.

How I broke free—and especially how you can too—is described in detail. Believe me, if I can do it so can you! Career-wise, you may have to do something different than what you do now in order to reach your goals of freedom and prosperity, but probably not. People who follow the WTS strategy become super efficient, and most of them keep doing what they have been doing all along as they suddenly break the chains and leave their competition in the dust.

Let's go "one layer deeper" and question some of your foundational assumptions of how your enterprise should function. Let's dig out the waste and drive your company forward. Let's make you and your operation incredibly efficient.

Despite the book's sly title, there is nothing sinister in these pages and there's nothing that won't seem logical. There are no gimmicks or mysterious theories. No Six Sigma-type complexities. No hype. No BS. What I discuss, including the get-it insight you will experience, is simple and will make perfect sense.

Sound interesting so far?

Here it is, the simple mechanics: there are an infinite number of independent puzzle pieces out there, and for each of us to get what we want in our lives it's just a matter of seeing those pieces accurately, making a proper selection, and then assembling them in a way that produces the results we desire.

And no, in focusing on the mechanical you won't lose your humanity.

Work the System is not rah-rah, pumping you up but giving you nowhere to go. It will guide you to achieve the "systems mindset" perspective and provide you a template for advancement. Then you will determine your own specific steps for creating the prosperity and peace that you've always wanted in your life.

Contrary to popular opinion, the workings of the world make perfect sense. There is an inherent order that is stunningly evident if one drops preconceived notions and quietly observes life as it is. By internalizing this new insight, by going one layer deeper, it's an easy matter to arrange things in order to "get what one wants."

The most satisfying outcome is that life theory and hard reality become congruent. This means one is no longer swayed by peers, public opinion, what feels good, or by moment-to-moment expediency. There is no knee-jerk tail-wagging-the-dog decision-making. Addressing raw reality head-on, one confidently makes up one's own mind about things and then consistently applies that certainty to the real world—and it works! It works because reality operates in the same way everywhere, all the time.

It's been thirteen years since the first edition of *Work the System* was published, and at the time I hoped it would help readers get better control of their businesses and their lives. At the risk of braggadocio, that has happened. In the last nine years, my business associate Josh Fonger, sole licensee of the Work the System Method, has directly contracted with and revitalized more than 1,000 small-to-medium-sized businesses in the Unites States and around the world. And since the book was first published, hundreds of thousands more have forged ahead on their own.

I'll say this here at the beginning: each of us has a mechanical aspect and an emotional aspect; and contrary to much pop-psychology theory, I say it's a good thing to separate the two. If we don't, things get muddied and neither aspect turns out so well. And I take issue with the presumption that the road to freedom and prosperity begins with the elimination of personal emotional hang-ups. *Work the System is about straightening out the mechanics of a life first: get the machine right, and emotional improvement will tag along naturally.* Can one have emotional hang-ups together with wealth and freedom? Of course. We all know people like that. But hang-ups or not, obtaining wealth and freedom will go a long way toward improving the emotional end of things.

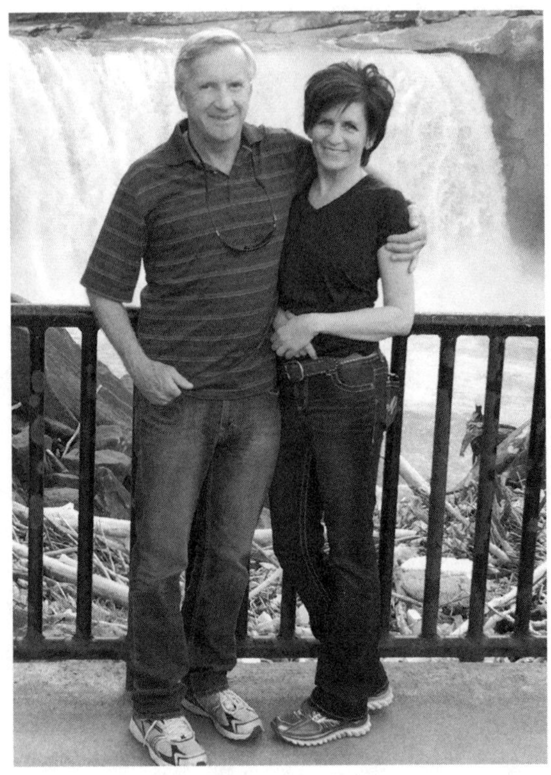

Sam and Diana Carpenter

In any case, yes, *you can flip a switch and your life can all of a sudden become what you want it to be*. This is because the switch is located in your head and therefore is readily accessible.

Ninety percent of people struggle. On the surface, it seems this is because they don't set direction, they don't get organized, and they spend too much time on fire killing and trivialities. That's true enough. Yet when the mechanisms of life one layer deeper are seen, the causal reason for the struggle suddenly becomes obvious. But because most of us use up our days coping with too much that doesn't matter and in repairing bad results, we don't think about delving downward to make adjustments where those time-wasters and bad results are propagated. We humans just have a penchant for thrashing around on the surface, not paying attention to the simple mechanics down below.

We're driven to complicate what isn't complicated.

We've found that not everyone is interested in making more and working less. Some want to make more while working the same amount of time or to just become more effectual at work and at home. And many simply want to feel more in control of their lives, and to have their worlds make more sense. *Work the System* serves all these purposes because it's about becoming more life-efficient.

And, for the record, I love to work—to get mentally submerged in what I call "system-improvement." Hard work puts me in the zone. And this work I do is creative—in several businesses and on many personal fronts—mostly one-time "machine building" efforts that challenge and intrigue me.

Oh yes. My life is *not* boring!

Relative to the third edition, is there new core-material in this fourth edition? Some, but not a lot in the theory and practice, and my defense is that base reality doesn't change over time. Yet, although the fundamental message remains unchanged, I've made massive improvement in how *Work* reads and in more fully explaining the important points. It's a better-quality book. There are literally thousands of small enhancements, updates, and additions. I want you to "get it" easier and faster. In this, over these last months I've found enormous self-satisfaction in producing a better representation of what I believe.

I'll borrow a common descriptive term for one of the most important threads that weaves its way through the book: "bottom-up." In a business, bottom-up calls for system-improvement ideas to be generated at the customer service and production levels and then passed on up through management for approval. It's not a declaration of democracy—I like to think a business leader is more of a benevolent dictator—but rather, it acknowledges the obvious: the great ideas most often come from the people on the front lines, the people producing the product or service, as well as those dealing directly with customers.

And I'll go here at the risk of proselytizing: in group presentations, as I begin to discuss my mechanical take on business and life, there is always some initial head-shaking from the follow-your-bliss contingent (of which I used to be a card-carrying member), who feel they are called upon to rise above the mechanical world in order to focus on the spiritual. They believe the sacred pursuit of truth is noble and superior and shouldn't be hampered by the restrictive chores of dealing with the petty issues of the mechanical here and now. In fact, they believe that their impending spiritual purity will somehow lead to mastery of their physical worlds.

My response, which invariably gets them head-nodding in agreement instead of head-shaking in disapproval, is that we are all spiritual beings existing in a mechanical world; and until we learn to assertively steer the raw mechanics of our lives, we cannot get to a place that gives us the freedom to pursue what is beyond this concrete reality. Why? Because in our mechanical dysfunction we will always be pulled back into that concrete reality out of sheer necessity. So to these people I say, *The key is to get your personal physical world—with all its boring and base considerations—straightened out first, so you'll have the time and energy to focus on what is beyond it.*

Yet, having said that, this mechanical existence that we experience can be perceived as a beautifully orchestrated spiritual place if we can just, moment by moment, go deeper to see it for what it actually *is*. For ethereally inclined Westerners especially, it's a reverse tack to use the mechanical to enter the spiritual. Give it a shot if the opposite sequence hasn't met your expectations.

And back to the subject of producing a better-quality book: there is this "system-improvement" thing. It's *the* prime thread that weaves though these pages. *Work the System* is about the improvement of systems . . . and a book is a system in itself. *Like any other system, this book is an "enclosed entity with a multitude of spinning wheels, all contributing to the singular purpose of accomplishing a goal."* And like our lives, a book is never perfect; there is always room for betterment—for system-improvement. Herein lies a roadblock within the book-publishing industry that I have managed to bypass.

There is a lesson in this. Read on.

I have an interesting contractual relationship with my publisher, Greenleaf Book Group, based in Austin, Texas. The arrangement is fundamentally different from 99 percent of author/publisher arrangements because I have kept the rights to my manuscript. With this, I can tweak and improve my book to my heart's delight (of course, all the while paying close attention to the recommendations of Greenleaf's fine editors).

Normally, "getting published" means the author's rights to the work are forever forfeited to the publisher. New authors, frantic to avoid permanent residence in the dustbin of the self-published, sell their souls to the traditional publishing company. The consequence is that, for starters, the original manuscript is handed over to an editor who, depending on competence, style, personality, political inclination, attitude, mood of the moment, degree of belief/interest in the subject matter, and experience (often, in traditional publishing arrangements, editors for new authors are just out of college), will often render the originally submitted manuscript unrecognizable. There is no recourse for the author. The publishing company owns the manuscript and has the final say on the content and presentation.

"Here," says the new author to the publisher, "I want to be published so, yes, take my work and do what you want with it."

And beyond that profound abdication, good luck to the industrious scribe who wants to make further changes and asks the publisher for another printing or, heaven forbid, requests a new edition. There's no going back to improve and update the book without the publisher's approval, and most of the time that approval won't be forthcoming.

This is a shame because as the non-fiction author grows over the years and becomes even more expert at his or her special message—and while the world continues to quickly evolve—their owned-by-the-publisher book is going to remain static, very soon to become old news.

So, because I wanted precise control over this master statement of what I believe, I sought an alternative to the classic publishing deal. I think you'll find the following chronology of the book's development interesting for that reason, but especially for another: the developmental history of *Work the System* is a perfect illustration of the system-improvement thread that is, as I said, the centerpiece of the book itself. Follow along with me here.

I self-published *Work the System* in the spring of 2008. This first printing was softcover. I had spent two years and probably a thousand hours getting the book right. It was the very, very best I could do at the time. It was impeccable, I thought, as in early 2008 the manuscript finally headed off to the printer, sans publisher. I held my breath and waited patiently for my masterpiece to arrive at my doorstep in hard copy.

The boxes of new books arrived six weeks later. I excitedly opened the first box. I grabbed a copy . . . and *instantly* gasped at a horrible miscalculation: the cover was an embarrassing gaffe. As a first-time author, how arrogant was this, to splash my photo across it? Then I opened that particular copy and within seconds I blanched again because right there on the very first page I could see that *things could have been said so, so much better.* I continued to read. It was agonizing. There was clumsy sentence structure, flat-out grammatical errors, poor flow of thought, horse-following-the-cart assertions, and way too much repetition. It was painful!

Nevertheless, I put the book out there because it seemed to me the message was solid.

To my surprise, it sold pretty well, and a month later I could see there would have to be another printing. This was a relief because this would give me the opportunity to make things right, to institute some serious "system-improvement."

This time I would get it right. Finally!

Enthusiastically I went to work on the manuscript, endlessly tweaking, working day and night to fix the deficiencies, including getting rid of the cover photo. For weeks, I hammered. The message was unchanged, but there was a lot to fix in the delivery. It was a satisfying exercise because I was certainly going to get it right with this second self-published printing! This upgraded version would also be softcover, and I decided on a simple plain-white glossy cover this time.

Off to the printer it went.

The shipment arrived a month later. I opened a box with confidence that this would prove to be the penultimate representation of my beliefs about work and life. Whoops. For starters, my minimalist cover was amateurish. And inside, I found that despite the countless grammatical and sentence-structure revisions and the continued soundness of the message, it was still clumsy in its presentation.

Yet again, this second printing did well in the limited self-published marketplace. And with that success, Greenleaf Book Group accepted the manuscript. We signed a publishing deal and preparation for a second edition ensued. This time, with first-class professional editors and book designers via Greenleaf, the book's contents were shuffled around a bit, and literally thousands more adjustments were made. It would be hardcover this time, to be released in the spring of 2009.

When the books arrived, even though I now had a publisher, I was disappointed *again*! The new cover jacket was attractive, but the experimental glossy cover material was absorbent, instantly smudged by the fingerprints of anyone who picked up the book. And yes, so much inside could have been better said!

For the second printing of that second edition six months later—again hardcover—we fixed the jacket and made hundreds of internal enhancements. The books arrived, and sure enough, I was disappointed once more. The cover was fine but my message was *still* garbled.

Arrrrggghhhhh!

But what I haven't said until now—and this is the key point in all of this, so pay attention here—is that because of my disappointments in each printing, and the resultant jillion improvements that I made because of those disappointments, the book's quality had improved tremendously. Despite my nitpicky self-recriminations, I had to admit that the second printing of the second edition wasn't half bad.

Why was the book better? It was due to the incessant system-improvement gyrations of the previous iterations.

And yes, thirteen years later, this first printing of the fourth edition has literally thousands of readability and update tweaks, and Greenleaf has yet again come in behind me to smooth things out even further. (In particular, Elizabeth Brown, my copyeditor, has been incredible.)

From the very first edition back in 2008 to today, the message has remained the same. It's the delivery of that message that has incrementally improved with each printing.

I've grown, and so has my book.

As I look back, it's clear to me that I should have known *Work* would never be what I wanted it to be the first time, or even the second, third, or fourth time. *I knew better!*

In any case, I've repeatedly tweaked this book over the thirteen years of its existence, keeping it up-to-date and controlling the content while paying close attention to the advice of my publisher. The end result? Each new version of *Work* has been of better quality than the previous version. This first printing of the fourth edition is no exception. At this moment, it's the very best I can do.

I tell you all of this to make a point beyond self-aggrandizement, a point that has everything to do with you and your business: *Work the System's relentless evolution, in itself, is a perfect illustration of the system-improvement process that is at the core of its own message.*

Can you see how this system-improvement strategy can apply to your own business and life?

I'll also use this chronology of the book's evolution to point out the beauty of personal freedom—of not getting hamstrung, of being able to chart one's own course.

So with this book I want you to develop the capacity to *see* the individual processes of your world from moment to moment, and then to expend the bulk of your future work-time and energy tweaking those processes to higher and higher efficiency.

I want to help you make your systems incredibly effectual so they quietly yet powerfully churn out the results you desire.

Hunker down to relentlessly improve the systems of your world, and soon the fire killing will cease and you'll have the time and money to enjoy the life you have always wanted.

I hope you get that.

This book is printed in English, Chinese, Japanese, Russian, Korean, Arabic, and Romanian, with more than two million distributed in hard-copy, audio, and download formats.

Others have seen the value of my writing and have attempted to literally steal my work and profit from it. In 2014, I fought to preserve and protect my intellectual property by filing and prosecuting a copyright infringement case in federal court against Schefren Publishing, LLC. This action was resolved in my favor in late 2016 with the entry of a stipulated judgment that specifically confirmed Schefren's infringement of my book. (See more detail in Appendix K.)

Note that in a general system-improvement effort aimed at "life simplification," in 2018 I gifted the consulting/coaching branch of the WTS business to my long-term employee, Josh Fonger. (See Appendix D.) Also in 2018, I gifted the Business Documentation Software business (see Appendix H) to our European-based IT managers, Marcello Scacchetti, Centratel's CIO/Digital Marketing Manager, and Emanuel "Manu" Gug, Centratel's IT Engineer/Web Application Developer. These were one-time transactions so I receive no ongoing compensation from either enterprise. That's the way I wanted it: clean and simple. However, I am in near-daily contact with Josh, Marcello, and Manu, assisting them when they ask for my help, especially over these tumultuous years of COVID-19 and civil unrest.

In this fourth edition, Josh has gathered sixteen real-life case studies from his consulting/coaching clients. Each vignette is presented in short-story format, providing feedback from business owners who have gone through one of our Work the System training or consulting programs. Each case study describes where the owner was in the beginning, what they did with the Work the System Method to fix their situation, and their current life-result. You'll find these case studies in Appendix E. (And in 2020, Josh launched a "Work the System Certification" training program for those who wish to operate their own consulting business or to just get a deeper understanding of the methodology. See Appendix D.)

Six years ago, I wrote another book, *The Systems Mindset: Managing the Machinery of Your Life*. Published by Greenleaf, it's for people who don't own a business: job holders, students, the retired, the unemployed, and those working at home to raise a family. *Mindset* is shorter than *Work*, as it doesn't go into the details of business documentation; but the system-improvement message is the same. You can find out more about *Mindset* at www.thesystemsmindset.com, where you can download the first four chapters in pdf format. It's available in hardcover and audio, too.

To complete this Preface to the fourth edition, I'm thinking it would be good to explain the overall threads of the book, right here at the start. I'll keep it simple:

1. Reality is what IS, whether you like it or not.

2. Drop the prescribed menu. Cut loose. *Make up your own mind.*
3. Your life is a collection of linear 1-2-3-4 systems. The scary and wonderful thing about that? In this moment—don't argue with me—every condition of your life was preceded by an assemblage of step-by-step processes. And this means the processes that are executing right now—seen and unseen—are determining your future. *To create the life you want, you must intensely manage your systems in the present moment.* You must ceaselessly perform system-improvement. Do this, and great future results will come along almost spontaneously.
4. Spend the majority of your work-time in preparation and building, not personally executing the work.
5. What dysfunctional primary system is pervasive in business and personal life? It's one-on-one and group communication protocols, including frequency, speed, encapsulation, direction, and tools. The stupendous news? Bad communication is quickly repaired, and the instant return on investment is astonishing.
6. People say, "Everything happens for a reason." That's true enough, yet it's a sophomoric vision. Almost always the individual who declares this is referring to a prestamped life, a template existence in which someone upstairs is orchestrating every occurrence. Something bad happens? Something good happens? Either way, that event has been predetermined . . . so it's OK! But being a puppet is not the divine endowment we've been given. Rather, our God-given gift is the freedom to choose. To lighten up that concept, here's something Diana has off-handedly said more than once: "*Everything happens for a reason, and sometimes that reason is because someone did something stupid!*"
7. Point-of-sale. Get the wheels turning NOW! At first glance, this might seem platitudinous. It's not.
8. Create value for others, all the time.
9. "Mind the gap." Silence breeds paranoia. *Don't stop talking.*

10. In the kingdom that is your life, be very careful about who and what you let enter through your gates.
11. The more control you have over your life, the more productive and happier you will be.
12. *The magic of life is right here, right now, in front of our noses.* It's not out there somewhere.

The colossal human error is the assumption that there is a cosmic inclination to chaos. The mechanical truth? There is a default propensity toward order.

In my own way, I'm a believer now; and I thank God for every moment of this life.

One more thing: know that *business is art*. The ability to patiently ascend the learning curve, to relentlessly plow through obstacles, to keep improving things no matter what, to ultimately create something of beauty out of the miscalculations of the past—to weather the storm—are beautiful things. *A successful business is a self-sustaining entity of worth that creates value for all involved.*

As you stumble, walk, and sprint to that end, don't ever underestimate your accomplishment and your contribution.

—Sam Carpenter

PREFACE TO THE FIRST EDITION

It's Just Mechanics
(2008)

I work the system, but not just one. I work *all* the systems in my world—professional, personal, financial, social, biological, and mechanical. You have your own systems. Do you see them? Do you manage them? It doesn't matter whether you are an entrepreneur, CEO, employee, stay-at-home mom or dad, retiree, or student. Your life is composed of systems that are yours to manage—or not manage.

In the slang sense of the term, someone who works the system uses a bureaucratic loophole as an excuse to break rules in order to secure personal gain. But winning the life-game means following the rules, for if we don't, any win is a ruse. Be assured that you will find nothing deceitful or unsavory in these pages. Nor does the work-the-system methodology have anything to do with esoteric theory, politics, or religion. It's about common sense and simple mechanics.

I call it a workingman's philosophy.

Life is serious business, and whether you know it or not—or whether you like it or not—your personal systems are the threads in the fabric of your existence. Together they add up to *you*. And if you are like most people, you negotiate your days without seeing these processes as the singular entities they are, some working well for you, and some not so well.

In the complexity that is your world, what if you could distinctly see each of these systems? What if you could reach in and pluck one of these not-so-efficient processes out of that complexity, make it perfect, and then reinsert it? What if you could do this with every system that composes your being?

What if you could reengineer your existence piece by piece to make it exactly what you want it to be without having to count on luck, Providence, blind faith, or someone else's largesse?

The foundational thrust of *Work the System* is not to educate you in the ten steps to peace and prosperity or to warn you of the five most common mistakes in seeking happiness and material success. The Method digs deeper than that, causing a modification in how you see the elements of your world. And when this quiet yet profound mechanical shift in life-perception occurs—you will remember the exact moment you "get it"—the simple methodology will make irrefutable sense and you will never be the same.

I call this new way of seeing things the *systems mindset.*

This book also provides a framework—yes, an easy-to-follow map—in which you can channel this new perspective to get precisely what you want out of your life.

THE TOUGH TIMES

Readers who have experienced tough times will "get" this book. Those in their early years who have so far cruised along unscathed, may not. The tough times to which I refer include prolonged physical and/or mental crisis where one stands alone against the blackness: a nightmarish childhood, war, disabling injury or sickness, crime/incarceration, addiction, divorce (perhaps with an attending child-custody battle), personal or public betrayal, financial calamity, mental breakdown, or endless repetitious work that drains and demoralizes.

TWO APPROACHES

In the broad sense, there are two psychological approaches to finding a way to lead a full, positive existence. The first holds that the events of the past and the mindset we formed as a result of those events determine today's happiness. In this view we are victims of unpleasant circumstance and have a chance at peace only if we face and then disarm the psychic monsters planted in our minds long ago. That's the Freudian stance. Figuratively speaking, you could lie on a couch blathering away at a psychiatrist for the rest of your life and still see no improvement.

The second approach, the cognitive, maintains that the thoughts we feed ourselves today are what matter most, and the events of the past are just that—in the past—and gone forever unless we insist on swirling them back into the present moment.

The cognitive approach is more effectual than the Freudian approach because it's simple and clean and fast, enabling one to steer the thought process rather than wallow helplessly in mental negativity from years gone by. Adherents believe that what one does today will determine tomorrow, and blaming the past or the world or someone else is a debilitating way to travel through this precious one-time event called life.

Old-school psychologists who see endless dour complexity in the human condition will sniff at the simplicity of the *Work the System* message. Things are more complicated than that, they'll say. I thank them in advance for the oblique compliment. This is an elementary, dispassionate, drop-the-load dispatch that describes lives as they really are: simple cause-and-effect mechanisms that can be logical, predictable, and satisfying.

No PhD necessary.

So take the title of this book at literal face value, understanding you will be working *your* systems. In these pages, I will challenge you to see, dissect, and then refine them one by one until each is flawless. I call this process *system-improvement*. You will create new systems, too, while discarding the ones holding you back, the ones that have been invisibly sabotaging your best efforts.

Command the systems of your life and move to inner serenity, prosperity, and the best for those around you.

LEADER AND HIGH EARNER

Not too long ago I participated in the annual Cycle Oregon event, a week-long professionally organized bicycle tour. It was early September, and seventeen hundred riders pedaled an average of seventy-five miles per day through remote eastern Oregon. At night we camped in ad hoc tent cities planted at various locations along the route—rural high school football fields, small town parks, and wheat fields. Seldom did we have mobile phone coverage. That was just fine as we, en masse, divorced ourselves from the damn things for this seven-day break from the regular world.

At dusk on the last night of the tour, as my riding partner Steve and I were casually walking through the surrounding sea of tents, we encountered a group of young men, in their twenties, sitting around drinking beer, being boisterous. We overheard them laughing, waging bets about how many messages one of them would have the next day when he was back within mobile phone range and able to check his voice-mail box. Clearly, back in the real world these guys worked together in an office. In our quick passing, we heard one predicting the total messages would be 150. Another said 250. The young man on the receiving end of the jest was robust and confident. He smiled at the fawning. It was obvious he was important in his workplace. He was well respected, a leader, and most probably a high earner—a success. People depended on him.

For twenty-three years I have been the owner of a telecom business in Bend, Oregon. Centratel is profitable, has thirty-three employees, and nine hundred regular customers. The part I play in my business is also important. In my world, I'm likewise a leader and high earner. Many people depend on me, too.

When I checked my own voice mail the next day as I began the long drive home, there was just one message. Andi, my COO, had left an update because she knew I would want to get caught up on things when I was again able to pick up my messages. She reported that, no surprise, all was well in the office, and she hoped I had had a fun week away from things. "Drive home safely," she said. That was it. She didn't need to address the obvious: during the week, without an ounce of input from me and without a hitch, the business had functioned perfectly for staff and for clients, as it churned out thousands of dollars in profits.

It didn't matter that I was absent.

Who knows what that voice mail–inundated young man from the bicycle tour did for a living, but I tell you this: he was mismanaging things if his gig back home couldn't proceed for a single week without his direct influence—if the slew of processes in which he was involved all came to a halt when he was not available. Yes, all those voice-mail messages (and heaven only knows how many e-mail messages were waiting on his desktop) attested to his status and importance; but in the bigger picture he was a slave to his job, and the people who depended on him were slaves to his presence. They waited for his response and could not move ahead until he provided input. In his absence, because he failed to set up business processes that kept producing while he was gone, things came to a standstill just the way water accumulates behind a dam.

I'd say he was close to thirty years of age. I'm fifty-eight. People and circumstances change with time. Eight years ago my life was just like his.

NERVOUS GRATIFICATION OF THE MOMENT

Here's a more general observation. In the past twenty years, the lure of instant gratification has seized a huge chunk of our population. For members of the hooked-up generation, too many with the attention span of a gnat—addicted to cellular phones, headset-music, and dumbed-down by the silliness of much of the media and entertainment industries—it's a stretch to slow down to consider the root of things. *The nervous gratification of the moment is a distraction from the quiet contemplation of the reasons why events unfold as they do.* Today, unlike three decades ago, a good "now" is available by just plugging in and tuning out. For too many of us, slowing down to examine things is not entertaining, and that's too bad because *it's mandatory that we take the time to understand the machinery of our lives if we are to modify that machinery to produce the life conditions we desire.*

Yes, the work-the-system methodology is a throwback of sorts, back to an age when it was universally accepted that the path to success required careful preparation with no expectation of immediate payback. But having said that, know that an investment in the work-the-system strategy will show real benefits almost from day one.

CLOSED-SYSTEM LABORATORY

My primary business, Centratel, is a high-tech telephone answering service. For fifteen years it floundered, my personal life a reflection of its chaos. Then I attained the new mindset in a single moment, and immediately the pressure began to drop. As I persistently applied the protocols described here in this book, my workweek was soon dramatically reduced while my bottom-line profit increased geometrically.

Moreover, my time away from work is smooth and easy now. In the morning I awaken clear-headed and instantly alert, looking forward to yet another day of quiet, steady enhancement on all fronts. In the course of a week I spend far more time reading, writing, traveling, hanging out with friends, going to the movies, climbing mountains, and riding bicycles than working at my several enterprises.

My business and life are in control, proceeding exactly how I want them to proceed.

What I've learned is this: despite the almost visceral societal belief to the contrary, *there is a direct connection between happiness and the amount of personal control we attain.*

The nature of the telephone-answering-service business, with its multitude of interacting processes, both human and otherwise, made Centratel the perfect closed-system laboratory for developing the work-the-system methodology. Therefore it's logical and convenient to use my business as the explanatory platform for these chaos-to-order processes. And a business book can get too dry and theoretical without real-life examples, so describing the Method within the framework of Centratel adds some fun to the party.

The strategies described here are not just for the business leader; they're also for those who work in a managerial capacity for a business owned by someone else. There are lessons for those born with a silver spoon and for the self-made, too. And there is much for those who engineer family life at home. It makes sense: we're dealing with reality, and reality works in the same way for everyone, everywhere, all the time. So, when I offer a business illustration, read between the lines and find your own application.

When I refer to business and use the word "manager," understand that the label also applies to personal life. We are the managers of our lives and, as I've said, the fundamentals described here are universal.

The word "system" is a pointed and unique unit of language. It's so precise that it doesn't have many synonyms. But it has a few almost-equivalents that I like to use because they add spice in certain narratives. They are "protocol," "process," "mechanism," and "machine."

The principles presented here are simple, but it is not enough to memorize or understand them. They must be internalized deep down. There is a difference between learning something new and undergoing an epiphany. On a gut level, I want you to "*get it*," and for this reason some repetition will occur as I approach the concepts from different angles.

Trust that the epiphany will arrive soon and—this is exciting—probably when you least expect it.

A qualifier: I don't adhere to the work-the-system principles and guidelines every minute. I fall down on the job now and then. Nonetheless, because I have structured my existence around the Method, the details of the day continue to take care of themselves despite any temporary distraction or physical/mental slump.

I've carefully engineered my systems so they keep things moving forward no matter what.

The same will hold true for you, too, should you choose to take command of the systems of your life.

—Sam Carpenter,
March 2008

INTRODUCTION

The Simplest Solution

Out of clutter, find simplicity. From discord, find harmony.

—Albert Einstein

One should choose the simplest explanation of a phenomenon, the one that requires the fewest leaps of logic.

Or one could say, "Keep it simple, stupid!"

My wife, Diana, and I—and our coonhound, Justy—live in the small city of Bend, Oregon. The house is open and bright, furnished in a pragmatic people-actually-live-here way. It's everything we have ever wanted in a home. We have another house, too, in rural southeastern Kentucky in Diana's tiny hometown of Stearns. We built it three years ago and it's perfect for us too. Oregon or Kentucky? We go back and forth . . .

Today, in Bend, I sit at the dining room table in front of my laptop. Outside the big windows, the quiet of midafternoon is palpable. It's October. The lawn is still lush emerald green and is the launching pad for a half-dozen massive ponderosa pines towering above. This house, like our house in Kentucky, is atop a hill, and I occasionally gaze down on the city below. It's another crystal-clear, cloudless day. Yesterday was like that and tomorrow will be the same.

It's peaceful.

Down there in Bend, Centratel, my telephone answering service business, churns away whether I'm thinking about it or not, providing us more than a good living. It wasn't always this way. For a decade and a half, my business experience was a chaotic morass of endless work, fire killing, debt, health problems, and bad relationships.

Twenty-two years ago, at a time that I can pinpoint exactly, I experienced an unexpected shift in perception that began the transformation of my existence from chaos to calm—from a desperate financial condition to prosperity, and from endless toil to relaxed, occasional input.

Now, truly managing my several small businesses and the rest of my world, I am no longer enmeshed in minutiae. I'm an arm's-length observer of it.

Back then, after that mental shift, my health came back too. Since then I've been climbing, hiking, cycling, and skiing again, as I did in my youth. And Diana and Justy and I spend a lot of time hiking and climbing in both the mountain wilderness of Oregon and in the hills and hollers of gorgeous backcountry Kentucky.

As for the subjective? It's no stretch to say my life has a hundred times more peace and freedom than before. As the day slides by I feel confident, relaxed, and efficient. As I look at my existence now, I feel a certain element of incredulity because my natural comportment has always included some flakiness. I've had a hard time focusing, sticking to things. I've been purposeless. After high school I dropped out of college three times, got caught up in alcohol/drugs, worked countless dead-end jobs, moved from relationship to relationship, always dissatisfied—clear up until the age of fifty. But now, when it comes to the big things, my personal bearing is centered and deliberate. It's true, I can still display a certain surface distractedness, but on matters that carry weight and when working toward goals that are important, I am determined and focused until I obtain the results I want.

Getting to this place wasn't hard to do once my mindset shifted to view each day from a more intimate positioning, from a place I like to call "*outside and slightly elevated*." Since that singular moment when I seized this new vantage point, I've been able to channel my efforts to get precisely what I've always wanted. Did I have to work hard? Yes, for a short while. But in comparison to the nightmare of my previous existence, the effort was not much, and it was a pleasure to do it, especially as the results began to roll in.

How I did this with my business and my life—and how you can do the same—is the message of this book.

I especially direct this book to those who have the following chronic internal dialogue: "*There are things I must do right NOW, and there is barely enough time to do them. I will bulldoze my way through these tasks, and as usual they will be completed just in time—but the results will be of average quality and my body and mind will continue to be stretched to the breaking point. I'm tired and stressed and not getting any younger. There is too much chaos in my life and never enough money or personal freedom. My world is far from what I want it to be . . .*"

If you own or manage a business, have a job, are a student, or engineer family life at home, there's a good chance that narrative caught your attention. These days, this I'm-just-barely-hanging-on self-talk is endemic to every class and every age group.

I'm a low-key guy. Not a lot of flash, no frills, a working-class family background, and with no advanced college degree. I've run the gauntlet of ups and downs, successes and failures; and like a lot of folks, I've worked hard. It's clear to me that pragmatism increases with age, one's life improves by trial and error, and indelible lessons can be learned from being banged around.

I'm not afraid to face cold reality as I exhibit a knee-jerk suspicion of unsupportable theory—theory that is too often based on an ulterior motive.

My existence has a limited time span, and I treasure this life-gift.

My life is engineered now, planned and maintained. Work or play, the details of it get my full attention. No, of course I don't have everything neatly tied up in a bag (who does?). But I've found a way to take charge of things, to make my days orderly and calm.

COMPLEX JUMBLE?

What about you? How do you describe your typical day? Is it an amorphous and complex jumble of happenings, or is it a relaxed and ordered sequence of events? Is it chaotic, or is it under control? Do you have enough money? Do you spend enough time with family and friends? Through the day—and through your life—are you in an endless race around a circular track, or are you climbing slowly and steadily toward a mountaintop? Are you getting what you want?

If not, could it be because of your mechanical approach?

Could it be a personal chronic inefficiency rooted in a not wholly accurate perception of the fundamental mechanics of reality?

Don't confuse these questions with right, wrong, good, or bad. And don't inject some abstract theoretical, political, or religious bearing into your answers. Put all that aside for now and keep this mechanical, and—equally important—keep it simple. And take heart. If you tend toward defining your existence as a complex jumble, rest assured that you already have 100 percent of the resources necessary to eliminate this too-common story line.

The Work the System methodology is almost silly in its simplicity; but it's—and I risk hubris here—nothing less than profound in its capacity to transform. That's why I chose the words of William of Ockham for the epigraph of this book. To paraphrase, "The simplest solution is invariably the most correct solution."

Here, as I begin to discuss recognizable events and scenarios, habits, goals, successes, failures, and plain old common sense, you will relate to the Method because it's believable. It's about unassuming mechanical improvements that will combine to transform your existence.

Yet what I describe here is not apparent to the casual observer.

This book is not about feel-good, pie-in-the-sky promises. You won't find new-think premises, nor is there pseudo-intellectual blathering. You will not be asked to write down tedious lists, memorize odd platitudes, repeat affirmations, make daily journal entries, publicize your newfound direction to your friends and family, or, worst of all, be required to wait and see if yet another mysterious theory will make things better.

This isn't a matter of blind faith.

But if you think this new insight and, for that matter, sheer energy, clever thinking, a positive attitude, and hyper-enthusiasm are enough to secure the freedom and income you want, think a bit further. Certain structures—certain mechanical processes—must be in place before these important attributes can help deliver you to where you want to go. Independence and wealth can occur only *after* the system mechanics are put in good order.

So, is there something you must do? Some work you must perform? Yes, at first there is some written documentation. And if you lead people, you will teach them your new vision and strategy. But listen: you're putting in your time and working hard anyway, right? For a short while you'll simply channel a portion of this time and energy toward step-by-step, one-time building efforts that will lead to permanent freedom, prosperity, and peace.

And think again about racing around an endless circular track versus steadily climbing upward. Effort is required either way, but know it is the climbing you want. Instead of depleting precious resources on getting-nowhere, churning tedium (which is the hardest and most frustrating work of all), you will expend that same time and energy in a step-by-step steady ascent that will provide a geometric return on investment.

We'll be dealing with a perfunctory fact that most people overlook due to an almost universal can't-see-the-forest-for-the-trees myopia. The system-based protocols discussed here are quietly used in large, successful organizations everywhere, but they are not often present in small- and medium-sized businesses. And although the principles of the Method are scattered among thousands of time management, business, spiritual, and pop-psychology writings, here those basics culminate in this summary truth: *a life's mechanical functioning is the end result of the systems that compose it.*

And if it's true that a life's mechanical functioning is a result of the systems that compose it, then reaching your goals does not lie in coping with the bad results of unmanaged systems. Doing that is a wasteful distraction—a reflection of an I'm-just-trying-to-survive mentality. Rather, *getting what one wants requires delving one layer deeper to take control of the systems that create the results.* Hence the title of this book: *Work the System: The Simple Mechanics of Making More and Working Less.*

The first step—the "getting it" part—is to experience an awakening that will make you constantly aware of the separate systems of your existence. Once you truly *see* those separate systems, the job of "working" them—so they churn out precisely the results you want them to churn out—is just common sense. Thoughtfully work your systems and great results will spontaneously appear.

CAREFULLY PAYING ATTENTION

Each of us has recurring individual systems we employ to good advantage. We have a multitude of these processes down pat, and we perform them efficiently today because we have practiced them over and over in the past. We've become expert at walking, driving a car, preparing breakfast, and operating a smartphone. Why are we skilled in these small-system proceedings? Because sometimes they are simple, yes, but mostly because at some point we consciously paid close attention to the elements of the processes. We analyzed, adjusted, practiced, and learned the bit parts so that after a while we could execute the complete protocols with little effort, much of the time without thinking. (Remember learning to tie your shoes and to ride a bike?) But for most people there is no deliberate effort to dissect and then perfect the sequential workings of more complex, adult-world system processes within their businesses, careers, health, and relationships. Too many just churn along, wasting their days dealing with the same problems over and over again because they aren't focusing on the systems that are creating those problems.

Is this you?

So, to tackle the more involved challenges of your world—the challenges that have stymied you because of their invisible complexities—we're simply going to redirect the perceptive, investigative, and analytical skills you already possess.

You're going to focus moment to moment on the elements of a profoundly simple equation.

OVERVIEW OF YOUR NEW SYSTEMS MINDSET POSTURE

The systems mindset is not the mental paradigm ninety-nine out of one hundred people pack around day to day. Here's how it will be for you: instead of seeing yourself as an internal component of circumstance enmeshed within the day's swirling events, your vantage point is going to be *outside and slightly elevated* from those events. The day's happenings will be visible as separate and individual elements, simultaneously occurring in logical sequences. You'll be an observer looking down on your world, examining the comings and goings of the day as if they are physical objects spread out on a table in front of you. You'll clearly see the separateness of the systems of your world. The components will be simple and understandable. Wherever you look, the world's bustle will make sense. You will see that, step by step, one thing leads to another as the systems around you continuously execute, some under your control and some not under your control.

Your job will be to work your systems, the systems you can control.

One by one you will take your systems apart, analyze the elements, and then make them better. Over time, complexity and confusion will decrease and will be replaced by order, calm, and rock-solid self-confidence. There will be little fire killing and no confusion, and as you peer down at your handiwork, you'll feel self-respect and you will be proud of what you've accomplished. All by yourself, you will have created the life you've always wanted.

I COME TO YOU AS A PROJECT ENGINEER

With blue-collar roots, I have a mixed-bag background: land surveyor, heavy-equipment operator, union-man factory worker, door-to-door salesman, technical consultant, hamburger flipper, house painter, department store sales clerk, construction superintendent, design engineer, ditch digger, sales professional, builder, janitor, journalist, public speaker, book publisher, multi-book author and blogger, retail store owner, lab technician, logger, mill worker, gas station attendant, machinist, stocks and commodities investor, writer, photojournalist, telecommunications entrepreneur, internet marketer, real estate salesman, handyman, software developer, corporate CEO, business consultant, business owner, and survivor of two statewide political primary elections. I founded and continue to operate a nonprofit organization that assists earthquake victims in Azad Jammu and Kashmir (see www.kashmirfamily.org). Through my business, Centratel (www.centratel.com), my special expertise is telecommunications: taking information, processing it, and then passing it on.

My personal comportment? I'm a handshake, not a man-hug kind of guy. (And in this era of COVID-19, I find the demise of man-hugs a relief, elbow-bumping laughable, and the ban on handshakes calamitous.)

My overall life-role is as a project engineer. That is, I'm someone who accepts a problem, designs a mechanical solution, and either alone or in concert with others makes that solution work in the real world. I'm a project engineer in every aspect of my being, including my family-and-friend personal roles.

Metaphorically, here's my day: after a solid night's sleep, I bounce out of bed, shower, eat a big breakfast, and jump into things full bore. I *plunge* into the new day. Today I'm working with my crew to build something tangible out of the design I created on the drafting table just yesterday. On the job in a decent shirt, clean jeans, and work boots, my persona is relaxed. There is a slight smile on my face just under the surface of my focused comportment.

Again, metaphorically, I pull the levers and push the buttons of the unfolding day. My crew is lighthearted, relaxed, confident, and efficient—and we're fast. *Work feels good* and time flies as we cut a wide swath, making positive things happen as we convert yesterday's paper design into a touchable component of today's physical world. We're creating something worthwhile. We're permanently improving things.

If I can pull this off, so can you!

A NON-HOLISTIC APPROACH

Is there a holistic or "global" side of you that balks at separating things in order to scrutinize them individually? You may say everything is connected—that we're all one, and we must stop seeing ourselves as distinct from the world around us. Perhaps you think our lives are immeasurably complex and beyond human comprehension. That's fine for the big picture. I tend to think that way myself when relaxing and daydreaming. But for now, here on this material earth where we must physically navigate each moment, deep-six that perception and go with the case for separation and simple mechanics.

Try it on for size.

And understand that repairing an entire scattered conglomeration of a life in one fell swoop is impossible. It can't be done holistically, despite the feel-good rightness that word suggests. Fixing anything of complexity requires proceeding one step at a time, one component at a time—a decidedly non-holistic approach.

I don't care for the term "holistic solution." Instead, I like the term "holistic result," which suggests that each component subsystem within the primary system is functioning at peak efficiency, resulting in an entity that is superb in fulfilling its purpose.

So it's a very good thing to take your world apart to study it, to get things straightened out piece by piece. You can view things as a whole later, when you're not working on the details. There will be plenty of time for that.

CHANGES IN YOUR LIFE

Because this isn't a mystery novel, and because preparation is at the heart of the Work the System Method, here's a two-part summary of how it will affect you and what it asks.

First, here are four points about how acquiring the systems mindset will impact you personally:

1. **You will undergo an elementary yet fundamental shift in perspective.** It's probable that your systems mindset will arrive suddenly, as a stark awakening at a point in time rather than over a drawn-out learning experience. *After the mindset takes hold, moment to moment you will—without effort—dispassionately observe the separate human and mechanical systems that comprise your world.* These individual systems will stand apart from each other, starkly visible and sharply defined. You've turned a corner. You're one layer deeper.
2. **There will be no turning back.** You can't go back! Point two is a warning of sorts. *Because of the obvious logic of it, the systems mindset is something you won't be able to shake.* (But that's OK. You won't want to shake it.)
3. **You will no longer be swallowing unsupportable theories of reality.** This is because you will more accurately see the world's actual mechanical workings. There's plenty enough reality without

having to delve into unsupportable feel-good notions or doomsday qualms. *You will know the truth of the Work the System Method because life makes sense deep down in your belly.* And be assured that you won't sound flighty when you explain your new perspective to those around you. You're not going to lose your friends and family, because you are not going to ask them for anything. You have nothing to sell. Instead, should they ask what's up, you'll explain what this is about, and I promise they will be intrigued with what you have to say.

4. **At first there is some heavy lifting.** Yes, you will undergo an exciting change of perspective, but that is not enough. At the beginning of this rejuvenation of your business and your life there is some sit-down work as you create documentation in order to better define your targets and to keep moving efficiently toward them. *In all probability, it will be the best investment of time you will ever make*, because the end product will be a relaxed persona, plenty of money, and lots of free time. (Boring but true: What is the single major operational difference between the owner of a large successful business and the owner of a small struggling one? The successful business owner insists on intense system management that includes documentation of those systems. The owner of the struggling business does not.)

Here's the second part of this introductory nutshell summary, the three steps of the process:

1. **Separation, dissection, and repair of systems.** The incredibly satisfying exercise of exposing, analyzing, and then perfecting work, personal, and relationship systems. This ongoing effort includes creating new systems from scratch as well as eliminating the ones that have been holding you back.
2. **Documentation: creating written goals, principles, and processes.** These are tangible guidelines for action and decision-making for you and the people who work for you. This is not a feel-good exercise. It's the mandatory foundation for creating tremendous efficiency. This is the one-time heavy lifting, and it

won't take long to get your documentation up and running (and if you lead a team or department, you'll teach your people to do it).

3. **Ongoing maintenance of systems. Greasing the wheels.** It's easy. By this time, the positive results of the Work the System Method are motivating because it's so obvious the systems you've created are carrying the ball. You'll happily manage your systems in order to keep them operating at peak efficiency.

AND THREE ITEMS OF NOTE

First, at the end of most chapters I've placed real-life examples to illustrate various aspects of the new approach. Some relate to the previous chapter, some don't. The examples will remind you that *a critical element of the Method is to view your world from an outside perspective.* The systems-mindset vantage point is removed from the day's ongoing events. Only from an exterior position can system mechanics be properly seen and scrutinized. Then, from this observation post you will reach down to adjust those mechanics so they produce the results you want.

Second, as noted in the preface to this fourth edition, my business associate Josh Fonger has assembled sixteen real-life, "from the field" examples of how the Work the System Method has been applied in actual businesses. In the last decade Josh has, one-on-one, trained, coached, consulted, and advised more than a thousand business owners. (See Appendix E.) Josh has also written an Epilogue, focusing on the roadblocks and successes clients encounter.

Third, let's speak the same language. Here I'll define words and terms as they apply to the Work the System Method. Best to get familiar with them here at the beginning,

99.99 percent of everything works just fine: Look around! There is a penchant for efficiency in the world. The systems of the world *want* to work perfectly, and 99.99 percent of them do.

Bottom-up: The strategy of seeking the advice of front-line staff.

(A real) business: One does not have to personally show up in order to earn money.

Closed system: A self-contained processing entity, easily discerned from its surroundings.

Error of omission: A less-than-perfect situation that occurs because someone didn't do something.

Fire killing: Precisely what you don't want. It's the opposite of the systems mindset approach. The immediate gratification it delivers is highly addictive.

General operating principles: The second of the three primary work-the-system documents, it's a two- to four-page collection of "*guidelines for decision-making*" that is congruent with the Strategic Objective.

Job, profession, and a pseudo-business: One has to show up in order to earn money.

Linear: This is how systems execute, in a 1-2-3-4-step progression over time. Within its context, a process is not chaotic. It is logical, reliable, and simple to understand.

Mechanical system: A physical car, house, tree, etc. that, because of its materiality, doesn't fluctuate in its form or purpose. But also, within the work-the-system context, a formerly "organic" work system that has been made physical via written documentation.

Off-the-street people: These are the people who will do the work as viewed by business owners and managers. Depending on the situation, off-the-street workers can be novices or professionals.

Organic work system: A recurring human communication or work process in which the components (and therefore the outcome) vary according to personality, mood, time of day, etc. Not a mechanical system, it's the bane of most small businesses. Not a good thing.

Outside and slightly elevated: Your essential (and almost metaphysical) vantage point is external and above. Think of an eagle floating high overhead, looking for prey down below. Of course, the singular human advantage is self-awareness, so that view downward also encompasses the observer—you.

Perfect: In the work-the-system world, 98 percent accuracy is perfect because trying to achieve that additional 2 percent demands too much additional output. Of course, there are exceptions where 100 percent perfection is necessary.

Primary system or system of systems: An encapsulated entity with an ultimate purpose. An organism unto itself.

Project engineer: The role of a business owner or manager who adopts an outside, system-improvement posture rather than an inside, doing-the-work role. For personal life, it's a positioning in which one's systems are continuously contemplated, analyzed, adjusted, and controlled.

Recurring system: An enclosed process that executes over and over again.

Strategic objective: The first of three primary work-the-system documents. It's a single page that defines goals, describes methodology, lists strengths, and prescribes action.

System, subsystem (or process, mechanism, machine): An enclosed entity, with numerous spinning wheels, all contributing to the singular purpose of that entity which is to accomplish a particular goal. Within the work-the-system context, *we are especially interested in recurring systems*. The words *system* and *subsystem* are interchangeable depending on the application.

System-improvement: The heart of the Method. It's the never-ending search-and-repair effort of tooling a system closer and closer to perfection, all the while documenting and maintaining that system so its hyper-efficient execution will recur every time.

System management: A focus on maximizing the efficiencies of processes in order to prevent recurring problems, increase production and quality, and save time. It is the opposite of fire killing.

Systems mindset or work-the-system mindset: The embedded vision of the world as an orderly collection of processes, not as a chaotic mass of sights, sounds, and events.

Tweaking: The antithesis of neglect. The assertive, dogmatic, boots-on-the-ground work of making incremental subsystem enhancements that will produce a hyper-efficient primary system.

Work the System Method: The mechanical process of establishing goals and then perfecting the systems that will ensure attainment of those goals.

Working procedures: The third of the three primary work-the-system controlling documents. These are written instructions that describe how individual systems of the workplace are to operate. They are the end-products of the system-improvement process. Written working procedures are not often necessary for personal life.

Workingman's (or workingwoman's!) philosophy: A set of beliefs stemming from the hard, cold, sometimes messy realities of life's job site. The pragmatic view that a carefully composed blueprint directs the assembly of individual pieces into an excellent end product.

PART ONE

THE SYSTEMS MINDSET

CHAPTER 1

Control Is a Good Thing

My father says that almost the whole world is asleep. Everybody you know. Everybody you see. Everybody you talk to. He says that only a few people are awake, and they live in a state of constant, total amazement.

—Patricia (Meg Ryan) from the movie *Joe Versus the Volcano* (Warner Bros. Pictures, Amblin Entertainment, 1990)

For many, hearing a version of the adage "To get what you want, you must have more control" evokes the knee-jerk response that seeking control is a bad thing. They counter that one should relax and go with the flow, stay loose, and not worry so much about details . . . and that seeking more and more control can only mean one is devolving into a nervous control freak. There is an almost cosmological sense—a carryover through the generations from the '60s, no doubt—that "we're all one," and the problems in our lives and the world around us are created by people who don't share our brand of let-it-be spirituality. If my boss, my spouse, my parents, my children, my neighbor, and my government would just lighten up and be sensible—*like me*—then everyone would be happy!

Confident in the truth of it but confounded by reality, too many of us are eager to proclaim that the states of our lives—and the conditions of the world—are not good. We exhort that people are too uptight, too concerned with tiny details.

Allow me to retort.

Notwithstanding the possible at-the-atomic-level truth of "we're all one," it's my contention that *being in control of the details of our lives is mandatory if we are to find peace and success*—if we are to find happiness. Conversely, while we're focusing on those factors that are in our control, we must lighten up about those that are not. If we attempt to influence events that we cannot affect, we are in for discontent.

Is it difficult to determine what we can and cannot control? No, it's not.

My '60s generation emphasized a great and useful truth: what's happening now *is* the most important thing. But it's clear to me that any contentment I feel in any particular moment has much to do with details carefully orchestrated in days past. Yes, I try hard to be here now, but I spend some of that here-time focusing on actions that will ensure future moments will be what I want them to be.

WALLOWING

With my younger brother as an ally, I was brought up in my grandparents' house in the tiny impoverished town of Port Leyden in upstate New York. It was a chaotic, unsettled family.

At seventeen, I was out of there and on the streets of the Haight district in San Francisco. It was mid-1967, the Summer of Love, when I discovered an intriguing escape from the not-so-great family situation back home. For six years I was immersed in sex, drugs, and rock 'n' roll. (Well, maybe not that much sex.)

In the summer of '69 I ended up at Woodstock, the famous gathering of 500,000 in rural upstate New York. *Far out*, I thought. Afterward, I continued to fruitlessly seek a better state of mind, and three more years wafted by. I was the poster child for the freewheeling '60s.

In my self-imposed stupor, there was little I didn't complain about. I tried college but dropped out my second year, distraught in my loneliness and with my vision of a planet gone mad. In 1970, during a Washington, DC, political demonstration, I was teargassed. Literally, as the mist of gas swirled down in the middle of the cordoned-off street, I met the woman who was to be my wife and the mother of my two children. Then within weeks, with my new love in tow, I revisited the now dangerous streets of

San Francisco. We lived on those streets for two months and then returned to upstate New York.

Through it all I balked at everything that didn't align itself with my idea of rightness. I chafed at the unfairness of it all. I thought, *It's the system, stacked against me.* I ranted that too many narrow-minded, selfish people were manipulating things. They were conspiring to ruin my life.

Of course, I was a beacon of equanimity.

In truth, I was a pain to everyone around me. My life was a series of dead-end jobs and personal frustrations. Profoundly unhappy, dropping out of college twice more, I was a narcissistic complainer haunted by self-imposed psychic hooligans.

In the middle of all this, I married my teargas love. Not surprisingly, my bride was equally frustrated with the unfairness of things. We were two peas in a pod, loud and bold, convinced of our rightness and everyone else's wrongness.

Then, after too many years of floundering in this foggy, self-absorbed existence, the chains suddenly fell off one August morning. Hungover and depressed yet again, I sat at the kitchen table in our dumpy apartment in Inlet, New York. I was earning minimum wage as a seasonal worker at a State of New York recreational campsite, collecting garbage and cleaning public restrooms. I was late for work that morning, but nevertheless sat there immobile, looking inward. In that moment I declared to myself, essentially, and in not so many words, "*I'm twenty-three and I'm not living like this anymore. Until now my point of view has not been working for me. No longer will I try to change the world by whining about it. There is very little outside myself I can direct, so I will stop agonizing over events beyond my reach. I'll go back to school this fall to learn something that can be used to create a future for us. From now on there will be no more complaining. No more blaming. Rather than rejecting the world as it's presented to me, I'm going to get inside it—as it is—and see what I can do with the parts of it that are within my grasp.*"

Little did I know that my desperate acquiescence to "the system" in my early twenties would be the first step toward writing this book three decades later, a book that would point out the beauty of systems and—in their proper management—the freedoms they can provide. But unlike my preoccupations back then, what I write about here has nothing to do with fairness, politics, wishful thinking, or right and wrong. It's about simple mechanics.

That day I enrolled in a tech college, the New York State Ranger School,[1] to study forestry and land surveying. Two weeks later we moved to the remote campus town of Wanakena, New York, in the Adirondack Mountain foothills. My fourth attempt at higher education, I put my head down, worked hard through the winter, and graduated the next summer with a simple Associate of Applied Science (AAS) degree.

Continuing to pay attention to the details, for six months I drove heavy equipment on a nearby road-construction job in order to save up enough money to move west. In November of 1974, my wife and I and our five-month-old son headed to Oregon with $400 in our pockets and everything we owned packed into a homemade trailer attached to the back of the Plymouth. I had taken a stand. I was improving my life—and the lives of the two people who were depending on me—by expending my energy only on the details that I could control. The fog in my head had lifted due to an absurdly simple adjustment in my thinking process.

But despite those first steps toward dealing with the real world as it is, I had not yet recognized the next necessary step that would lead to solid control of my environment and thus the ability to forge freedom and wealth. It would be another twenty-five years before I took that next step.

PERPETUAL DISAPPOINTMENT

As I look back, my best explanation for my self-imposed hubris is summed up by a famous photo taken at Woodstock. It's one you may have seen. It's of a lovely, slender, long-haired girl who is maybe eighteen years old. She's beautiful and she's dancing in a farm meadow in a long sheer dress. There are flowers in her hair and she's laughing as she whirls with her arms stretched above her head in a casual way. Her handsome ponytailed boyfriend is dancing too. They share a peaceful ecstasy, and anyone who sees that photo would, at least for the moment, want to be one of those two young people.

---

1 Renamed shortly thereafter to SUNY-ESF Ranger School.

The image is a declaration of pure bliss with the clear message that happiness *is* attainable, and the path to that place requires no more than an uninhibited persona, hip music, and an unlimited supply of drugs. With a broad metaphorical brushstroke, the message that photo paints is that freedom will arrive as soon as we drop our uptight preoccupations and, metaphorically, dance in the meadow.

Let it all hang out. Stay loose. Go with the flow.

Back to the real world. The photo is an enticement for a state of mind that exists only for brief moments. Its message on how to live is a sham. One can't just lighten up and expect ongoing happiness! Life doesn't work that way.

But many of us who evolved from that era continue to think life *should* be that way.

We bask in wealth never seen before, but wonder why we are unsatisfied. Fifty years after Woodstock, that silly, self-absorbed perspective has carried over to a vast swath of our children and grandchildren. Generations of us live from day to day in perpetual disappointment within a world that refuses to conform to our expectations.

(Don't get me wrong. I don't like focusing on negatives, and it's a bit painful for me to discuss the unhappy contortions of my '60s generation. But it's a necessary discussion for presenting the work-the-system premise, so I have to start here—in the negative—in order to set the stage for the rest of the story, which I promise you will find uplifting.)

Too many of us—old and young—finger-point and complain and wonder at our dissatisfaction. It's too bad we do that because it's not just depressing, it's a distraction from what we actually need to do to find life satisfaction and to contribute. Excuses, generalizations about the alleged dire state of the world, and under-the-radar as well as overt attempts to change the people around us are ineffectual to the point of paralysis. These preoccupations are diversions from the personal actions we could take that would actually produce what we claim to want in our individual lives: peace, prosperity, and control of our own destinies. And pursuing peace, prosperity, and control are noble goals because the sure way to realize those goals is to contribute to the people around us.

And what about the generally accepted notion that someone who seeks firm control is an unpleasant personality, someone who needs to lighten up? I submit that this premise is wrong. Back in upstate New York as I sat at that kitchen table at the age of twenty-three, it dawned on me that happiness would not be found in control over others or in complaining about world conditions or in finding the perfect drug. It would be found by paying attention to the moment-to-moment details of my own existence.

But as the three of us drove west to Oregon back in late 1974, what I didn't fully see—as illustrated by the dancing girl photo—was that gaining command of one's life can't be found by manipulating it from the outside. Personal control will only occur after a mind shift inside.

Your Circle of Influence

A concept made popular by Stephen Covey, the circle of influence analogy illustrates one's level of control. In years past I was hardly able to direct my own comings and goings due to whatever psychological funk was eating me up in the moment. As I stood in the center of it, my circle of influence felt like it was inches in diameter. Today my circle feels as if it's miles across as the days effortlessly sail by and I am able to accomplish nearly all that I set out to do. This gives me great satisfaction as I grasp that *the wheels of today's personal progress keep turning due to the work I do inside my circle—not because I have spent time railing at conditions outside of it.*

Take a moment to imagine your own circle. How large is it? Is it just six inches in diameter? If it is, when you look down upon it is the top hidden underneath your feet? If the tiny circle is a cone and just twelve inches in height, you can barely balance on it. Do you spend all your available energy and attention just trying not to fall off? If this is your situation, your tenuous balancing effort doesn't leave much time for anything but complaining. Instead, what if you could channel the time and energy expended in this constant balancing effort into making your circle larger?

Whatever the size of your circle, focus on making changes inside it, not outside. Don't spend precious time agonizing over big-picture issues you can't control while neglecting the elements of your own life that you can easily modify. Expend your life's limited and precious allotment of time and energy on the matters you can adjust, the matters within your circle. Do that and your circle—and therefore your influence—will expand.

LIFE IS A STREAMING VIDEO, NOT A SNAPSHOT

Outside of brief moments within that encapsulated era, the unbridled approach of the '60s was just another great idea that didn't work. It was a theory of living that didn't consider how we actually are, but instead declared how we should be. If the Woodstock meadow-dancing photo had been a documentary movie, the hours and days surrounding that dance would tell a different story.

The truth of Woodstock? The nonstop music was good, but few bands played their best due to the confusion and extensive drug ingestion. Yes, it was peaceful, but after that first glorious day it was cold and wet and we sat in the mud shivering, drenched, hungry, and thirsty. Huddled in the rain, a half million of us worked hard to relax, insistent in our success at finding freedom and joy outside the system. Peace, brother! In the downpour, over and over again we told ourselves that all we needed was love. Yes, we really had jumped outside the everyday troublesome world, but in our T-shirts, jeans, and little else, we were utterly unprepared. We shivered, as the cold, relentless torrent hammered down.

It was no contest as soft theory met bare-knuckled mechanical reality.

With the inevitability of a wave washing onto shore, the enthusiasm faded as the filth that comes with neglected crowds began to accumulate. After forty-eight hours of this, a general paranoia swept through the cowering drug-addled horde, and my friend John and I got out of there. We left before Jimi Hendrix had taken the stage. It was that bad.

Listening to the radio as we headed home in my beat-up wreck of a car, we were reminded of Vietnam, racial unrest, and political deviousness. And beyond those negatives, both college dropouts, we each worked graveyard union jobs in a local paper mill; and as we drove home through the night, exhausted and depressed, it was clear that the joy we experienced at Woodstock fell within just a narrow sliver in time.

John was eighteen years old. I was nineteen. We were party guys and proud of our chaotic lifestyles. We never thought of the relationship between our undirected lives and our unhappiness. As I think back and analyze, it occurs to me that the ones who were creating something worthwhile were the ones we called the "straight" kids. They were not immune to down times, but in their willingness to conform to the reality of planet Earth and to face existence head on, they were more in control, more courageous, and yes, happier.

The lure of dancing in the meadow is an invitation to illusionary bliss. Truth is, orderliness and attention to detail are the roots of peace. Proof? Consider the indisputable reverse logic: in any setting, the opposite of peace—disorder—always leads to desperation. It's this way for any out-of-hand situation: a natural disaster, riot, war, car accident, or family argument. Bedlam is never a pretty sight.

Too many of us are paralyzed in the static snapshot of how we think our worlds should be instead of facing the truth of our own unpleasant flowing realities. Life is not a snapshot. It's a real-time streaming video—and the video plays on, whether we affect it or not.

DISTRACTED

So, all these years later, what is the relevance? For those who still buy into the '60s mystique, an unfounded assumption smolders. It whispers there is chaos all around, that systems and organization are bad and that Big Brother is right there behind the curtain, always steering things in the wrong direction.

This thread of paranoia leaves too many of us obsessing about conditions that are not in our control, and that obsessing distracts us from taking the personal actions that would truly make us free! It's not "the system" that holds people back. It's a flaw in individual perception.

Back in 1974 as I moved my small family west, what I still didn't understand was that freedom and peace lay in seeing the mechanisms of life and then attending to them. Back then I didn't know there could be a breathtaking internal shift in perception that would not only allow me to see the machinery that was producing the results of my life, but also the immense power I had over my own destiny.

It didn't occur to me that by being blind to personal systems, the mistake of a lifetime could be waiting just around the corner, ready to flatten me when I least expected it. And less dramatic but more endemic, that small inefficiencies could quietly accumulate and take me to the same dark place. The logic that this churning flow of life would be at my command only by paying close attention to the nuts and bolts that composed it was beyond me.

Back then, I didn't understand that peace and prosperity arrive *after* the mechanics are put in order.

Mood Adjustment

In the Western world, 10 percent of adults are alcoholics, 80 percent drink copious amounts of caffeine, 20 percent are addicted to tobacco, and more than 10 percent rely on antidepressants. Throw in the other legal and illegal drugs, and it is safe to say that each day, 98 percent of us ingest at least one mood-altering substance in our search for better states of mind. Of course, many of us are multi-substance users—for instance, consuming caffeine in the morning and alcohol at night. One addictive substance counters the negative effects of the other, in the classic endless loop of Western chemical mood adjustment.

A DEARTH OF USEFUL SYSTEMS

From a systems perspective, what happened at Woodstock? One system that worked well was the one that delivered the music. The technicians were adept and the equipment functioned adequately. And despite the logistical complexities, the musicians showed up, which meant the transportation process worked—the entertainers were delivered by helicopter. The location (Yasgur's farm) was perfect.[2]

---

2 Diana and I showed up for the fifty-year Woodstock anniversary celebration in August 2019. The museum and grounds were a spectacular representation of what went down in mid-August 1969, with one exception: the centerpiece theme—the unbridled drug ingestion—was not just downplayed, it was utterly omitted. Just sayin'.

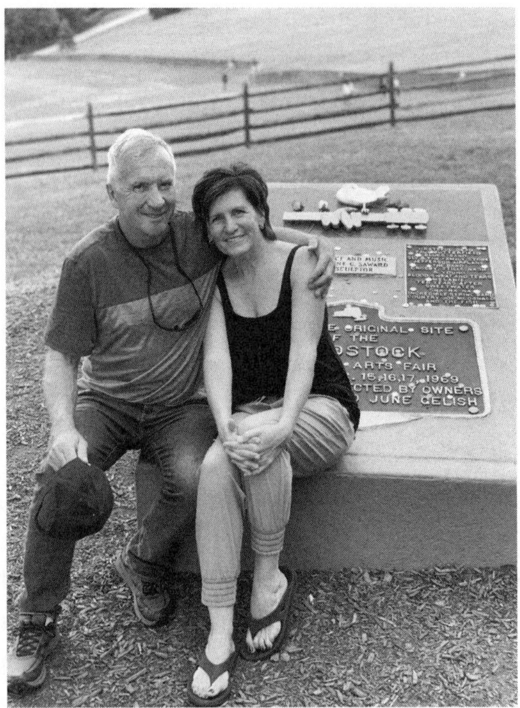

Woodstock, 50 years later

What systems did *not* work? You name it. The ticketing process failed, with all the surrounding security fences coming down the first day of the event—a disaster for the promoters. The sanitation and medical systems were overwhelmed. There was little food and water. And if overt police protection had been required, it would have been mayhem because there was little more than a tiny contingent of informal, untrained private security guards.

Of course, few in the audience were physically prepared, even in a rudimentary way. To compound the external challenges, drug use was hampering rational thinking. Everyone was in the middle of everything and chaos was a breath away, held back by no more than the luck of the draw.

One day of peace and music? Yes, OK, that's true. Two days? Well, the drugs helped maintain a certain calmness, but circumstances were deteriorating quickly. Three days? Whew! It was an exodus out of there! If there had been four days? For those diehards who might have remained it would have been a sordid, nasty affair.

For a while it was the love and goodwill of the people that made the festival work. But that sliver of bliss was narrow and can't serve as an example of how a life can be lived day to day. "I love you man" is not nearly enough for the long term.

A Potent, Visceral Reminder from the Folks at NASA

The space shuttle was arguably the most complex machine ever built by man, and a launch was perhaps the most magnificent display of human system control. I never missed an opportunity to watch the event on TV in real time.

The shuttle program ended in the summer of 2011, but one can still consider the precision of the countdown, which relied on thousands of simultaneous and automatic monitoring processes, all created and overseen by engineers and technicians. Launches were executed and tens of thousands of active processes, both on the craft and on the ground, operated independently and in concert. Each system was a precision entity unto itself.

There were a total of 135 space shuttle missions, two of which were spectacularly horrible failures. Yet, considering the incredible complexity of the undertaking, and acknowledging the human predilection for error, one could legitimately wonder why there were not more catastrophes than this.

Like countless minor failures of the past, the two tragedies provided space shuttle engineers with information they used to prevent future problems. As time moved on, the chances of failure decreased steadily as all those tens of thousands of individual shuttle systems were tweaked ever closer to perfection. Each launch was a keynote celebration of human potential and a visceral illustration of the beauty of the countless systems that comprise our existences.

CHAPTER 2

Events Did Not Unfold as Anticipated

King Arthur (Graham Chapman), after chopping off both of the Black Knight's arms: *Look, you stupid bastard. You've got no arms left!*
Black Knight (John Cleese): *Yes I have! . . . It's just a flesh wound!*

—From the movie *Monty Python and the Holy Grail* (EMI Films, 1975)

One reason I use my business, Centratel, to illustrate the work-the-system framework is because it is an easily understood primary system that is composed of easily understood subsystems. It's a closed "system of systems" that provides simple cause-and-effect depictions of the principles. As I go through the details of my business, read between the lines understanding that the picture I paint, as an analogy, is completely applicable to your own personal life.

For its first fifteen years Centratel struggled for survival, always at the brink of disaster. Why did this primary system begin to prosper in year sixteen? Yes, focused attention, terrific staff, targeted marketing, and a consistently high-quality product went a long way, but they were not the *cause* of the turnaround. Instead, these were by-products of the cause. The reason for the turnaround was the discovery and application of the principle that *leadership must focus on improving processes, not on performing the work or on repeatedly snuffing out brushfires*. Quality products or services, a stable staff, and profitability are the result of the quality systems that underlie them, not the reverse.

Centratel is a high-tech national telephone answering service (TAS). As a third-party outsourcing business, a telephone answering service employs telephone service representatives (TSRs) who process incoming telephone calls (from *callers*) for various businesses (*clients, or accounts*), who pay us.

Essentially a private 911 dispatch center, an answering service's purpose is to take messages from the clients' callers and then deliver those messages to the client. Clients include medical and veterinary clinics, hospice and home health care services, funeral homes, public utilities, property management companies, HVAC operations, high-tech firms, and the like. These are businesses that must provide 24/7/365 human interaction to their customers or patients. Since these businesses can't cover their phones 24/7, they must employ an answering service to screen and process their after-hours calls. And a significant number of our accounts use Centratel during daytime hours when incoming phone traffic is more than can be handled in-house, or if the company is very small and has no physical office.

At Centratel, up to thirty TSRs at a time (depending on call traffic) sit at workstations and field one call after another, with the incoming calls arriving randomly from any one of approximately fifteen hundred client accounts. When call traffic is heavy, they come in to our TSRs like machine-gun fire. One will be from a nervous husband whose wife is on the way to the hospital to have a baby, the next one from the panicked owner of a racehorse stricken with colic, the next from an apartment tenant who has accidentally locked herself out of her unit. You get the idea.

TSRs take messages, record them in a database, and then deliver them in a variety of ways, including mobile phone, voice-mail box, e-mail, text, and/or fax. It's a complex enterprise with a multitude of human and mechanical processes executing simultaneously. Caller, client, and TSR communication is almost always time-sensitive. Each account provides unique and exact instructions on how to handle their callers and how to process messages. No two accounts are the same. So, within a TAS business, there is much opportunity for error; and without strict systems protocol and superior staff, it's an understatement to say it can be a breeding ground for chaos.

The TAS industry stretches back to the first days of telephones. As they were then, today's answering services are around-the-clock operations. This all-the-time activity engenders another interesting challenge: odd working hours for TSRs. It's a tough way to earn a living, and a major challenge for those who field calls after hours and on weekends. Our more senior TSRs have worked themselves into daytime shifts, but new people must earn their stripes, enduring the tougher schedules until they can move into better slots that open due to staff attrition and company growth. In any case, the pay and benefits are very good at Centratel, close to double industry averages.

(I'll add here that since the COVID-19 crisis that began in February 2020, 90 percent of our TSR staff now work from their own home offices, with the other 10 percent preferring to come into our HQ/operations center in downtown Bend. This is exactly the reverse of how we have operated for the past thirty-six years when nearly all TSRs reported to work at our downtown location. And for those 10 percent who report to work downtown, we have radically changed our physical operational structure in order to accommodate the six-foot distancing requirement. This was a near-instantaneous yet monumental change in how we operate. At the end of Chapter 20 I'll talk about how we met the COVID-19 emergency that resulted in Centratel's continued growth, rather than its demise. Plenty of competing answering services instantly folded when the COVID-19 frenzy took hold.)

In 1985, the total number of TAS businesses in the United States was more than twenty thousand, most of which were small, local mom-and-pop operations. Now, survivors are larger and they offer service nationwide—but there are only eight hundred total. The root of the decline is because as a percentage of the overall population, the number of TAS clients has decreased considerably. Smartphones, voice mail, the internet, and advanced telephone company switching options have cut deeply into the potential client base. Nonetheless, plenty of businesses still require a real-live human being to process their incoming calls, and the relatively small industry will not be disappearing any time soon.

WHY DO IT?

Thirty-six years ago, I contemplated entering the TAS industry for four reasons (and these reasons are still good general considerations for anyone thinking about going into business).

First, it is all about people and constant one-on-one communication. That's a compelling combination.

Second, revenues would be passive. If managed properly, I would not have to be physically present in order to receive income. Back then I was new to entrepreneurial business ownership, but it seemed to me that making money without having to show up to do the work would beat being a doctor, attorney, teacher, psychologist, working man, or any number of occupations where a specific individual is the centerpiece of the endeavor.

Third, revenues would be recurring—clients would continuously use our services and pay us over and over again. Because clients paid monthly, generating new income would not be a full-time daily challenge. I reasoned that if the product was superior, clients would stick with us and the income would constantly flow.

Fourth, it seemed to me that if there was an economic or other emergency, a TAS business would survive or even thrive.

OVERVIEW

So, in Bend, Oregon, on December 1, 1984, at the age of thirty-five, I bought Girl Friday Telephone Answering Service. It was an ailing TAS on the verge of failing. The total purchase price was $21,000. The down payment was $5,000. There were seven employees, 140 accounts, and 400 square feet of office space. A financially sinking operation, monthly revenue was $5,500. (Today, that figure exceeds $500,000.)

Now the owner of a business, I changed the name of the company to reflect the evolving times, and—per my arrogant cockiness in those days—announced to anyone who would listen that we would someday be the highest-quality telephone answering service in the United States. Despite my bravado, I had no idea how we would achieve such a goal. (And as I think back on those days and how I presented myself, the words "brash" and "clueless" enter my mind.)

Events did not unfold as anticipated. The new business came to me as a disorganized nightmare with a red-ink bottom line, and in the chaos of it all, my personal world quickly devolved into a shamble. Within a year there was a divorce, and then I proceeded to do my best to bring up my two children as a single custodial parent. All this was compounded by a deep economic recession that had especially affected the Northwest, which was still reeling from the recent virtual destruction of the supporting regional industry: timber products. (For my beautiful hometown of Bend, Oregon, however—and lucky for us—tourism would soon fill in the gap and the local economy would boom while the rest of rural Oregon gravely suffered economically, with much of that suffering continuing to this day.)

Even though Centratel was always on the brink of disaster, we benefited from Bend's powerful economic growth and we grew in volume—but profits never increased. It was an epic struggle, and as the first years passed, the best-in-the-US goal disappeared behind the cloud of disarray.

For a decade and a half I endured moment-to-moment turmoil, working long, long hours—consistently in excess of eighty hours a week—always just scraping by financially. I got sick from the pressure but powered on anyway. The only thing that would stop me would be if I dropped over unconscious from stress and sheer fatigue, and after fifteen years of relentless pressure, this became more than a possibility.

Then I had an unforeseen insight. An earthmoving event, the new vision deeply affected me as it changed the way I perceived the world. Per this mini-enlightenment, I immediately began to interact with my surroundings in a completely different way, and instantly the turbulence began to subside. Over time, Centratel became a better and better business because I was more precisely viewing how it—and the world—actually worked. And yes, we would ultimately become the best in the US.

Just after my awakening, I brought a minor partner into the business—a good man, an acquaintance I had always respected who said he knew about my company and thought it had a future—and I was no longer in it alone. Now, with this stock sale of 9% of the company, Centratel had a substantial financial boost. Interesting that as I began to delve deep into the mechanics of my business and my life, odd synchronistic signs emerged. For one, my new partner's name? Sam.

The next few chapters describe the odyssey in detail. As you read, think of parallels in your own life.

Installing a Preventative System

Sometimes we install a system that doesn't do much. We achieve the desired effect by the mere existence of it. At Centratel, we knew that a few of our TSRs spent time surfing the internet while on duty. For security and focus reasons, that's not a good thing. We had no way to track these sleight-of-hand excursions, and the closest we could get to managing the problem was to walk around a corner and find a TSR covertly closing a non-Centratel window upon our approach.

So we installed software that tracks and logs all internet activity. This new system solved the problem instantly and completely.

Have we ever tracked down bad behavior with it? Yes, when we installed the software without announcing what we had done, the expected suspects emerged. Did we say anything to them? No, it wasn't necessary, because we knew that once we revealed the installation and noted it in our Employee Handbook, the people who were violating the rules would change their behavior. Did they? Yes. In routinely checking the monthly logs have we had subsequent abuses? No. Never.

In our society, other examples of preventative systems include drug testing, the police, the military, and laws. These mechanisms provide consequences for bad behavior, but of course are mostly intended to halt problems before they occur.

Think of preventative systems and mechanisms in your personal life: the seat belt in your car that doesn't just protect you from injury but reminds you that a defensive driving posture is paramount; the cloud backups on your computer; the small courtesies you show to loved ones and strangers alike. As you go through your day, think of systems you can implement that will prevent problems down the line while they keep things smooth in the present.

CHAPTER 3

The Attack of the Moles

Gwen DeMarco (Sigourney Weaver): *They are so cute!*
Guy Fleegman (Sam Rockwell): *Sure, they're cute now, but in a second they're gonna get mean, and they're gonna get ugly somehow, and there's gonna be a million more of them.*

—From the movie *Galaxy Quest* (DreamWorks SKG, 1999)

All telephone answering services perform the same function for their clients, and my newly purchased TAS was no exception. At all hours of the day and night, our TSRs took incoming calls from our clients' callers. When clients called in, TSRs read their transcribed-by-hand messages back to them. It was the mid-1980s, when word processing and electronic database management platforms were in their infancies. We were one of those mom-and-pop answering services, and for a flat rate of $35 to $45 per month we processed as many incoming calls as the client could send us. During the day, two TSRs handled calls; after hours, one.

From the beginning and for those fifteen subsequent years, I called the shots on all aspects of the operation. From the first day of ownership, it was a madhouse because most of our business accounts had taken advantage of the flat-rate arrangement and used our TSRs as their full-time telephone receptionists. We were overwhelmed with call traffic, and so the quality of call handling was abysmal: incorrect phone numbers, misspelled names, incomplete messages, and subsequently, angry clients. At first, all I could do was watch and wonder because I had no understanding of the internal mechanics of an answering service. That first day I didn't even know how phone calls were mechanically routed to us through the phone company.

When I bought the business, the monthly total gross revenue was not enough to cover wages, rent, telephone company costs, and everything else, including supporting myself and my two children. The business had been mine for only two months and disaster was already at hand. ("Disaster is at hand" was to become a serial catchphrase over the ensuing years.) In month three, standing by and not taking some kind of action would be the quick ticket to failure, so with my staff and with my eight- and ten-year-old children depending on me, I had to do something immediately. Here, my brashness would be useful.

It was ironic that although the business was in terrible shape when I bought it, some positive aspects ("gold") lay hidden. After just a few weeks the major problem was obvious even to me, someone with zero knowledge of the industry. It was clear we must immediately correct the most glaring inefficiency: a customer-pricing schedule that was way, way too low. It was fortunate that our service rates were extremely low—we could raise them significantly and still remain competitive.

So, I informed our clients by letter—there was no internet in those days—that service rates were going up and we would start charging for the actual call traffic we handled for their individual accounts. I told them that a large price hike was the only choice if we were to stay in business. So for each client, we eliminated the monthly flat-rate billing plan and began charging for the actual number of messages we processed.

On average, this *tripled* our customers' monthly costs, and immediately one-third terminated service while others dramatically cut back the call traffic they forwarded to us. The decrease in incoming calls allowed our TSRs to spend more time on each call, and because they were less rushed, the quality of service improved—the first of many incremental quality improvements that were to accumulate over the years ahead.

As a sidelight, and to illustrate just how low our service rates had been, even with the 300 percent increase, our prices remained lower than our much larger local TAS competitor.

Despite losing more than a third of our total client base, our monthly gross revenue doubled overnight to $11,000.

The dramatic increase in income was awesome, but equipment had to be upgraded and wages raised. So even with the additional cash boost, the company was still not profitable. We raised rates again in six months and then again six months after that. One year later we did it again! It didn't matter. We continued to struggle.

The just-barely-hanging-on predicament endured. Over the next decade and a half, we couldn't get ahead, even though we were able to multiply our initial gross income by a factor of twelve. Our revenue growth was due to the rate increases, a booming economy, and new clients that we gained because of our growing reputation for quality—quality that had risen from terrible to marginal (but marginal quality was better than our local competitors, who remained at the terrible level because of their own self-perpetuated chaos). It was uncanny: the increase in income was always matched by increases in operating costs. The largest hikes were in wages, health insurance, retirement, and other benefits to the TSR staff.

Within three years we moved to a larger office space. We stayed in that location for twelve years and then moved to an even larger space. We continued to grow, but there was little profit, and the turmoil and cash-flow problems mounted.

In all those years, my small salary didn't change, and my 80- to 100-hour workweeks continued unabated. I had no life outside the business, and any off-work time went to my two children.

As the years passed I thoroughly learned the ropes of the business, priding myself on being expert in every facet. I was able to perform any function and address any challenge. Within moments I could move from scheduling staff to handling customer complaints to solving telephone company problems. I could interview a job applicant for a TSR position one minute, and in the next minute put together a plan for adding a computer. I could prepare payroll while signing up a new account and then head to the bank to plead my case for yet another small loan. I did it all, including being an effective single parent to my kids (the task-juggling at home rivaled the task-juggling at the office).

What a feeling of power as I simultaneously solved multiple unrelated problems! I was a master of survival, a fire killer extraordinaire. How heroic! But in my blind arrogance, I was swept up in endless fire killing. I was headed for destruction and I didn't even know it.

The Numbers Are Gloomy

Statistics show that of one hundred new business startups, only twenty will survive five years. Then, in the next five years, only four of those remaining twenty will still be functioning. In another five years, three of those four will disappear, leaving only one out of the original hundred. That's a 99 percent small-business fatality rate over a fifteen-year period. This is in accordance with my admittedly anecdotal conclusion that the vast majority of small businesses are mismanaged.

Gauge your own situation and look ahead. Are you an employee of a small business? If so, the numbers are not on your side. Or do you own a small business? If so, there is hope because you have the power to direct it.

Too often, what ends a business or a job, or what casts an onerous spell on a life, is death by a thousand cuts. This is inexorable erosion caused by recurring inefficiencies and their toxic offspring: fire killing and distraction. These time wasters undermine efforts to create and sell a good product or service to a viable market. And in personal life? You've seen it in those who can't seem to break out of the bad-luck syndrome. It's not mysterious tough luck that takes people down. It's serial inefficiency. The great news is that inefficiency is easy to correct if one can see the cause of it.

THIS SURVIVAL THING IS KILLING ME

With the exception of whatever happened to be going on in my mind on any given day, there was no direction for the company. Centratel grew because of the booming local economy and my knack for foiling the reaper at the last minute. Long-term planning didn't happen and routine maintenance was a vague concept for the future.

My days spiraled downward into ever-deepening chaos. I leaped from one predicament to the next. Crises multiplied. The days were crammed with cash-flow crunches, chronic staff absenteeism, and innumerable customer complaints. The office temperature was too cool—or too warm. We would run out of critical office supplies and not have the time to leave the premises in order to replace them. Turnover among TSRs was incessant, and scheduling was haphazard, put together at the last moment. In year ten, we went through more than sixty new people—and my total number of staff was twelve! TSR trainees would start work, stay for a week, and then quit. My employees who were sticking it out were unhappy, and the same held true for our clients as they endured a still marginal quality of service.

Making payroll was always a challenge. Every two weeks it was a last-minute, hold-your-breath epic as we gambled that payroll checks would clear. Twice they didn't, and I went to employees' homes with cash to cover their bounced checks, pleading with them to give me another chance; to please come back to work.

Through it all, I was the heroic save-the-day entrepreneur, the master fire killer who would work as long and as hard as necessary.

The years streamed by. My teenagers would wait for me at home as I flailed around at the office late into the night. When I finally got home, I would check to see if they were sleeping OK and then stumble into bed myself. I would lie there exhausted with a deep, deep fatigue way down inside my chest.

Bills were late, both at home and at Centratel. Collectors called day and night. Checks bounced and NSF fees accumulated, sometimes over $100 at a time. There were multiple federal and state tax liens. The people at the bank felt sorry for me, marveling at both my ineptitude and my endurance.

We lost our house and then my truck. My kids shared the office space with me because we couldn't afford a place to live. They went to high school during the day and at night slept on bunk beds in the back room of Centratel's small office space. When I could, I slept alongside them on a cot.

The years rolled by.

After my two teens had gone off to college, in one long stretch of seven months, seven days a week I answered calls as the sole TSR on the midnight to 8:00 a.m. shift. Here's the kicker: during those seven months, Monday through Friday of every week I also worked the daytime shift from 8:00 a.m. to 5:00 p.m., taking care of all administrative tasks. This meant that each weekday my shift began just before midnight and ended no sooner than 5:00 p.m. the next day. Weekends were a relief because I only had to work the midnight shift. My workweek exceeded one hundred hours, and so of course there continued to be no time for a social life or personal relationships.

During those long months of graveyard shifts, I was sleeping just a few hours each night and never in a single stretch because, as the lone TSR, I had to wake up each time a call came in. Throughout the shift the medical and veterinary emergency calls arrived at a steady pace. There was the occasional straight hour of sleep as I lay on the floor on a single mattress with a pillow and blanket. After that long stretch of graveyard shifts ended, it was impossible to sleep through the night because my body had become hardwired to expect only three hours of nightly catnap rest.

Financially, those midnight shifts as a TSR helped, and after those seven months I was finally able to go back to my regular eighty-hour weeks. The kids were OK. They were out of town, off to school.

But I was still working eighty hours a week. There was no relief, due to my critical involvement with every aspect of the operation, and I wondered how soon my physical and/or mental collapse would occur. Of course, that would be the end of things because the business would immediately fail if I wasn't there moment to moment.

For the body and mind there is little worse than long-term sleep deprivation. Those seven months of 100+ hour workweeks had damaged my physical and mental health more than I knew. It was an exhaustion and depression that inhibited every thought and action. My performance became clumsy in the face of the escalating problems. The situation was getting worse by the day, and after a decade and a half of accumulated trauma, I finally realized the end was near.

If things were so bad, why didn't I give up the business and get a regular job? Because I was terrified of rejoining the workforce as someone else's employee. The thought of having a traditional job sent shivers down my spine. After all those years of being on my own, I knew for sure that working for someone else would be a nightmare for me *and* for my employer. I rationalized that if I was in hell, at least it was *my* hell.

PLAYING A GAME I COULDN'T WIN

I had no idea what to do other than what I had always done, to dig in and take care of whatever came up. It was horrible and the fire killing got worse. I kept at it. My existence was like playing the Whac-A-Mole game in which little grinning-faced mechanical moles keep popping their heads out of any one of a dozen holes. I would whack one mole with my rubber mallet and two more would emerge from two other holes. My mallet would respond in a flurry, and with a twisted satisfaction I'd ram those mole heads back down into their tunnels, one after the other.

Even with my declining health I imagined that my craving for multitasking/fire killing was a good thing, that it was a beautiful performance, a remarkable demonstration of dexterity, resilience, and power. Truth is, and of course I could not see it at the time, *the immediate gratification of multitasking and fire killing is as addictive as a powerful drug.* (Indeed, adrenaline and cortisol—human stress hormones produced by the body itself—are chemicals.)

But despite patting myself on the back for the heroics, the mole-whacking was not just killing me, it was distracting me from seeing what was necessary to actually fix my business and my life. The incessant disaster control was blinding me to the fact that I was playing a game I could never win.

The problem wasn't how I was playing the game. The problem was the game I was playing.

The Whac-A-Mole Game, per Wikipedia

According to Wikipedia,

"Once the game starts, the moles pop up from their holes at random. The object of the game is to force the individual moles back into their holes by hitting them directly on the head with the mallet, thereby adding to the player's score. If the player does not strike a mole within a certain time or with enough force, it will eventually sink back into its hole with no score. Although game-play starts out slow enough for most people to hit all of the moles that arise, it gradually increases in speed, with each mole spending less time above the hole and with more moles outside of their holes at the same time. After a designated time-limit, the game ends, regardless of the skill of the player. The final score is based upon the number of moles the player struck."[3]

---

3 Wikipedia, https://en.wikipedia.org/wiki/Whac-A-Mole.

Jim Morrison and Mick Jagger

Jim Morrison and Mick Jagger are arguably the best lead singers rock has ever produced: Morrison's comportment and lyrics, Jagger's energy and flair. Jim Morrison's short, wild ride was fueled by his enigmatic stage presence and brazen thought images, built around a mystique of chaos. He existed in a haunted darkness, enamored with the great unknown beyond death. He lived in chaos, too, awash in alcohol and drugs, abusing his physical and mental processes. He died at the age of twenty-seven after just five years of performing and recording. His band, The Doors, quickly dissolved. Morrison's too-short existence was the perfect opposite of systemization and order.

In dramatic contrast, Mick Jagger has been hammering away for nearly sixty years, more than ten times longer than Morrison's stint. Not just the Rolling Stones' lead singer, Jagger is essentially the band's GM and CEO, carefully attending to the operational detail of the incredibly sophisticated touring/recording machine that is the Rolling Stones. Eschewing drugs and alcohol in his early thirties, and now approaching eighty, he is as fit as a thirty-year-old. Whether he's creating music, performing, recording, or managing the complexity that is his world, he is a systems management genius.

CHAPTER 4

Gun-to-the-Head Enlightenment

It is often darkest just before dawn.

—Sojourner Truth

For fifteen years I carried on like a perpetual motion machine, pounding my small business into some kind of subservient yet mocking submission. But of course, it was tenuous. Everything depended on me, and if I let up for one moment, everything would come crashing down.

Then, a few months after my seven-month double-shift epic, I hit a brick wall. In my arsenal of last-minute bailout strategies there was no solution to the looming deathblow—my inability to cover even part of an upcoming payroll. My staff would walk out when there were no paychecks, instantly ending Centratel as our clients raced elsewhere to find another answering service to handle their urgent calls. In a single moment, my business would close its doors, and everything I had built in the past decade and a half would be lost, not to mention that my staff of sixteen would be jobless and my three hundred loyal clients would be in crisis.

I was a mentally and physically wrecked fifty-year-old single guy with kids, facing financial and career oblivion, and it was more than an interesting coincidence that Centratel's imminent demise was dovetailing with my almost certain physical and/or mental breakdown. I was desperate—and for the first time, angry—and the doomsday clock was ticking toward midnight.

DAWN

The payroll was due in just three days when I yet again lay awake in bed, utterly exhausted. But that night, for the first time ever, I stopped thinking about work details, business philosophies, elaborate theories, or some last-minute divine intervention. It was the end, and there was nothing left to ponder or ruminate about, nothing left to salvage—except one small thing. In a last gesture of raw defiance, I could at least end this long sad epic with some small bit of self-respect. As a final last-gasp effort, I would go down in a satisfying blinding flash. This would not end with a whimper.

Since everything was lost anyway, why not go a little crazy and seize a last resolute moment of control?

This time there was no salvation and I lay there in the 3:00 a.m. darkness reviewing the blinding-flash possibilities. I remember feeling a morbid amusement in conjuring up a final death throe. What would it be?

But something was odd. In finally giving up, in my utter exhaustion I was suddenly at peace. How could that be? Then, without coaxing, two simple pragmatic questions emerged out of the blackness: *What have I been doing wrong all these years? And since the end is coming, what is there to lose if I abandon past assumptions and look at my world from a completely different angle?*

My what-is-there-to-lose posture was the catalyst. The certain end of Centratel gave me the freedom to consider *anything*. No matter how outrageous, any new idea was an option because there was no further possible downside. I had a few more days to stretch into unknown territory and do some experimentation, maybe even relax and have some fun with it, because . . . what did I have to lose?

Then, prostrated in bed that night, answers came out of nowhere.

I underwent an enlightenment of sorts. It sounds corny, but in my dream-state I rose up and out of the jumble that was my life. I was no longer an integral part of it. Floating upward, just above the chaos, I gazed down at the details of my business spread out neatly as individual physical components on display on a tabletop. I was reminded of my grandfather's workbench when he was in the middle of a project: a tool here, a mechanism there, a component over there, all separate from each other but all essential to whatever it was that he was trying to accomplish.

I can still see Grandpa hunched over that workbench, disassembling and assembling.

(Do you get a sense of where I am headed with this?)

From this bird's-eye perspective, it struck me that Centratel was a simple self-contained machine! It was—and is—nothing more than the sum of an assemblage of separate sequential components: answering the phones, sales presentations, payroll preparation, scheduling, handling complaints, etc., with each protocol executing in a linear fashion whereby one step follows another step until the sequence for that particular process is complete and there is a result. I knew immediately that the rest of my life operated in the same way, as a collection of separate and independent processes, each one functioning in reliable 1-2-3-4 sequence according to its own construction. (Yes, I thought, of course these systems intermingle and affect each other—an integrated assemblage to be sure. But that integration can't mask the wonderful separateness of each process, the beauty of each one's individual existence.)

Yes, in Centratel there were actual physical components such as TSR consoles, desks, chairs, copy machines, etc., but these were accessories to the fundamental offerings of the company that had to do with processes and human-to-human interaction.

Late that night a new, deeper vision of reality gripped me, never to let go.

My thoughts raced at lightning speed as I marveled at the simple beauty of it. I understood that my previous view of the world had been wrong. The planet Earth is not a gigantic, amorphous, seething mass of people, objects, and events swirling in disarray. It's a place of order and logic, a place of predictability. The world is a collection of logical systems!

Whether those systems produce what we consider good results or bad results is not the point here. For right now, the point I want you to get is the simple mechanical reality of it.

For the first time, I saw Centratel as a closed package, a primary system—an independent, stand-alone mechanism, a machine—a separate entity, like a human body, an airplane, a tree, or a city. And I knew that the primary system I called Centratel shared a commonality with all other primary systems in that it was simply the sum of the numerous separate subsystems that composed it.

The logic of it was crystal clear, exquisite. I felt a quiet joy. To this day, I remember every wonderful nuance of that night's vision.

And from that night, I can remember that a line from an old rock song by The Fixx reverberated in my head as I lay there: "One thing leads to another . . . one thing leads to another . . ."

In my head, I looked down on the items on that tabletop and saw that my leadership in the business had been reactionary and therefore horribly inefficient. *I had taken the wrong stance—a backward stance—because the mechanics had been invisible to me! All I did was kill fires, unaware that those fires were the products of dysfunctional individual subsystems that were not being managed.* The subsystems had lives of their own and were acting out their 1-2-3-4 linear sequences without supervision, constantly producing random bad results—bad results that had to be fixed or covered up or somehow absorbed.

The primary system that was my business was out of control because it was composed of undirected subsystems!

My world was chaos not because I was some kind of loser or unfortunate victim of circumstance, but because so many of my subsystems were not being controlled. Unsupervised, these chaotic 1-2-3-4 processes composed the dysfunctional primary systems of my existence: business, health, and relationships. Nothing more. Nothing less. Very simple . . .

WHO IS IN CHARGE OF ALL THIS?

Exhausted yet exhilarated, I lay in bed floating above it all, looking down on my world. I remember that in those moments I savored the delicious new vision. It was borderline mystical, a sort of near-death experience but without the tunnel and bright light. Transfixed, for the first time in my life it was clear to me that my perception of reality had been murky and undefined. How does the Biblical quote go? "One thing I know: once I was blind but now I see."

From depths beyond my physical and mental exhaustion more questions surfaced, questions I had never considered before: "Who is in charge of all this?" And, "How does this world continue to function day after day, year after year, millennium after millennium?" The answers came fast and hard.

I was startled to grasp that there is no human King of Everything who directs the goings-on of the world. On its own and no matter what, this earth keeps turning and life carries on in an overall structured and organized pattern, and . . . no one here on earth is in charge! The indomitable laws of nature ensure systems work perfectly according to their construction. On this earth, gravity works all the time, everywhere. Over here, one plus one equals two, and over there, one plus one also equals two! The incontrovertible laws of nature cause the mechanics of the world to be dependable and predictable, and the God-given gift with which we humans have been blessed is the ability to get in the middle of those mechanics, to manipulate them, to direct our lives to be what we want them to be, to use the infallible laws of nature to our advantage.

Deeply submerged in the vision, I wondered at the silent and invisible organizational strength that keeps this earth chugging ahead like a freight train despite our human race's best attempts to derail the process. Cyclically, relentlessly, and for whatever reason, this complex world moves along on its own, adjusting, balancing, and counterbalancing. And at the root of it all, and in the middle of it all, uncountable separate linear systems are at work. I thought: *It's a beautiful thing.*

AN INCREDIBLY IMPORTANT DISTINCTION

I will interject this important point here because I don't want it to remain an underlying subtlety that you miss. I want this fact to be your stone-cold understanding. Here we go:

In these pages, I am not suggesting you "add systems into your life in order to get your life under control." I'm not saying that "your life-problems are the result of your lack of systems." Get that *your life is already a collection of systems.* These life-systems have determined your life condition in this moment, whether your life is going well or not; whether you have managed those systems or not! Systems really do compose life itself! *Now your job is to manage them: to fix the broken ones, to discard the ones that are dragging you down, and yes, to introduce some new ones.* Don't say, "I never had systems in my life and that is why I have failed." Rather, say, *"I've been failing because I have not been managing my systems, the systems that have been there all along."* Get the subtlety? Make sense?

THE WORLD CHURNS AHEAD WITH POWER AND PURPOSE

This systems rationale is not another feel-good, think-positive invocation, and it's not even about faith. It's about grasping stone-cold mechanical reality. Think about the processes of our lives and then do the numbers. Across time we wake, shower, dress, eat, go to work, and proceed through the day to return to our loved ones in the evening . . . or we come home to an empty house or apartment. Then we watch TV, read, and go to bed early—or stay up late. We go to sleep and then we awake again the next morning.

And, whether we're "happy" or not, everything around us works fine 99.99 percent of the time.

That's the cursory overview. Break it down and sequentially track the specific system components of the day's chronology. It will be thousands of items long. It includes contributing elements to the day such as the coffee maker that works every morning; the car that—despite all of its internal intricacies—operates with the turn of the key and then goes down the road with the manipulation of the various controls; the office we occupy; the complexities of the work we do; the incomes we receive for doing that work. Walking across the room or driving across the country! Computers! Smartphones! Consider the processes of sharing information back and forth with those around us: one-on-one, voice mail, cell phone, e-mail, text, and the written word. Junior high school band concerts and professional football games. A piano. A power drill. Each is a stable and predictable system. Each working flawlessly 99.99 percent of the time!

Envision the system we call a TV. By simply pushing a button, this incredibly complex mechanism jumps to life every time! Beyond the physical TV itself, consider the myriad organizations that put together the programming that appears on it. Then switch gears and think about the lawn mower, the water that flows from the kitchen tap, the electricity that comes to our homes to animate a host of devices, each a complex system of its own.

Contemplate the clothes we wear, the shopping we do, the pet we love so much.

Consider the gas pumped into our cars at gas stations. In some faraway place, sophisticated mechanisms extract oil from far beneath the ground. Then it's transported via high-tech ships, trucks, and pipelines to refineries, where it is converted into gasoline via esoteric refining processes. Next, that gasoline is delivered to an uncountable number of convenient locations so we can pump it into our cars whenever we feel like it. We never think twice about the intricacies of the drilling/refining/delivery systems, just a few of the millions of systems that touch us through the day . . .

And what about the human body? Try to fathom the amazing complexity of chemicals and mechanics that make it work. For each of us, as we progress through the day billions of cells simultaneously cling to each other making us who we are. And as we function moment to moment, trillions of concurrent electrical signals execute automatically.

Incredible!

Consider the miracle of what you are doing this moment, viewing and translating the characters on this page—or perhaps you are listening to my words in the audio version. You are transferring my thoughts to your mind where you instantaneously interact with what I am saying, making immediate judgments, agreeing or disagreeing, line by line. This is happening *now*, in *this* instant.

So far, I have especially focused on human systems, which are just a fraction of the total systems at work in any given moment. Uncountable natural processes add to the numbers and dwarf what man has created, and they all work perfectly according to their scripts.

And once one finally sees the world's beautiful systems-dance for what it is, the mystery of it goes even deeper. Consider that primary systems depend on subsystems, and those subsystems depend on sub-subsystems branching downward and outward, further and further, to subatomic levels.

See that these processes repeat themselves over and over, as they incrementally create new forms and dissolve old ones. And know these systems, in their own various ways, vigorously protect themselves from oblivion.

The world is *alive*, and all by itself churns ahead with power and purpose!

Stop for a moment and attempt to draw it all in. The depth and intricacy of life's fabric is astonishing beyond comprehension. Grasp the beautiful complexity of life's workings and know that all by itself this world gurgles and percolates along with no overall human supervision. The countless stable systems that comprise life surge on and on while most of us remain oblivious to the colossal mystery of it—unaware of the sheer elegance of it.

The relentless flow of life carries on no matter what. The sun comes up and later goes down. Grass grows in the spring and lies dormant in the winter. The tides rise and fall. We catch a cold and our immune system quietly rescues us. The microwave works! The car works! Love comes, love goes, and then it comes again. We live and then we die, and another is born.

It's interesting that the two most opposite groups of people imaginable share a similar wonder of the world's enigmatic workings: scientists and the religious.

Systems, systems, systems—everywhere and always!

We Are Machines

Fourteen years ago, as I was charging down a Bend city street on my mountain bike headed for home, a sixteen-year-old driver in her dad's SUV veered across my path. I slammed into the side of it and was launched over its roof to land on the pavement on the other side. To this day, I don't remember either of the impacts.

Knocked unconscious, I came awake only as I was loaded into the ambulance. On the way to the hospital, the paramedic asked my name. I answered correctly. Then she asked me where I had been on my bike and . . . I just couldn't remember. It was several hours before I could recall the details of my long ride before the accident.

With a slight concussion and some bruises, I was released from the hospital a few hours later.

From this experience, a lesson was hammered home. *Our minds and bodies are elaborate machines, machines that perform—or don't perform.* Each of us is an indescribably complex collection of subsystems, operating via countless sequential and cooperative protocols. Our impossibly intricate minds and bodies work well most of the time, but because of the occasional mechanical glitch within a subsystem, sometimes they don't work so well, or yes, they fail altogether.

We should never be complacent about our connection to the world around us; never underestimate the tenuous grip we have on our individual existences. We must handle our bodies and minds with care. We should be careful about upkeep and maintenance, yet challenge them so they stay strong. We must attend to them and never take them for granted.

THE COLOSSAL MISPERCEPTION

Late that night, entranced in my systems epiphany, I asked myself, Could it be the common presumption that the world is functioning badly—that it's a mess—is *wrong*? Yes, I instantly realized that if we look at the numbers, that presumption *is* wrong, because in any given life, on any given day, countless systems work flawlessly. We don't notice them and so we take them for granted. We seldom appreciate their impeccability. We hyperfocus on individual, mechanical, and geopolitical systems that are not to our liking and conclude that dysfunction is the default way of the world. Blindly locked into this limited vision, we see perfection as an anomaly and imperfection as the norm. That conclusion is backward.

Overall, the systems of this world work absurdly well. It's really true that 99.99 percent of everything works just fine. And even the parts we consider imperfect are that way only because we personally think those parts should be different from what they are. (In truth, this world is 100 percent perfect . . . if we discount what we want. However, for our purposes let's *not* discount what we want. Being pragmatic, let's characterize it as 99.99 percent perfect.)

That night, I lay in bed in wired stupor, thinking about how life insistently plunges ahead within a framework of countless efficient processes.

And I thought, since there is no human King of Everything, there has to be an underlying cosmologic urge toward efficiency and order. Some incredibly powerful force out there prefers events to go smoothly, and in fact has inserted itself everywhere. It's holding the world together. It's *making* it work . . . *God?*

This new understanding was the reverse of my previous vision of existence in which I saw my world as a place of barely controlled mayhem, tenuously held together by its human masters. The colossal misperception of my life was that I had visualized perfection as an occasional harmonious chord in a universe more comfortable in its cacophony.

Oh yes, I thought. Indeed, there *is* a God.

Back on that night in 1999, my mind raced on, and it struck me that if the universe has a predilection for order, it should be a simple thing to climb on board. And *since system inefficiencies comprise such a small percentage of my life's events—there wouldn't be that much to fix—I should be able to isolate those problematic systems and then, one at a time, adjust them to produce the outcomes I want.* It should be easy to get things straightened out because cosmological bias is on my side—and let's go one step further: this bias isn't just rooting for efficiency, it's demanding it!

OVERWHELMING STRENGTH AND INEVITABILITY

Is there a real-time analogy for the single-minded power that propels the processes of the world? Yes. Find railroad tracks and stand nearby while a freight or passenger train slams by at full speed. Feel the overwhelming strength and inevitability of it. As the colossal mass of the train surges by, feel the invincibility. This is an in-the-guts sense of the universe's mechanical potency and purposefulness. It's *that* deliberate.

The world's turning is powerful and relentless, and *that* is the point. Why it behaves that way is the human mystery—the ultimate question—but it is not the issue at hand here. *What matters right now is that you "get" that despite the common assumption that chaos reigns, the truth is that the mechanics of the world work incomprehensively well.* And if we can proceed with the premise that there is a proclivity for powerful efficiency—rather than blindly buying into society's almost universal notion that all is chaos—we will stop fighting events. Instead, confident and deliberate, step by step we can descend one layer deeper to go to work to construct the exact lives we want.

GUMMING UP THE WORKS AND THE ENIGMATIC POWER

Of course, it must be said that although there is a regulatory force disposed to keep things flowing smoothly, human free will enables us to wreak havoc on personal and global scales. When a process or mechanism doesn't produce the outcome we want it to produce, because of something we did or didn't do, we must recognize that this is the logical downside of the human race's gift of being able to influence and manipulate.

Dysfunctional systems may constitute just a small percentage of all systems, but for the record let's state the obvious: we humans are inclined to disrupt things, and for this reason there has been horror in the world. The worst of it? In the last century, in fits of narcissistic insanity, tens of millions of people were slaughtered by Hitler, Mao, Stalin, Mussolini, and Pol Pot. These were human systems gone haywire. And still the agony continues, at its most virulent in third-world, nondemocratic countries.

Then there is the self-generated personal pain that resides within our own individual thought processes. Add to this the self-inflicted damage caused by the neglect and abuse of the body mechanisms that we inhabit, not to mention no-fault setbacks such as accidents and genetic irregularities: the Forrest Gump "shit happens" scenario (a terse yet profoundly meaningful phrase).

Large or small, cultural genocide or a missed appointment, the life events that go wrong are due to component flaws within systems. When a process does not produce what we want it to produce, something within the process is not as it could be. Something is gumming up the works.

Despite all this, and notwithstanding the general media's allegations otherwise, the majority of lives move from beginning to end with a minimum of true, overt pain. When there is trauma it is most often short-lived. Because of the universe's inclination toward stability and efficiency, real discomfort is a small slice of the pie; and when it happens, it is most often the result of self-inflicted mental anguish and fear—negative constructs within our own thinking.

Yes, as I said, of course there are the notable exceptions. I am not a Pollyanna.

In any case, *systems want to be efficient.* If a system could talk, it would say, "My single goal—and I am passionate about it—is to accomplish the task that I was built to accomplish!" This means that our efforts to improve circumstances are aided by an enigmatic power that works hard to propel those efforts to success. So, within one's life, getting things to work swimmingly is not a difficult task if one deals with the actual mechanics of it.

Late that night, lying awake in bed, I realized the force *is* with you.

Safety, Comfort, and PC in the First and Third Worlds

Why are there major differences between life in the Western world and, say, Afghanistan or rural China? Why is life in the West easier than in the East? A part of the answer is that in the West, there are significantly more safety protocols than in the East. Therefore, lives are less in jeopardy. A simple example: In the West, we wear seat belts in our cars 100 percent of the time. It's the law—and the law is a system. In the numerous times I have been to the rural Far East, I have seldom seen a driver or passenger buckle up. In many third-world countries, there are no enforceable seat belt laws. Are seat belts actually *in* the cars? Yes, they usually lay buried in the seat cushions—but sometimes the driver has altogether removed them.

Another example: Here in the developed world there are quick and severe penalties for anyone's unprovoked, assertive aggression toward another. In the third world sometimes there are few protections, and meager justice mechanisms can be corrupt and impotent, encouraging undeterred person-to-person crimes.

And the flip side? It is telling that the annoyance of the politically correct is nowhere but in the West. This is a result of people trying too hard to regulate other people. It is systems-thought taken to the extreme by people whose basic needs are satisfied and who therefore have the time and energy—and proclivity—to attempt to channel the thoughts and actions of others. Busybodies.

For the backcountry African, there is no PC thinking, as life is negotiated via just a few systems, systems that have to do with survival. People there don't have the luxury of expending energy on silly PC gyrations.

(And, I'll go ahead and say it here: East or West, and for whatever reason, neurotic/power-hungry people are drawn to political leadership. For the big systems that we all depend on, that can be a very bad thing.)

For a Westerner, it is a good thing to live for a while in a third-world household. It's a crash course in discovering fundamental priorities and humility.

FLOAT THROUGH THE DAY IN FASCINATION

For me, one plus one equals two. For you, one plus one also equals two. The natural mechanics of planet Earth are reliable and can be trusted. And human-devised systems will also operate reliably if they are properly put together and maintained. If they are not put together correctly and/or not regularly coddled, they will fail to produce the results we want.

Few people think their problems are a result of personal process failure. Most see their troubles as isolated outside events, blaming fate, horoscopes, bad luck, karma, God, the devil, neighbors, competitors, family members, the weather, the president, liberals, conservatives, climate change, too much money, lack of money, the educational establishment, or just a world gone bad. And most see problems as overwhelming in number, an onslaught from *out there*, only to be fended off by superhuman efforts. For too many, the excuse/blame list is endless. I had long been a resident of that camp, but when the new systems-mindset vision engulfed me that night, there was zero chance I would ever live in that place again.

I now navigate through the day in fascination. Instead of being swallowed up in a hodgepodge of unpredictability and fire killing, I see events and objects as part of one structured system or another. This real-time, outside and slightly elevated perspective has channeled peace and prosperity into my life and into the lives of those who depend on me.

I call it a spiritual awakening.

Negatives will sometimes worm their way into my day, most often due to fatigue. It's not often, though. Not anymore.

This bears repeating: *the colossal human error is the assumption that there is a cosmic inclination to chaos, when the mechanical truth is that there is a default predisposition toward order*. It's a beautiful thing! I'm a believer now, and I thank God for every moment of this life . . .

THE FABRIC OF YOUR LIFE

By perfecting your life's individual systems—by identifying them and then rebuilding them one by one—order and peace will accumulate incrementally. However, the enhancements in these rebuilt systems must be made permanent or the systems will slip back into dysfunction due to random outside influence. In the workplace, permanence happens first by creating written descriptions of how systems are to operate. And second, by getting responsible parties to willingly follow the steps described in the documentation. Third, involved parties must be encouraged/rewarded for constantly improving their systems. We'll get to those details soon.

Once systems are studied and flawed components are exposed and repaired, they will produce desired results. Creating necessary new systems and eliminating unnecessary ones will add to success. And since this is all mechanical, when the changes are made, improvements will be instant.

For your own situation, not only can you count on an overwhelming bias toward efficiency, but you probably won't have a whole lot of systems to adjust, create, or delete. It won't take long to get your circumstances straightened out.

Now we are at the heart of the Work the System Method.

Whether an outcome is to your liking or not, the underlying process is performing exactly as constructed. You are not at the mercy of mysterious conspiring forces or the swirling backwash of chaos. If it is in your power—and so much that affects you *is* in your power—you can fix things! *You can make your situation exactly how you want it to be.*

BE READY TO WALK AWAY

What about those systems you can't repair because they are out of your influence? Relax. If you can't fix something, don't worry about it. Do what you can or walk away, but certainly don't spend time or energy agonizing over it. If you live in a democracy, vote and/or run for office, but then don't complain about the aftermath.

If you have a problem with a coworker, talk to him or her and then don't obsess about the outcome. Metaphorically speaking, if you don't like the TV program, change the channel or turn off the set. Save your energy for efforts that will provide actual positive results within your circle of influence.

AN OBJECTIVE

Back to my story and the looming crisis at Centratel. Late that night, yet another realization struck. My business needed at least one solid objective. From my new vantage point I could see we had been operating without any pointed purpose. The closest I could come to a reason for the existence of the business was that I hoped we would make money and be successful. That is the single objective of the typical small-business owner or corporate middle manager. It is not concrete and directed. It's ambiguous and wishy-washy.

Not only had I never considered its individual components, I didn't have a grasp of the *why* of the organization. It had no direction! This particular insight prompted the birth of the Centratel Strategic Objective document. I'll talk about that in Part Two.

THE CRUX OF CONTROL

Without prodding or willing it to happen, I stepped outside my life and rose above it. I looked down, never again to settle back into the quagmire that had been my previous existence. There was nothing airy-fairy about this. The new vantage point was mechanical and logical. I saw that the solution to my business problems did not lie in becoming more proficient at whacking moles—the solution was to find a way to eliminate those moles altogether. I had to put aside the hammer and dig down into those tunnels to find out exactly where those moles hid. And when I found them, I would ruthlessly strangle them one by one. Their grinning little furry faces would not deter my genocidal mission. And while I was down there taking care of mole extermination, I would find a way to prevent any mole relatives from returning later.

Ruthless? Yes!

Late that night I understood way down deep inside that perfectly executing systems were at play everywhere and all the time, and that imperfection was the anomaly. And I realized that my business—and for that matter, my whole being—was the sum total of the results of the efficient and inefficient processes that composed it. Confident and strong, I would look down on these systems and isolate them one at a time, viewing each as a separate autonomous entity. Per a solid directional plan, one by one and over whatever period of time it took, I would disassemble and then rebuild my subsystems so that each contributed to Centratel's clearly stated goals. Yes, in addition to the repair work, I would add new systems and discard useless ones.

I finally realized this: *the leader's role is to first see the wheels of the machine, and then figure out how to get those wheels turning fast and with maximum efficiency.*

It was simple logic. Creating efficient subsystems would of course cause the primary system—Centratel—to be efficient too. And to take this a step further, it seemed to me that if the individual subsystems could be made more than efficient, if each were to be made potent and powerful, then my primary systems—my business and my life—would become potent and powerful too.

Once I clearly defined an objective, I just needed to optimize the individual components to meet that objective. The primary system would be super efficient, the end product of the super efficient subsystems that would compose it.

I hadn't been looking for a revelation, but in my desperation, I got one. It was a vision that revealed the simple mechanics of the world, mechanics that had been cloaked by the dissonance of the day. *It was a permanent shift in perception, and I would never again be a master fire killer. Instead, I would specialize in fire prevention.*

The crux of control? I would never again deal with the bad outcomes of all those underlying inefficient systems. Instead I would expend my energies on perfecting and managing those systems—and good outcomes would prevail.

For a decade and a half, although the simple truth had been floating right there in front of me, the mental turbulence of my fire-killing approach had relegated this simple yet earthshaking reality to invisibility: a life's condition is not the result of luck or of being good or bad. And it's not about intelligence, karma, attractiveness, education, social class, political stance, or even about how hard one works. A life's condition is determined by simple, cold-blooded mechanics—the mechanics of the systems that compose it.

And what I instantly understood that night was the simple difference between happy people and unhappy people. Unhappy people's lives are out of control because they spend their days coping with the random bad results of their unmanaged systems. Happy people's lives are *in* control because of the good results of their managed systems.

My new perspective was not just an interesting new concept. It was an electric, life-changing revelation. Late that night, the moment the switch flipped in my head, there was no going back. I was a changed man.

CENTRATEL WOULD BECOME A MACHINE

It was uncanny. My middle-of-the-night reveries surged on into the dawn. Supported by indisputable logic, an entire strategy unfolded as I lay there.

I thought, *If Centratel is an organism—like a human body, or a car, or a TV—smooth and efficient operation will depend on a multitude of simultaneously functioning efficient processes that operate automatically.*

In other words, the business mechanisms I would fix and/or create would function without direct moment-to-moment supervision by me, the owner, GM, and CEO of the company. Other people would be watching the details. The watchers would be employees who would supervise the mechanics of the business without the need for my constant over-the-shoulder intrusion. Centratel would become a self-perpetuating organism.

Centratel would become a *machine.*

Further, this particular machine would be the highest-quality telephone answering service in the United States. We would accomplish this in five steps:

1. We would exactly define overall direction and strategies. It would be done on paper by creating strategic objective and general operating principles documents.
2. We would break down Centratel's workings into subsystems we could easily grasp: processing calls, staff management, client services, equipment, quality assurance, the protocol for handling client and customer requests, bookkeeping, purchasing, customer services, etc. Then, each of those subsystems would be broken down into even smaller contributing sub-subsystems, including receivables software, customer complaint resolution protocol, employee recruitment, equipment maintenance schedules, and so on.
3. Once isolated, exposed, and understood, we would refine and improve those systems—one by one—so each would contribute 100 percent toward the stated goals of the strategic objective. As needed, we would create new systems from scratch. We would discard useless ones. We would document each process into a working procedure, thus making perfected systems permanent. The execution of the perfected systems would recur without prompting. They would be perfect systems executing perfectly 100 percent of the time, automatically.
4. We would implement fail-safe recurring maintenance schedules. We would set alarms to point out systems that were not functioning properly. And along this line of thinking, we would prepare for unexpected external economic or physical hammer blows.
5. "Replacement" employees would be identified and trained. Every employee, including me, would have someone in the wings who could instantly take over, should that become necessary.

FROM ORGANIC TO MECHANICAL

Why does a car perform the same way every time? Why does a city remain in the same place without spontaneously moving to a new location? Why do we, throughout our lifetimes, continue to be ourselves? The reason is hard mechanical reality: physicality. With the obvious exceptions of fluids and gases, physical objects don't morph into other physical objects or dissipate into the ether. They are mechanical—dependable and predictable.

On the other hand, human communication processes—organic systems—are the antithesis of physical substance. For example, the execution of a non-documented recurring communication protocol not only varies among the individuals executing it, but also changes for any one person, depending on the time of day, the weather, or mood. Untamed, these organic systems are feathers in the wind.

In the workplace, the challenge and the solution is to make these organic human processes as solid and reliable as the mechanical objects that surround us. On planet Earth, we accomplish this with documentation!

The Essential Formula

The base fact of life is this: every single life-result is preceded by a sequence of steps executing over time.

Here's the simple formula: *1→2→3→4* = Result.

Therefore, the secret to "getting what one wants" lies in spending the majority of one's efforts in managing the left-hand side of the equation, the *1→2→3→4* part.

The painful truth? *Most people never see the left-hand side of the formula.* Instead, they expend their energies on the right-hand side—the Results segment—endlessly shuffling, reorganizing, and repairing the random bad results created by those unseen and therefore unmanaged systems on the left-hand side.

Read that last paragraph again. It's the key to all of this.

And remember this rule of thumb: *unmanaged systems produce random results, and random results always add up to chaos.*

STRENGTH AND RESILIENCE ARE BY-PRODUCTS

In the process of rebuilding Centratel system by system, strength and resilience would evolve as by-products. Outside events would continue to challenge us with unexpected shake-ups, but the business will have become rugged and adaptable. Potential earthquakes would be anticipated; but because we would be prepared, they would be reduced to tremors. Until this point, earthquakes had been earthquakes and there had been too many.

And if what I saw for the business was true—that it was a primary system composed of component subsystems, each of which could be brought to high efficiency and strength—then it was logical this would be true for the other primary systems that were in immediate crisis: my physical self and my mental self. The process for fixing my body/mind difficulties would be the same process I was using to fix Centratel, and the results would be the same: my body would become powerful and resilient; my mind steady, calm, and efficient.

Again: *the systems mindset is super effective in every life situation because it deals with fundamental cause and effect—the basic truth of how the world mechanically operates everywhere and all the time.*

AN ANALOGY TO PACK AROUND

Imagine a cutaway view of a single-story house. See the first floor, full of belongings. You are there. Your TV is there. The refrigerator, sofa, your job, and your relationships are there. Everything in your life is there. You didn't know it until now, but down below is a basement full of machinery that never stops working. These silent machines are the systems of your life. They have been producing your life results, upstairs. Until now, because the machinery has been unseen and therefore unmanaged, it has been producing random and, many times, bad results. But things are different now. Your new systems mindset makes these machines visible. Now you will be eager to spend time down there in the basement—the basement you didn't know existed—adjusting that machinery to produce the exact results you want upstairs.

HOW MOST
PEOPLE SEE
THEIR LIVES

THE
SYSTEMS
MINDSET
VIEW OF LIFE

It's a very simple thing.

This is *it*! This is the systems mindset!

Learning How to Sleep

So, for any recurring problem there is a path to getting things repaired. Take the inefficient process apart and fix the separate pieces one by one.

Earlier I mentioned my problems with getting enough sleep. Sleep intertwines with numerous other biological, social, and relationship processes, but in that broad context one can't begin to find a solution to improving it. What did I do via systems methodology to cure this problem? I envisioned sleep as an independent primary system composed of subsystems.

This new approach led me to a doctor who specialized in sleep disorders. The doctor's recommendations had a strong theme—reduction of stress—and this led me to the subsystems of yoga, more sensible exercise, and meditation. Also, I would substantially reduce my intake of caffeine and sugar. There were other subsystems to modify, including changing the layout of my bedroom, removing the clock from the nightstand, and going to sleep at the same time every night. I would adopt a more consistent routine for preparing for bed. Another thing: testing indicated my requirements for sleep were less than average—six hours was enough—and so I should avoid long hours of tossing and turning in bed, vainly hoping for eight or nine hours. Lying in bed wide awake, mentally churning away, was stressful in itself, so when that happened, the sleep doctor said I should get up and read, work, or even exercise.

With the help of my regular doctor, I found my blood chemical subsystems were out of balance. Those imbalances affected my sleep in a bad way, and I began to fix that problem with supplements.

I had to reduce my hours at the office, and that meant getting the company to run itself without me having to be there every minute. Of course, that transformation was already underway, using precisely the same systems thinking.

continued

I got back to a healthy sleeping routine over the course of just a few weeks, literally doubling each night's sleep duration.

I attacked the overall problem by isolating the primary sleep system and then breaking it down into subsystems that could then be analyzed and manipulated. By taking an outside and slightly elevated vantage point, I was able to tweak my sleep process to become more and more efficient, one component at a time. This was pure mechanics.

Now if my sleep is less than what it should be, I can quickly identify the errant subsystem, tweak it back to normalcy, and instantly get back on track.

CHAPTER 5

Building the Machine

If there's a bustle in your hedgerow, don't be alarmed now,
it's just a spring clean for the May queen.

—From the song "Stairway to Heaven," written by Jimmy Page and Robert Plant and performed by Led Zeppelin (Atlantic Records, 1971)

Until that night when I had my awakening, my vision of Centratel was of an amorphous mass of interrelated and confused sights, sounds, and events. Unraveling had been impossible because of my presumption of chaotic complexity. Observing the workings of my business in a holistic way, I could not detect the simple internal subsystem inefficiencies that continually churned the business into bedlam.

THE SIREN SONG OF HOLISM

On a subliminal level, the feel-good holistic precept that everything is related to everything else so we should consider each of our actions in a global way encourages paralysis while it masks mechanical disarray. Any possibility of internal enhancement is subverted by the assumption that tampering with things over here will upset things over there. Inaction prevails. The notion that a butterfly flapping its wings over the jungles of Brazil will have an impact on the weather patterns over the mountains of New Hampshire is an interesting concept, but it induces a nonsensical paranoia. Although the precept illustrates the interrelation of life elements, taking it literally casts a spell of impotence over an individual's inclination to make changes.

In anyone's day-to-day existence, the Brazilian butterfly doesn't make a damn bit of difference.

The reason I had felt helpless to fix my business was because I had seen it as hopelessly complex and impenetrable. I never considered dissecting Centratel into simple subsystems that could be optimized one at a time. *Instead of fixing the individual mechanical inefficiencies within faulty subsystems, I had been spending my time cleaning up the recurring problems the faulty subsystems created.*

The first fifteen years at Centratel had agonizingly crawled by as I whacked the moles. It had seemed there was no other option but to stumble around in the middle of it and hope for some kind of magical, overarching solution. Maybe securing another loan from the bank, or landing the perfect employee, client, or consultant would do the trick.

I could have spent my whole life like that!

A NEW WORLD

My mini-enlightenment arrived just days prior to the payroll I was going to miss, and so I had to immediately find the money to pay staff and keep them working. Fire killing! But my new life quest was to begin the repair process. The gathering of cash to make the payroll had been reduced to an annoying, temporary hurdle.

With newfound emotional energy, I convinced my credit card company to raise my credit limit a bit so I could draw some cash. A friend gave me a loan. Offering a discount, I talked a high-volume client into paying for a year of answering service in advance. Several staff members agreed to delay cashing their paychecks.

We made it through the payroll crisis and I immediately turned my attention to creating three sets of documents that would get Centratel on track. *First, I would create the strategic objective, which would define us and set our direction. Second, I would put together the general operating principles document, which would serve as our "guideline for making decisions." Third, we would begin to write out working procedures, which would exactly detail every recurring process of the business.*

These documents would be the end result—and the tangible evidence—of our system-improvement quest. (I've been asked where I got the idea for these three specific written instruments. Truth is, they sprang up instantly and out of nowhere, late that night back in 1999. I have not modified their names or their intent since that moment.)

I completed the first draft of the strategic objective and began the principles document. Then I explained the new vision to my staff, outlining what we would do next and how they were going to assume new leadership postures. Tentatively at first, to get the hang of it, we began creating our working procedures: isolating, fixing, and documenting processes one at a time. For examination and repair, *we first selected the most damaging process and then moved on to the next most damaging one.*

From the moment of my late-night epiphany we were on a new path—and there was no turning back. Marching ahead without pause, we quickly began to see actual results. Confusion subsided and cash flow came under control. In the first few months my workweek dropped from over eighty hours to sixty. Then, in the next months it fell below forty.

Much of our early success had to do with the improvements we made in our internal communication system. Every moment, each of us knew what was going on in other parts of the business, and each of us could make decisions without stumbling in semantics or bureaucracy. You'll read more on communication in Part Three.

We made all critical human and mechanical systems redundant. The first year passed and we confidently hammered on. Customer and staff complaints declined dramatically, and chaos dissolved into serenity as we relentlessly improved our processes and mechanisms, one by one.

Our central focus was on working our systems.

This is key, so I will repeat: precisely channeling our efforts via the Strategic Objective and Operating Principles documents, *we tackled the most dysfunctional recurring systems first*, eliminating inefficiencies by generating working procedures. Plunging ahead relentlessly and refusing to be distracted, in that first year we rebuilt and documented several hundred existing systems. At the same time, we created new systems from scratch and discarded useless ones. Whew!

Through it all there was some employee turnover. A couple of managers wouldn't accept the new systems protocol and attending documentation. They were replaced by fresh faces who understood the systems-mindset approach. (Today, we attract and keep smart, goal-oriented people because of *how* we operate. Also, because of our hard-boiled approach, we are expert at precisely sizing up people in job interviews. Another reason we have great staff is because our compensation/benefit package is much higher than that of other similar businesses in our region and in the TAS/call center industry nationally. The high wages we pay are possible because we are internally super efficient. We have just a few people accomplishing a lot of work. More on staffing in Part Three.)

As error rates plunged, the overall quality of service dramatically improved, light years better than industry standards. The growth of the business went into high gear, and within two years of instituting our new paradigm we bought out all three of our local TAS competitors (and we bought five nonlocal ones as well). We absorbed both of our local voice-mail service rivals, too. And in that period, our TAS client base grew from three hundred to seven hundred.

It was system-improvement at its finest. And although we finished the heavy lifting long ago, today we still spend most of our time working our systems.

It took a long five years to fix Centratel. That's partly because we were figuring out the details of the new methodology from scratch. We invested—and sometimes inadvertently wasted—time and money as we experimented with new concepts, tried to find the right management people, and stumbled with the documentation.

But also during this period, our relationship with a third minor stockholder had a huge negative impact on our transformation. Unrelated to our new internal direction, this partnership began in the middle of the rejuvenation and included outsourcing some of our call-processing chores overseas. The quality of that outsourced work was horrible and resulted in a heavy loss of clients. In turn, this led to full-blown legalities. In the end, we were able to buy the partners out of the company, based upon a settlement agreement, but it's my guess that the bad partnership and resulting litigation cost us between two and three years of progress and a loss of 20 percent of our client base. Over those years, our new growth and bottom line were nearly swallowed up by this aberration.

If we were to do this again without having to develop the work-the-system process from scratch, and without having to deal with a messy partnership dissolution, I'm guessing it would take less than a year to fix things. (And through our WTS consulting business, we know a one-year time frame for fixing things is probably too conservative. For the business owner who's ready and willing to make changes, things move fast.)

There was a lot of work to do because in addition to the rebuilding efforts and the litigation, we had a business to run. But there was enough capacity to do what was necessary because of the tremendous time savings and heightened service quality we instantly realized.

It was a long five years, but despite the trial-and-error and experimentation necessary to institute this sweeping new approach—and the distracting legalities—I recall those years with satisfaction and nostalgia.

As mentioned, despite the setbacks and the additional system-improvement workload, my physical involvement with the company's daily operations continued to decline. Today, as mentioned before, I spend less than an hour a month working on Centratel business. Some of that hour is for the occasional quick remote management staff meeting and the rest of the hour is working with Andi, my CEO, attending to various R&D and long-term planning efforts. Most recently my surface involvement has had to do with the COVID-19 infrastructure rebuild we've had to make. But then again, Andi and Marcello have handled 99 percent of those details.

The Price to Be Paid

Abusing personal systems too often means introducing foreign substances into the miraculous mechanism that is the body. Perceiving themselves to be unhappy, people complicate their already flawed thinking processes by contaminating themselves. The ice-cold truth? One plus one always equals two, and with the same utter reliability a drunken night out on the town equals days of subpar physical and mental performance as the human body works overtime to repair itself from the chemical assault. We make our worlds worse in the long term by violating bodily systems in the short term, ignoring the simple truth that disruption of an efficient process always has its price. One could say that substance abuse is a criminal attack on one's own self.

ISOLATE-FIX-MAINTAIN

In parallel with the business resuscitation, there was no time to delay in regaining my health. As with the business, I personally had to change course right away and it was obvious what had to be done. I would handle my physical problems with the same systems methodology we were using to fix the business. Here's what I did:

1. I changed my vantage point. What exactly was making me ill? My doctor thought it was depression. But after belaboring that theory for way too long (and ingesting too many anti-depressants), it was suddenly clear to me this was not the source of the problem, but merely a symptom. My so-called depression stemmed from chronic lack of sleep, way too much stress, and the intake of foreign substances that were making things worse. Short-term gain. Long-term pain. I thought, *Of course I'm depressed! Under these hundred-hour workweek circumstances, anyone would be depressed!* I got outside, looked down from above, and saw my body was a collection of subsystems. My physical being was not a jumble of random happenings to which I could only react. It was a logical collection of systems, and some of those systems could be adjusted or altogether eliminated. And I could add new ones. So, I modified and removed a number of internal and external stress-inducing systems in order to prevent stress events from occurring in the first place. The biggest relief was in cutting back my office hours through the retooling of Centratel's processes.
2. I created a personal written plan by writing a simple one-page management document in which I described my goals and guidelines—my Personal Strategic Objective. I also created a Personal Operating Principles document that included a series of stress-reducing action items. Both documents had an uncanny similarity to the ones I had created for Centratel. They came together quickly.
3. Once circumstances got better, I continued to perform the stress-reducing action items on a dogmatic, routine basis. I still do. Always

working toward the ideal but not always reaching it, this preventative maintenance is what I have to do to stay healthy. That's it! The credo is to isolate-fix-maintain.

Stress-Reducing Action Items

It started with a simple list on a folded-over piece of paper. I wrote down five or six actions that would reduce anxiety. I carried the list in my pocket for a couple of weeks, jotting down additional ideas as they came to mind. My final list on this by-now crumpled page included fifteen action items, each a separate subsystem of its own. These points were not special in any way. Most people would agree that any one of them would help eliminate stress.

Here's the original raw list (I still have it): work fewer hours; lose ten pounds; go to the sleep disorder clinic to find out how to sleep (and actually *do* what the doctor advises); stop ingesting caffeinated drinks; learn and practice meditation and yoga. Exercise vigorously but not excessively at least four times a week. Eat good food. Drink lots of water. Ingest less sugar and salt. Get a full-screen blood test every three months and per those tests, take supplements until my blood chemicals come into balance. See friends at least once a week. Spend more one-on-one time with my family. Read a hard-copy book a minimum of one hour each day.

While I compiled the list, my thought was that when it was completed, it would be sensible to choose just some of the items on the list, whichever ones seemed best. However, when the list was complete I decided to implement all fifteen items, leaving nothing out. Why should any of them be dismissed if each one contributed to my well-being? It was a challenging list, difficult to fully implement, but I gave it my best shot, viewing each of my action items as a separate subsystem and incorporating every one of them into the primary system that was my life at that time. But even so—because I had become such a physical and mental mess—it took two years to get completely healthy again. Decades of stress damage was not unraveled overnight.

Today, do I live every minute by these standards? No, but I get close.

An Example of System-Improvement: Paying the Bills via Bill-Payer

Note: this is an example of replacing a haphazard and error-prone recurring chore with a highly efficient, predictable system. I describe a series of events that occurred fifteen years ago. Back then, only a small number of business owners were paying bills online. Now it's pretty much universal.[4]

For years, a nagging problem at Centratel was the time and effort it took me to pay bills. The time I spent performing this function contributed nothing to profitability, and each month required ten to fourteen hours of my time to process the sixty to eighty payables to our various vendors. I wrote the checks, entered the transactions into the check register, stuffed the checks into envelopes, and mailed them.

Then there was the filing and the bookkeeping entries. As we grew, it became too time-consuming for me, and in my new systems quest to automate, delegate, and delete, I hired a part-time bookkeeper to do the task. But that created an unintended consequence. The expenditures were not being questioned by our bookkeeper with the same intensity that I, the owner of the company, would study and question them. There were double payments as well as payments for services that we no longer utilized. There were late fees, too, because some bills simply weren't paid on time. (And yes, I ultimately dismissed that bookkeeper.)

The solution: our bank's online bill-payer feature and a new bookkeeper. These days, we seldom write checks. Ninety percent of recurring monthly bills are the same amount each month, and the bank software is programmed to pay these bills automatically. QuickBooks automatically logs these monthly payments too, so there is literally nothing to do in order to cover these bills.

For a payable in which the billed amount changes monthly, it's easy for our bookkeeper to review the statement and then insert the exact amount both online and in QuickBooks.

---

4 For this fourth edition, I've left this story intact because it very simply illustrates moving from chaos to control via a relatively tiny amount of one-time system-improvement work.

This is a good example of investing time to set up a new mechanism and then benefiting forever from the effort. When this transformation happened so many years ago, it took me maybe fifteen hours of additional work to program vendors into the bank bill-payer software—the same amount of time that had been required *every* month to pay bills with the old routine.

Today I spend zero time processing payables and there is never an error, never a late fee. (I know this because I get a monthly report showing every expenditure.) The overall time savings for me has been staggering: fifteen hours per month multiplied by fifteen years. That's equal to almost a year and a half of forty-hour workweeks!

At home I use the same system to pay our personal bills, but of course I do it myself. And now bill-payer is enhanced by bank auto-withdrawal features. Homeowner association dues, water, electricity, and everything else—for two homes, one in Oregon and one in Kentucky—are paid on time with little input from me. In a couple of quick sit-down sessions, it takes maybe fifteen minutes per month to open the bills and make sure everything is OK.

Bill-payer is the quintessential illustration of systems thinking, a colossal time saver and efficiency enhancer both at work and at home.

The following note is from our in-house CPA, Cheryl, just before publication of this fourth edition. (Note that today, Centratel is grossing 100 times what it was grossing back at the beginning when I was personally paying the bills.)

Sam, this is what we are currently doing:

1. *We moved the bulk of our monthly recurring bills to autopay on the (air miles) credit card. Then, when the vendor statements are received (either by mail or email), they are reviewed for accuracy.*
2. *Each month, we do manually pay 8 to 10 bills by check because the vendors charge us to use the credit card as payment. These are set up as Memorized Transactions in QuickBooks, so to pay by check basically takes a couple of clicks to print.*

continued

3. *We also pay 3 to 5 random payments per month by check (refunds, referral fees, seldom-used services, etc.).*
4. *Checks are cut only on the 10th and 25th, unless for some reason there is an urgency.*
5. *All in all, it is a very streamlined system, maybe taking a total of a couple of hours per month.*

—CT

CHAPTER 6

Systems Revealed, Systems Managed

A person needs new experiences. They jar something deep inside, allowing him to grow. Without change, something sleeps inside us, and seldom awakens. The sleeper must awake!

—Duke Leto Atreides (Jüregen Prochnow), from the movie *Dune* (Universal Pictures, 1984)

Note: *You must "get it" if this new system-improvement approach to life is going to stick. So, if you're still trying to make sense of all this, I present the next two summary chapters in a meditative, slightly rambling tone. There is repetition, too, as I metaphorically and directly render the core of the mindset. I want you to get it!—SC*

CONVERGING ROOTS

Your day is under your command. Chronic shortages of time and money, emergency decision-making, and dealing with less-than-amusing people are history. Starting with a subtle yet penetrating shift in perspective, you have done the necessary work to eliminate chaos from your life . . .

You discovered that the pathway to control is to objectively observe and then optimize your mechanical and biological processes. You adjusted your systems carefully, one at a time.

One dictionary's definition of *system* is "a group of interacting, interrelated, or interdependent elements forming a complex whole." That's perfect.

You've learned that systems don't operate randomly. Like computer code, they relentlessly execute in linear 1-2-3-4 sequence according to their construction. In your world, like everyone else's world, they are embedded wall to wall. And now you know that for sure.

These systems *are* your life! Sometimes your systems work alone, but things are best when they work together.

You wake, study, read, exercise, and eat. You breathe, walk, and digest your most recent meal. You go to work, talk to friends, drive to the store to pick up groceries for dinner. You put gas in the car. You earn money and put it in the bank. Later, you pay the bills.

You're always aware that every one of these accomplishments was a 1-2-3-4 process that executed over time.

Some of your systems are aligned to help you reach your goals, while a few others silently—or loudly—still sabotage your best efforts.

Today, you're making refinements in those few dysfunctional systems that still pull you down, manhandling them into efficiency, pointing them in the directions you want them to point, producing the results you want them to produce. (You are, of course, creating useful ones from scratch as you work hard to discard the remaining bad ones.)

Often during the day, even if it's just for a second or two, you quietly contemplate the primary system that is your life. In your quick, on-the-fly meditative moments you remember that your life is composed of subsystems, and that each of those subsystems is composed of sub-subsystems. You explore your way down further, through the multiplying, expanding, and intertwining roots. Then, still in your head, briefly ruminating, you turn around and work your way back up toward the top. As those roots come together and thicken into a single trunk, you see that they add up to the ultimate primary system that is you.

You are a system of systems!

And you always remember that the essence of your work, health, and relationships lies within systems; and although they are veiled behind the buzz of everyday consciousness, there is nothing complicated about them—or about their management.

You see life more accurately. You're one layer deeper than the people around you. In this more concise view of reality, you spend your days extracting, examining, and improving your systems one by one, and you know absolutely that the reward for this incremental approach is that peace and prosperity have quietly entered through the side door.

OH. YOU'RE NOT *THERE* YET?

OK, so you're not *there* yet. Then take a minute, slow down, and find a place where you won't be distracted. Let's work together toward the thrilling instant when the systems mindset takes hold.

Visualize each of the following processes and note the commonality: *sequential execution over time to produce an end result.*

In this moment, consciously concentrate on your world of systems . . . but trust that soon you will effortlessly carry this perception through the day, always living in this place of one layer deeper, easily observing the real-time mechanical processes that generate the happenings of the day.

Suspended in this deeper layer, this *right here, right now* place, you're going to discover the spiritual wonderment you have been seeking.

Here we go. Follow me here: Consider your mechanical world. Start by imagining the closed set of sequential actions over time necessary to drive a car from point A to point B. (Open the door, get in, put the seat belt on, press the start button, carefully check your surroundings, put the car in drive, head out toward point B, etc.)

Describe to yourself the specific linear steps—both mechanical and human—involved in finding a potential customer, making a presentation, and closing a sale. Think about the process of interviewing and hiring a new employee and then what you must do to keep this person for the long term while maximizing his or her contribution. Think about nurturing an intimate relationship, coping with the terminal illness of a parent, giving birth. Then there are the mundane processes of preparing a financial report, writing a paper for a college course, raking the yard, cleaning the house, dumping the trash, doing the wash.

Now ponder your own miraculous human body-mechanism that propels you through this material world moment to moment. Observe its innumerable individual biological and mechanical subsystems, nearly all of which function without any conscious guidance by you.

Use your imagination, and in your immediate proximity—right now—look around, wherever you are, to see the uncountable sequences that are in motion, most going unnoticed until now. You see that some of these processes don't matter too much, but others have a large effect on your happiness and the happiness of those around you.

Yes, systems intertwine and affect one another. Yet first they are separate entities.

Although almost all of your life processes are automatic, there are many you perform consciously. By focusing on the systems that are within your circle of influence you'll see that tweaking them to higher efficiency is almost always possible.

You'll know when you get it because within your moment-to-moment experience you will clearly and without conscious effort see the individual systems around you. You will know for sure that they are all separate from each other—on the street, at the airport, at home, in the mirror . . . and that they are all in constant motion. No longer will you feel suspended in a swirling and chaotic conglomeration of sights, sounds, and events.

And you know that all of these systems are propelled by a mysterious force, a force that many of us choose to call God.

The new vision will be natural and unforced, and you will wonder why you didn't see with this clarity before.

Yes, the moment you *get it*, you'll know it!

It could be right now, as you read these lines. Or maybe next week . . .

The Systems Mindset Is a System

Located in your head, the systems mindset is itself the master management tool used to direct all your other personal and business systems. It's the key mechanism for making the right moves, moment to moment, so you can engineer an efficient life: one of serenity, prosperity, and contribution. Focus on the mindset. Study and experiment with it. Internalize it. Wallow in it.

SYSTEM MANAGEMENT IS WHAT YOU'RE AFTER

You can list a multitude of minor individual systems that are necessary for just getting through the day, not to mention major primary systems such as running a business or holding a job, coping with college, raising children, making retirement vibrant and meaningful, or just staying level-headed while balancing a household, negotiating with family members, and providing an income. (I was a single parent of two children for fifteen years and—so many of you know it's true—this role is the supreme test of a human's ability to simultaneously kill fires, build something for the future, and stay sane.)

Each of your personal systems has direction and thrust. Each is headed somewhere, attempting to accomplish something, driven by an enigmatic power.

Will you manage your systems or will you let them operate randomly?

Your system trajectories are affected by genetically determined patterns, learned formulas, cultural codes, bias based on race and gender or whatever, humanitarian predilections, simple self-interest, and of course the standard physical predispositions for appetite, sleep, sex, and survival.

And again, here is the rub: your unmanaged systems are headed in oblique directions, randomly dissipating or outright opposing your efforts to reach your conscious goals.

At best, a system combines with other systems to help you reach desired objectives. At worst, an errant system invisibly creates problems that manifest themselves subversively, contributing to a gnawing anxiety that you are not in control of your life.

That anxious feeling is not rare. *Most people are not in control of their existences, especially if the definition of control includes the qualifier "I am getting what I want in my life."*

Living can seem complicated, but that complexity doesn't leave you helpless to get a grip on circumstances, because one at a time you can take action on relatively simple subsystem components that you pluck out of the chaos. Or maybe there are systems that are truly fouling up your life, in which case your best bet is to altogether eliminate them from your existence.

This is system management in its most elemental form, and the beautiful aspect of it is that neither your perception of the intricacy of it nor your tendency to lean in certain directions will stop you from improving these mechanisms.

I'll add this here: In our culture, it is common to call the simultaneous handling of the day's umpteen events *multitasking*. This is a flawed expression because it suggests that the conscious, hands-on command of multiple concurrent undertakings is some kind of laudable accomplishment.

Instead, the term *system management* is what we're after. It defines a thought-out life-orchestration in which one has a firm grip on details and is not living at the edge of crisis, floating along on hope, fingers crossed, prayers recited, and obsessions indulged.

So, drop the idea that life is convoluted and mysterious and get to work repairing the simple underlying inefficient mechanisms one by one!

And know this for certain as you consider your own management abilities: trying to find peace and life-control through drugs, food, work, money, silly psychobabble, fanatical adherence to religious or political dogma, running away, or excessive preoccupation with the extraneous—or any other obsession—is an abomination of the simplicity of it all. It's not management. It's evasion and masking and avoidance. These are wholesale quick-fix applications that falsely promise to soothe life's complexities in one fell swoop. Easy buttons! Instead, you'll go deep inside and fix building-block components one at a time. You'll go to work! This is about making small, mechanical betterments in subsystems that over time will add up to a primary system made of steel. This is how you will get where you want to go.

AGAIN: THE SUBVERSIVE HOLISTIC THOUGHT PROCESS

The concepts of holism and globalism are intricately woven into the fabric of our culture. With that, we often suppose an entire mechanism is faulty and so we think we must completely replace that mechanism. This overreaction is too many times rooted in feel-good emotionalism that obscures a more sensible path in which one simply studies a primary system's mechanical construction and then fixes a faulty component. From the start, the primary system is probably better than OK, working well in most situations. Rather than starting from scratch, which in itself introduces a whole host of challenges and unintended consequences, could we just make a simple internal adjustment?

You know the clichés. "Don't throw the baby out with the bathwater" and "Don't cut off your nose to spite your face."

THIS IS HOW SUCCESSFUL PEOPLE NEGOTIATE THEIR DAYS

If you are like most people, you have not *consciously* considered the involvement of systems in your not-so-perfect daily life. Therefore, you have not considered *consciously* tweaking those systems in order to eliminate problems from occurring in the first place. *For most people, whacking emerging moles is how life is played out. There is no thought of burrowing deep into the mole hole for some serious mole extermination.*

The little moles are furry, cute-faced decoys that distract us from the critical moves we should be making. Let's burrow deep inside their tunnels and ruthlessly eradicate them all. And then, before we leave, let's do what we have to do so no more moles show up later. After that, confident they will never distract us again, we'll climb back above ground and start working the other processes of our lives that will take us where we want to go.

Here is a mechanical truth: *one can compensate for the negative outcome of a recurring problem, but without repairing the errant process that caused it, the problem will undoubtedly occur again.*

Few people understand the systems approach of successful leaders who intuitively grasp that a seemingly isolated problem is not isolated at all. These system-improvement specialists see a problem as the result of a flaw in an errant system—a system that can be tweaked. For these leaders—yes, way more often from the private sector than from the public sector (don't get me started . . .)—a problem is not a setback just to be corrected and then written off. It's a wake-up call. It's a "red flag for improvement." This posture dictates that *once the immediate negative outcome is fixed, there is a mandatory second step. It is this second step that is key: the problem's cause is traced to the errant subsystem that caused it, which is then modified so the problem won't happen again.*

This is how successful people negotiate their days!

And through the astute business leader's observation, this problem in the primary system calls not just for a subsystem modification, but also for the corrected subsystem's documentation. The unanticipated positive consequence of this work? *The enhancement and documentation will not only prevent the error from happening again, it will cause the primary system to be incrementally more robust and reliable than before the problem occurred.* Taking the second step to fix the cause of the problem distinguishes people who are in control from people who are not in control—the successful from the unsuccessful.

In a business, *the improvement of a system is a system-improvement, and the documentation of that system-improvement is a working procedure.* We'll get to that in Part Two.

The documentation of each revision is critical. In a business, *it has to happen.*

Again, by focusing on repairing problems in this way, the primary system becomes ever more efficient. Rough edges disappear. It's a wondrous thing because as time passes, the mechanism gets better and better. *Imagine a mechanical system that improves with time rather than wears out!* Effective leaders understand this.

FOR YOU, NO MORE FIRE KILLING

At the start, these one-by-one efforts can seem daunting. You work at them for a while and then ask, "When will all these problems cease, and when can I stop fixing and documenting?" But you carry on. After plugging along for a short while more, you notice the pace and quantity of incoming glitches has decreased. You see the demands for fire killings aren't coming so fast . . . and this is the moment in time when a potent conviction takes hold. Now, with fervor, you accelerate the repair process so even fewer errors occur, and your organization and your personal life become ever smoother and more efficient. Profits improve while the vitality and resilience of both your business and yourself increase.

Now you're consciously managing your life, working your systems, no longer a victim of circumstance.

You'll never go back!

Once your new documented processes and procedures are in place and functional, you will perform routine reviews of the entire collection. What will be the end result of these ongoing reviews? Your operation's increased efficiency and bottom line will be maintained over the long term. And for you personally? No more fire killing as a way of life, and much more free time. (We'll talk more of routine maintenance in Part Three.)

Your Job

Your task is to optimize one system after another, not careen through the day randomly taking care of whatever problems erupt.

Your job is not to be a fire killer. Your job is to prevent fires.

HEAVY SEAS

For Centratel, the system-improvement process continues twenty-one years after the implementation of the Method. Now, problems are so few that when one surfaces, my staff pounces on it with a vengeance. It's hard to describe the deep satisfaction of leading a company that operates this way. Like Centratel, my personal existence still has its occasional unexpected ups and downs, but now it's tremendously more resilient and I am well prepared to absorb high pressure and unexpected blows.

This is what I want for you.

For the apple vendor, an overturned apple cart is a disaster, but an apple falling off the side of the cart now and then is a small, easy-to-deal-with occurrence. There is no getting away from random problems that are caused by an unexpected circumstance or unpredictable human error. That's life!

In organizations and in individual lives, outright mistakes account for only a small percentage of total errors. Most problems stem from nonexistent process management and show themselves as "errors of omission." Your new positioning will dramatically reduce this form of inefficiency. (Errors of omission are addressed in Part Three.)

What about the unexpected heavy seas of a debilitating injury or the loss of a loved one? Here it is again: strength and resilience are by-products of the Work the System Method. A life that is stronger and more resilient will be better able to navigate the inevitable dark and turbulent waters.

Business Is Art

The following hypothesis was suggested to me by a reader who explained it beautifully, and I paraphrase from memory: "Who says art must include a canvas, sculpture, or musical instrument? *Art is creativity, and is there a better example of a creative endeavor than building a successful business?* Indeed, business is art in its purest form! The painter and the musician shouldn't scoff at the entrepreneur or corporate chief who must take hard, cold life itself—sights, sounds, events, things, people—and stir them into an efficient enough mixture to produce a successful business, something beneficial for all concerned."

Business IS art. It's a heroic undertaking, and within a successful business lies two wonderful by-products: real and useful value to others—employees and customers—and personal income for the creator.

NOTICING POOR SYSTEM MANAGEMENT

When you get a feel for system management in your daily life, you will notice when it isn't happening around you. As you interact with the world you'll find yourself critiquing what works and what doesn't. You'll be hyper-aware of the processes others control—or don't control. This new posture as an informal service-quality observer will go with you everywhere.

You will understand the real reasons why people who promise to call don't call. Why there is lousy service in certain restaurants, retail stores, and hotels. Why there is haphazard communication with a service provider. You will develop a knack for instantly recognizing shoddy workmanship, missed deadlines, promises not kept, bad attitudes, and sloppy execution. You'll know for sure that these dysfunctional human performances are the logical end result of poor process engineering and/or maintenance, both organizational and personal. Human dysfunction is pervasive; and as soon as your new systems-vision takes hold, you will see these inefficiencies all around you. But when you encounter silky-smooth proficiency in an organization or another individual, you will notice that too, and you will appreciate it for the splendid thing it is.

When you're at the receiving end of poor service, remember that the ultimate problem is not with the person who is facing you, who may indeed be rude or uncaring, but with the individual at the top of the organization who is not managing properly. Even so, be sympathetic with that leader. Most people don't understand the system-improvement methodology or even that there is such a thing. With best intentions and working hard, they stumble along, batting off the fastballs as they come hurtling in from all directions. I was like that.

PERSONAL RELATIONSHIP SYSTEMS

What about selfish people who circumvent the rules and don't consider others? Be careful here, too. Don't confuse someone's personality flaw with their mechanical problem, which could be a simple lack of attention to the details of individual relationship systems. How one goes about cultivating good relationships is also a system, and the methodology must be set up with care and executed with consistency. *For thoughtless people, the base problem is not usually a personality flaw, but the lack of a functional relationship-maintenance protocol.*

This error of omission creates a vicious circle. These people do not return calls or remember birthdays, say hello to strangers, spontaneously smile, send thank-you notes, extend invitations, or really listen while in a conversation. They don't show interest in the vicissitudes or successes of the people right in front of them. They are often know-it-alls. The consequence is they receive little positive attention in return. These lonely people feel rejected and alienated, yet they dig themselves deeper and deeper into loneliness, getting sourer on life as the years pass by. Is it their fault? Well, mechanically speaking, yes it is.

It sounds antiseptic, but it's the simple truth: lonely people don't apply the recurring-relationship fundamentals necessary to make and keep friends. Maybe they don't care enough, or more likely they just don't understand the mechanical reality that having friends requires forethought and routine effort.

Despite the near perfection of our natural world, look around right now and notice that the human qualities of dependability and consistency are in short supply. And because they are in short supply, people accept that condition as normal. Actually, people *should* accept it as normal. It *is* normal! And happily for you, this means standing out from the crowd won't take much effort. The people around you will start to notice your quick execution of detail, your consistent reliability, and the congruency between what you say and what you do. They will especially feel your calm, confident comportment, especially that you are in control of your existence. People can depend on you and know what to expect and this makes you attractive to them. New customers, great employees, and reliable friends will be drawn to you because you doggedly adhere to the simple system-management tenets for cultivating great relationships.

YOUR LIFE: PROBLEMATIC OR ORDERLY?

So, how do you perceive your life? Do you see it as problematic—unfair, unpredictable, and inhospitable? Or do you view it as orderly and directed? Yet again, this isn't a matter of having a positive or a negative attitude or adopting some philosophical stance based on feel-good theory. This is about logic, simplicity, and mechanics.

How do you see your life?

A Certain Billionaire

My companion and I were on vacation in Siena, Italy. We'd been there just a few days, and at night the jetlag of crossing ten time zones had me entertaining strange dreams. A lucid midnight sojourn inspired this 2:00 a.m. writing session.

In my dream, a famous multibillionaire asked me to take the equivalent of the chief operations officer position for his conglomeration of several hundred international corporations.

Upon receiving the offer in this tycoon's ad hoc boardroom located on the tarmac of an airport somewhere, my central dream-thought as I faced him was that I would succeed. I would succeed despite my small-town heritage, my lack of an advanced academic degree, and the shortage of other seemingly mandatory background requisites. My challenges would be prosaic, limited to dealing with frequent travel, the inevitable corporate personality clashes, and whether or not being a part of the enterprise would cause me to feel trapped in a cage. (My current world is smaller, but without restraint I roam it as I please.)

Why was I confident in this dream? It was because my new position would entail dealing with the same simple mechanical realities of cause and effect that I deal with now, just on a larger scale. I would successfully work my systems in this gigantic corporate-conglomerate structure where, symbolically speaking, one plus one would equal two, just like everywhere else. Other than the scale of the endeavor, my tasks would be no different from the day-to-day tasks I already handle.

CHAPTER 7

Getting It: A Room Full of Boxes

I'm trying to free your mind, Neo. But I can only show you the door. You're the one who has to walk through it.

—Morpheus (Laurence Fishburne) to Neo (Keanu Reeves), from the movie *The Matrix* (Warner Bros. Pictures, 1999)

First you work your systems. Then your systems do the work.

Imagine the following metaphorical scenario.

Recently it became clear that one of the managers in the company where you work had neglected his department. It showed in the lack of output and the general chaos.

Yesterday he was fired.

It's too bad the department manager lost his job, but you understand why it happened. This sometimes occurs and when it does, you usually see it firsthand. You are a troubleshooter for your organization and your role is to get the apples back on the cart when they fall off.

You make your way to the department, which occupies a single large room in your building.

Into the dimly lit room you walk. You've been here before. The room is empty except for several dozen wooden boxes, varying from shoebox to refrigerator size. The boxes, each with a hinged wooden lid, are scattered haphazardly around the room. You know that inside each box you'll find a mechanical apparatus, each unique and each made up of an assemblage of gears, wires, and levers: small machines.

For sure these devices have been neglected. Some need repair. They all need maintenance.

You begin by replacing the burned-out light bulbs in the ceiling so you can see what you're doing, and then you push the boxes around so they are in order. You take time to organize them so you can perform your work on their contents in a systematic way.

It's just how you do things.

Besides the replacement light bulbs for the room, you've brought spare parts, your toolbox, and of course you have written technical instructions should there be questions about the devices within the boxes. The instructions are understandable and well thought-out. You know this because you are the one who supervised their creation.

Because of the long-term neglect of the contents of these boxes, you knew before you came here that completing this job would require a long day. You hunker down and get to work.

You open the lid of the first box, the largest one. You see the device within, and because you are trained in the operation and repair of such machines, it all makes sense: it is clear to you what this mechanism does and how it is put together. Peering deeper into the box to carefully view the intricacies, it is apparent that adjustments are necessary. You patiently and systematically reach in and make those adjustments.

In the course of your work on this machine, you notice an obsolete component. You replace it with an updated version. (You always carry spares.) This revision will make the machine operate faster—more efficiently and reliably.

Then you clean and oil the moving parts.

You thoroughly test the machine to make sure it's working flawlessly. It is.

On the inside of the lid of the box, you write your name and the date, along with a brief summary of what you did so when the new department manager shows up for the first day of work, next week, he or she will know what you've done and when you did it.

Gently closing the lid, you move on to the next box, one that is just a bit smaller. You repeat the process. One by one you move through all the boxes, ending with the tiniest one. You've made sure the unique mechanisms within all the boxes are operating perfectly.

It indeed took the entire day to complete your work, but the time went quickly—it was fun and satisfying as you spent your hours in a creative, constructive flow-space.

You've finished, and now you stand in the doorway and take a last look around the room. The boxes are in neat rows, their lids closed, and you are confident the devices within each of the boxes are all working perfectly.

You know the department's output will be very good now because each of its prime mechanisms is working flawlessly. How could it be otherwise? And you know the new department manager will be system-improvement oriented, watching over the details, not allowing things to fall back into disarray. There will be routine maintenance. And you will be called in again if there is a major problem.

As you turn off the lights and walk out the door, you are pleased with your work and with yourself.

Your day has been zero-defect.

There it is—the systems-mindset approach in which one sees life as a collection of individual systems (or call them processes or mechanisms or machines) that are to be, one by one, isolated and then made perfect. And once perfected, routinely coddled for maintenance and upgrading.

Here's the no-brainer that eludes most people: in the course of a day and in the course of a life, each movement we make is a single step in a linear sequence of steps intended to accomplish one or another goal. *Each thing we do is a component of a system, a system that has a purpose, whether it is managed or not.*

You are going to be a project engineer, directing the events of the day, not a feather in the wind blowing around at the mercy of whatever wind happens to be blowing.

My intention here in Part One has been to present illustrations and evidence from a variety of angles so you will see the mechanisms of your life on a visceral level. I'm being repetitive, hammering the concepts home. Are you there yet? If not, continue to be patient as I replay the elements of the new perspective while introducing some how-tos.

If you don't experience the aha! moment soon, don't worry about it. It's OK. The fake-it-'til-you-make-it routine is a potent way to get there.

But let's quickly go through this again.

THE MOST SENSIBLE THING TO DO

You know this by now. First, make the various systems consciously visible. Second, bring each to the foreground for examination and quick initial documentation. Third, examine. Fourth, adjust and document to final form. Fifth, maintain.

By plucking individual systems out of the amorphous mass of your real-time existence—that intense conglomeration of sights, sounds, and events that has been your life—you can assess and then precisely manipulate their workings. But first you must see them.

Again, *reaching the point where you see the systems around you is the first and most significant step*. It's a mini-enlightenment. When the epiphany arrives, you will have internalized the fact that systems make up your life and you will know that assertively directing them is leadership at the most fundamental level. You will view your existence with new clarity. Details will be sharper and more vivid, the colors more vibrant. Never again will you perceive your world as a confused assortment of people, objects, and situations.

What seemed complex before will now be revealed to be elementary.

Certain in your new vision, you will change your strategy from fire killing to system-improvement because it is the most sensible thing to do. Will you become addicted to system-improvement the way you were previously addicted to fire killing?

Yes.

YOU MUST STAND OUTSIDE OF IT

If you want to see where you fit within the machine that is your life, you must observe it from an external vantage point. *You must stand outside of it if you are to see how you are a part of it.*

There is nothing shadowy in this. This is about seeing your existence more precisely.

There is no need for me to list a ten-step process for making the Method produce results. You must simply see the processes in your life with the same clarity with which, in this moment, you perceive the physical objects around you. Once that happens, the rest will be fill-in-the-blanks sensibility. The days will slide by like a waltz.

After you've lived with your new mindset for a short while, you will ask yourself, "Why couldn't I see this before?" You'll look back on your previous life and observe that, embroiled in minutiae, you were blind to the processes that lay beneath the happenings of the day. You'll remember the moment the shroud lifted, when sequential life systems became visible and your perception of the world's workings shifted. You will remember your first inklings of the potency of systems methodology and how quickly it proved itself in action. Tangible rewards came fast. And you'll remember that removing the shroud didn't take a whole lot of faith or hard work, just some quiet observation.

IT'S WHAT YOU DO

Now you know, and thus you will act. Consider the following associated points.

First, *it's what one does that counts.* Good intentions, a positive attitude, and passionate enthusiasm are not nearly enough. What matters are the physical actions one takes.

Second, *getting things right most of the time is good enough.* And the things that don't come out well are just part of the overhead: the cost of doing business, of taking risks, of uncontrollable external confusion, of coping with events that are sometimes one step ahead of your best efforts; of being alive. *As by-products of your advancement forward, accept that less-than-perfect events are going to happen. Three steps forward and one step back is the way it goes.*

Remember what Forrest said . . .

Third, remember that *most people don't fail by making overt mistakes. They fail because they don't take action.* If you fall into this category, prepare to change your ways.

YOUR DAY WILL NEVER BE THE SAME

It is incredibly satisfying to have control—for the world to make sense, and to be able to determine your own destiny. And as time marches on you'll become tenacious about maintaining this new command because life just keeps getting better.

I belabor this point because it is key: *once the work-the-system methodology is internalized and applied, you will be a different person living a different life.* No more feeling anxious in the morning, your head filling with encroaching worries even before you get out of bed. During the day, no more long hours spent killing fires. No more evenings spent buried in paperwork or sitting exhausted, zombielike in front of the TV with zero hope of relief tomorrow.

Instead, at the end of the day you will look back to see that you spent your hours immersed in one-time creative projects and productive conversations with staff, customers, friends, and family. You'll feel gratification that the day's efforts were further incremental steps toward even more freedom and prosperity. You'll no longer pine for the big break, because it's clear the big break is already occurring piece by piece, step by step.

In charge of your life from dawn to dusk, you'll know you are building your destiny in a solid and honorable way.

In your day, you will have not just made incremental progress toward your most important goals, you will also have spent time with the people who matter most to you.

There's plenty of money. Your circle of influence continues to expand.

You are happy with yourself. You know why your life is what you always wanted it to be. It's because of you: *you did that to you!*

The systems mindset is logical, but it's magical, too, as the world you used to take for granted erupts into magnificence: simple and beautiful and predictable.

Violating a Social System

In Italy, we were staying in a small guesthouse in the tiny coastal town of Monterosso. One early morning I sat alone at a breakfast table in the corner of the dining room. Other tourists surrounded me, quietly enjoying their cappuccinos and pastries. I worked on my laptop, putting the final touches on the first edition of this book, my breakfast dishes pushed aside.

The manager of the guesthouse approached. In halting yet perfect English she asked, *"Are you finished with your breakfast?"*

I answered, "*Sì.*"

Then she said, *"Please. To work, take your computer to the lobby downstairs. This is a place of breakfast."*

That elegant phrase—this is a place of breakfast—was perfect. In her wonderfully nuanced English, my host got directly to the point and I instantly understood. There was no quibbling with the logic. I was working in a place of breakfast, and working in this place was wrong. Italians consider eating a semi-sacred process that should never be sullied by work.

My incursion was callous. I was not respecting a process that had been operating for scores of generations.

I moved downstairs to the lobby, a place where many things—including a busy American with his laptop—were welcome.

It's understandable how Europeans can sometimes consider Americans crass, as we too often fail to leave our overbearing quirks at home. It was a humbling reminder that I must always respect the systems of others.

PART TWO

MAKE IT SO

CHAPTER 8

Swallowing the Horse Pill

There are some people who live in a dream world, and there are some who face reality; and then there are those who turn one into the other.

—Douglas Everett

In your business, having your protocols written down is as important as what you think or say.

Here in Part Two, I describe the fundamentals of work-the-system documentation. They are presented here as we use them at Centratel, but you are welcome to copy and customize them. (And to make the process simple and thorough, investigate Business Documentation Software in Appendix H and at www.businessdocumentationsoftware.com.)

With your documentation you will transform ephemeral, feather-in-the-wind organic processes into iron-clad machines that do your exact bidding every single time.

Here's an analogy for the three work-the-system documents (and it will especially resonate for residents of the United States). The strategic objective is your Declaration of Independence, your mandate for a better future. The general operating principles document is your Constitution, a set of guidelines for future decision-making. The working procedures are your laws, the rules of your game.

Can you imagine a representative government not having its foundational canons recorded in written form? Why would it be any different for your business or your job? (Does a dictator want documented guidance/structural documentation? Not so much. It tends to get in the way of the tyrant's self-serving, free-form manipulations.)

First you will create the strategic objective. Then, the operating principles. These documents establish your bearing. They will keep you sailing straight. Putting them together won't take long. And then you will begin your working procedures, and it is here that you will spend most of your future time.

Again, the enhancement of a system is a system-improvement, and the documentation of that improvement is a working procedure.

THE UNASSUMING NATURE OF WHAT MUST BE DONE

One day not long after the light bulb switched on in my head, I realized that creating the necessary documentation would not be flashy. The mission would sometimes be tedious as it was clear that cataloging all of our systems would take time. The working procedures would not fall into place as easily as the first two controlling documents, the strategic objective and the general operating principles.

I saw firsthand that within my own TAS industry few owners perceive their business from an outside and slightly elevated perspective. They thrash within the inner workings, self-satisfied in their frenzies, endlessly smacking those moles. I realized immediately that my industry was not unique. Few small-business owners document their direction, and still fewer chronicle their processes.

Why is that? I thought. If this documentation methodology is so simple and potent, why aren't more small-business owners doing it? Could it be because documentation work is perceived to be too boring? Too tedious? *Too bureaucratic?* Yes, most business owners consider documentation to be all of those things! And so this bleak characterization camouflages the viability of it, and for this reason few small business owners undertake the quest. They don't do it because it's not dramatic! And there is this: *last-minute fire killing is not just dramatic, but it also satisfies a powerfully addictive craving, providing the business owner an instant ego boost fueled by adrenaline and/or cortisol.* (Can one be addicted to cortisol? Yes.) [5]

I suddenly realized that, yes, the *unassuming nature of creating documentation masks its viability!* This revelation instilled in me a passion to tackle the cataloging tasks that lay ahead. I kicked into high gear.

In any case, if I was to establish solid direction, hone processes to perfection, and then expect those processes to continue to be perfect in the future, it was logical the direction and processes would have to be written down. And then—there was no getting around it—the next prosaic task would be to ensure that my staff precisely followed the documentation.

My next moves were obvious, but creating the documentation would take time away from the nonstop efforts of keeping the business afloat day to day. Business demands would not step aside while we improved processes and wrote up attending paperwork, and I wondered if we could actually find the time to write everything down. But then I realized this was a moot question. Accomplishing the work was mandatory because if we didn't do it, the company would fail—and my guess was that if we *did* do it, the company would flourish. So I swallowed the huge horse pill that there was some serious work to do—unexciting yet potent documentation work—and plunged ahead full steam.

Motivating Yourself

To get off the mark, remember there will never be an easy button you can push to make everything instantly better. *Documenting systems takes time and focus. But you are already working hard and long, so what's the big deal?* Simply tell yourself that you must continue to work hard for just a bit longer. And think about heroics. Yes, documentation can be seen as boring, but conjuring up the fortitude to accomplish it is courageous.

5 "Just as you can be addicted to meth or heroin, you can be addicted to high cortisol. . . . The signs of addiction are often more subtle than track marks: perhaps you have workaholism, or just feel chronically depleted from working so hard or giving so much, or you are experiencing wandering attention." Source: wanderlust.com, https://wanderlust.com/journal/are-you-addicted-to-stress/.

PREPARATION LEADS TO COMMAND

Yes, the one-time heavy lifting necessary to create your documentation will be intensive at first, but once in place, your ongoing workload will dramatically and relentlessly decrease. In my case, I transformed one-hundred-hour workweeks into ten-minute workweeks. That's one way to look at it. The other view is that if you wish to keep working your long hours—or for whatever reasons you *have* to keep working them—why not significantly increase the quality and quantity of your output? For the salesperson, this means more sales. For the corporate manager, it means a faster climb up the ladder.

This sounds convoluted, but think it through: You will generate extra time, so you will have more time to prepare. And proper preparation leads to better command of future events, which leads to higher efficiency in your business and your life. Higher efficiency produces more available time—and some of that available time you will reinvest in additional preparation.

This is the opposite of a cycle of diminishing returns. It's a cycle of increasing returns that builds upon itself to ever-higher positive results.

So, the largest obstacle to better preparation is the reluctance to invest the necessary time to better prepare! At the beginning, even if you have experienced the insight that systems make up everything in life, you must be patient and self-disciplined. Keep your head down and grind out those working procedures until prosperity and free time begin to arrive, thus confirming deep down in your belly that this is a smart thing to do. When the results begin to materialize—and it won't take long—I promise you will become a fanatic for documentation.

Note that some documentation will be useful in your personal life, but it will be informal and less intensive.

As a preview, here is a 1-2-3 summary of what you'll create (there will be good detail on all three of these key documents in the following chapters):

1. **Strategic objective.** The one-page strategic objective will provide overall direction. You will create it yourself. Spread out over several sessions, it won't take more than six to eight hours to complete. (Caution: This is not a job for a committee. It's a job for the

leader, you.) Once the first draft is finished, you will get feedback from your staff. Over time, you will adjust it here and there. Yet as the years pass, it won't change much. Go whole-hog and create a separate one for your personal life, too. (In Appendix A you will find Centratel's Strategic Objective.)

2. **General operating principles.** Upon completion of the strategic objective, you will begin to put together a list of general operating principles. Just two or three pages long, this condensed "*guidelines for decision-making*" document requires, I'd say, ten to twenty hours to complete, but these hours will be spread over a period of a month or two as your Principles come to light in the course of your day. (Yes, the creation of this document is also a job for *you*, although you'll want input from others.) You will extract these principles from your everyday experience while formulating them from the perspective of your new systems mindset. *These principles are what you believe.* Don't rush them. Be thoughtful and patient with yourself. Put them together carefully and your principles, like your strategic objective, will change little over the years. You'll want a thorough set for your business and a more informal set for your personal life. Yes, the two lists will be similar in content as they are a reflection of *you*. (Centratel's "Thirty Principles" document is in Appendix B.)
3. **Working procedures.** *Instead of killing fires, you will spend your time creating a fireproof environment.* Your working procedures will be the blue-collar centerpiece of this effort. This documentation will be a collection of protocols that outline exactly how the systems of your business will operate. (Working procedures are not often necessary for your personal life, although the concept should always be in your head.) Brief, concise, and authored at first by you and later by other key people, 95 percent of your procedures will follow a simple 1-2-3-4-step linear format. The other 5 percent will follow an open narrative or checklist format.

Every system process should have its own written working procedure. As you did with the general operating principles, you will begin creating your working procedures documentation just after you complete your strategic objective. You will start with the most troublesome processes and then work down through dozens if not hundreds of additional ones, depending on the complexity of your enterprise. But even over this initial period, it won't be a full-time job. And if you have staff, remember that this is a bottom-up strategy: soon you will train your best people to do the legwork. Responsive to your everyday business experience and adjusted with evolving circumstances, working procedures are fluid (see samples in Appendix C).

Lifestyle Requirements

If you choose to live a certain lifestyle, that lifestyle has certain requirements. There are tasks that *must* be accomplished. *These are task requirements, not when-I-get-around-to-it or when-I-feel-like-it undertakings. To achieve your desired lifestyle, you must accomplish these undertakings, whether you enjoy doing them or not.* No matter how onerous the task—or how little you want to do what is required—the payoff will arrive as long as you take the steps! Carry this thought around with you: *I do not have to like the steps I must take. I just have to take them.* Nine out of ten people don't understand this. They think, rather absurdly, "If I don't enjoy what I'm doing, then what I'm doing must be incorrect." Bad presumption.

The documents you will create are mechanical aids. However, there is something else that is important about them. They are on paper and therefore concrete. Their physicality makes what you are doing and where you are going REAL. With written guidelines you can put your hands on your work and your future. In these documents, every day you will see your direction and goals, and this will be a reminder to stay on the path. Always remember that surging thoughts, desires, and hopes are ephemeral, and they can divert you, but documentation is real and it will keep you straight.

(For me personally, the Centratel Operating Principles document was perhaps the most satisfying document of all. What a wonderful exercise, to write down exactly what one believes!)

Your controlling documents do not have to be impeccable in the first drafts. They can be grammatically incorrect, the sentence structure can be less than optimal, and they can be brief. What is important is that you begin to create and use them. Just begin! You will clean them up later.

INEVITABLE EMOTIONAL SLUMPS

Like bedrock, your three master documents will stand against the storms that blow across your world. And what storms create the most havoc, reversing forward progress? Your own emotions.

Documentation lays out everything that is important for getting you to a place of control in your life. You'll be covering what matters: your beliefs about how the world works, what is most important to you personally, your goals and how you will achieve them, not to mention how you will operate. Because of this work, your forward progress will ebb only slightly as you encounter the inevitable emotional slumps and random hammer blows that are part of the human condition. With the new methodology in place you will minimize the impact of your personal downtimes. It may be slower progress during those times, but it *will* be progress.

THE KEY: GET OUTSIDE YOURSELF

There will be times when you think you are sinking, and when those times occur your documentation will reach down and yank you to the surface before you drown.

The strategic objective, general operating principles, and working procedures are your self-created guiding lights. In the tough times, they remind you that your business is a system of systems and that tweaking those systems is what you must do. When you are not feeling strong and/or your emotions are negative, your guidelines are right there, ready to get you back on track or at least keep you from straying too far.

As Mick Jagger says, "It's alright to let yourself go as long as you can get yourself back."

When you realize you are watching your temporary depression from the outside, you will know you have reached a higher level of control. This is cognitive self-command, the ability to monitor and then adjust your own thinking from an external vantage point. You see your thoughts as independent of you, mechanisms unto themselves, singular, almost touchable entities just like any of the other external system mechanisms under your direction.

Your new perspective will remind you that the reasons for the downtimes are usually quite simple: too little sleep, low blood sugar, excessive work or TV, negative people, gloomy environment, the payback for ingesting a mood-altering substance, and so on. Get outside these influences. Look down on them to see them for what they are. Then minimize, delete, or adjust them so they will no longer drain energy or create depression.

In my own life, being tired drives me downhill faster than anything else. Like clockwork, every afternoon between 1:00 p.m. and 2:00 p.m. I go into a physical and mental downturn and I either nap it off or crawl through the mid-afternoon, understanding all the while that my physical body—and my thinking process—is at low ebb. My mood is low ebb, too . . . and so I also remind myself that my general outlook can seem utterly hopeless when my body is drained.

I never make important decisions or handle sensitive issues in that afternoon time frame. But by 4:00 p.m., I'm fine again.

Discover your own cycles and work with them (more on this in Chapter 19).

STORMS OF THE CRIMINAL MIND

The criminal mind has a certain grasp of the base mechanics of the world, maybe more so than the average law-abiding citizen. In the classic colloquial sense, the criminal works the system as he or she strips away the niceties, assesses the raw mechanics—but without concern for others—and manipulates those mechanisms to selfish benefit. Yes, the criminal approaches life with a malefic bent, but one can't deny that it's a systems approach.

Criminality is a losing game because it's an imperfection in the overarching primary societal machine, a machine that automatically works hard to eliminate flaws one way or the other. Consider the plight of the chronic lawbreaker who gyrates outside of common expectations, ignoring accepted notions of how one is expected to act. For greedy/lazy reasons, the criminal takes shortcuts, exploits exposed system components, and makes small-time gains. As the societal system is manipulated without regard for fairness and compassion—the bulwarks of a just culture—personal pain arrives in an overt way: jail time, for instance, or more covertly, constant inner turmoil. *The criminal is afloat in a stormy sea.* The TV series *The Sopranos* perfectly illustrated the paranoia of fighting the system. The characters were diabolical, tormented, ultimately doomed. If you are a criminal, the force is *not* with you.

If one is working outside the system, what is the solution? It is to make the decision to step back inside, to accept the general human process as it is, to play the game as an adult—to follow the rules. Things are just smoother that way. The universe welcomes manipulation if it results in a more efficient process, but it will fight manipulation that is disruptive.

In the free world there is plenty of opportunity to fit in and to get ahead. One has unlimited options to succeed without going outside the boundaries.

A BACKBONE MADE OF STEEL

Look forward to this: in the midst of a less-than-awesome day, from your outside and slightly elevated vantage point and with the emotional uplift your documentation provides, you will watch yourself drag your emotions out of that black hole rather than allowing it to eat you up. Later, you will witness this self-rescue again. These incremental successes will strengthen you, and after a while this even-keeled response will come effortlessly. Soon you will find you won't be inclined to resort to the old antidotes of avoidance. No longer will you bludgeon your way through the downtimes with overwork or excessive alcohol, caffeine, food, sugar, or drugs—the temporary fixes that used to rescue your mood in the moment but guaranteed more intense declines later on.

The strengthening cycle will continue upward until you have a solid grip on your world and one day you realize you have become one of those rare individuals whose backbone is made of steel. It seems odd that dispassionate documentation could lead to this outcome, but as you can see, there is much more to this than the written word.

A PERSONAL CATACLYSM IS NOT NECESSARY

At Centratel, when we took action from our new external stance, turmoil evaporated and was replaced by order. Once we began the new methodology it was easy to continue to implement it because great results accumulated quickly. The more we invested in system-improvement and attending documentation—working the system—the more positive results we experienced.

Centratel is highly profitable now and I spend very little time managing it because the business is self-propelling. As its chief project engineer, I watch over it from a distance, nudging here and there to keep it traveling in a straight line and at full speed. *Centratel is not successful because of my presence as some kind of a heroic fire killer. It's successful because we spend the majority of our time perfecting the mechanisms that compose it.*

Of course, another critical element in our success is my staff's enthusiasm for the Method they helped put into place. They are project engineers, too.

Centratel is a pleasant place to work. Calm efficiency pervades. And along with the systems-mindset business strategy, the systems perspective flows through my personal life where I have the same levels of efficiency and freedom. Mentioned previously, I regained my health two decades ago and today consider myself more than robust.

One might think my adoption of the new perspective came about because I was courageous, but that wasn't the case. It was fear and exhaustion. It took impending doom to see life was not going to conform to my wishes just because I thought it should. It was gun-to-the-head enlightenment.

Why weren't the answers obvious to me *before* there was a gun to my head? Part of the reason was that although the year-to-year struggle was killing me, it was more comfortable—more convenient—to acquiesce to predictable day-to-day pain than to candidly question and then examine my overall vision and strategy. Don't make that mistake.

There was also pretentiousness. It was easier to posture myself as a hero, facing and then overcoming incredible external odds, staunchly marching on, rather than to question my presumption that the world would someday get a clue and adjust to my personal requirements. But when catastrophe was finally upon me, everything distilled down to the simple realization that I was not managing the processes of my life.

Am I happy the insight came as the end result of trauma? If that was what was required, yes. Do *you* have to have a gun-to-the-head experience to get to the same place? No!

Late that night twenty-one years ago, when I first got outside and looked down, it struck me that although there was some work to do, it would be simple to repair my business and my life. All I had to do was identify systems, isolate them, and then fix them one at a time! Does this make sense now? Do you see there is no need to undergo a personal cataclysm in order to change your perspective and then get your circumstances straightened out?

A sobering facet of my outside and slightly elevated enlightenment was the realization this was not some kind of divine blessing bestowed upon me alone. This perspective is already permanently etched into the minds of those who direct successful organizations everywhere. Yet many of the people who innately embrace the approach, as simple a concept as it is, can't identify it as the critical factor of their own success.

Devil's Advocate System Questions

By dispassionately dealing with stone-cold reality, the odds of getting what you want are infinitely higher than waiting for a ghost to communicate good tidings, a horoscope or tarot card to predict a prosperous future, or a multimillion-dollar lottery winning to land in your lap. Be mechanical. Can you imagine how you will feel as you watch yourself get a grip on life and make it what you want it to be due to your own actions and not because of improbable fate, magic, dumb luck, or someone else's benevolence?

There are down-and-dirty system questions—system filters—you can pose to yourself in order to really see the hard facts of any given situation. For example, *"Without regard for my personal preference, what exactly is going on here?"* Carry that question around with you everywhere, and when the necessary action is obvious but you are still hesitant, ask, *"Is NOT wanting to take action in this moment enough of a reason to not take action?"*

FLOW

You watch in fascination as the world's endless processes ripple on. It's simple mechanics and it's flow, and you like being part of it. You view your existence from this very nearly metaphysical perspective that is a step away and a little bit above yourself and your world. In your life, your job is to modify your systems, gently goading each to more and more efficiency. (Regarding systems that are outside of your control, you make no attempt at adjustment because it is a waste of time and energy.)

This world operates at 99.99 percent efficiency because there are unalterable physical laws that are powered by an unfathomable strength—a strength that hungers for order and efficiency. In the systems that make up our lives, results occur in a cold-blooded way, and that's a good thing. Outcomes don't mysteriously conform to our individual desires just because we want them to. And that's OK because this mechanical reality is predictable. It is something we can depend upon and therefore can confidently wield to our own benefit.

When you understand the utter dependability of the world's mechanics, and then carefully adjust those mechanics, you will get what you want in your life.

THREE LARGE STEPS AHEAD

In the middle of my business and health rejuvenation I was pounded hard by two unexpected, earthshaking blows. One was the nasty legal battle mentioned earlier. The other was a bone-crushing personal family loss. Those two nightmares arrived at the same time. The first lasted two years; the second, three. It was painful during those dark times, but I was able to roll through the days with sanity and effectiveness, watching the goings-on from my outside and slightly elevated vantage point.

The new posture is natural and unforced. Here is how it will be for you from this point forward: You wake up in the morning with an immediate focus on what is most important for the day ahead. The day's tasks will be one-time creative efforts, each aimed at carrying you closer to the objectives outlined in your two strategic objective documents—one for your business, one for your personal life. Although you will minimize stepping backward, there is no avoiding it because that is what getting through the day includes. You accept these backward stumbles as part of the overhead that comes with the much more significant movement forward—three large steps ahead for every one small step back. And the inevitable earthquakes? You'll be ready.

And at the end of the day you feel satisfied because there has been measurable advancement toward your prime objectives. Working or relaxing, you don't float or obsess anymore. You direct, build, watch, and enjoy. It flows.

Ingesting that big horse pill was well worth it. Three steps forward. One step back. That's the way it goes . . .

The Giant Machine

The world's largest manufacturer of computer printers keeps a factory running 24/7/365. It's in Italy. The nonhuman mechanical and electronic workers don't take breaks and they toil their entire lives in this fixed location. A daily line of transport trucks delivers raw materials and carries away the fully packaged products.

A few cars in the tiny parking lot indicate there is merely a small contingent of human workers present.

Given proper security clearances that are issued from the lone guard minding the front gate, a brave person can walk through the center of this monstrous mechanism. Doing so, one quickly learns that even human visitors are under the machine's governance. Standing at one end of this system of systems, one can barely make out the other end. It's a giant *machine*, as wide as it is long. Approaching a well-defined walkway, the human intruder is warned by flashing red lights to stop while a part of the mechanical line physically retracts in order to allow passage. Once the visitor passes, the track closes and the mechanical component restarts. It continues for a few moments at an accelerated pace to make up for the time lost by the encroachment.

This is not a place for the faint of heart or the claustrophobic. There are no escape routes. Should the machine fail to detect your presence, there are no humans readily available to intervene on your behalf. Yes, you are free to leave, but only at the mercy of this massive primary system and only at a pace that doesn't compromise system protocols.

The colossal machine is made up of subassemblies, and those subassemblies cooperate with one another as the completed products continuously roll off the end of the line. The fully tested printers are packaged and shipped to a local store near you, and in all likelihood the first human hands to touch the printers are those of retail purchasers.

This is a primary system with a clear goal—the production of objects of value. And where are the human masters? Removed from the actual process, of course, monitoring, adjusting, and maintaining.

CHAPTER 9

We Are Project Engineers

Management works in the system. Leadership works on the system.

—Stephen Covey

As an ad hoc synopsis—by now you know how much I like to drill home the simple principles from different angles—the essence of the Work the System Method is to:

1. Acquire the mindset, deeply internalizing the fundamental perspective. *Get it.*
2. Pinpoint and describe goals for your business. Briefly define the approach you will use to achieve those goals. This is your strategic objective.
3. Create a collection of general operating principles, your guidelines to decision-making.
4. Identify specific systems for improvement. You will deal with the most problematic ones first.
5. Dissect each system into its most elemental components. In detail, in your working procedures, describe each on paper in a 1-2-3-4-step, checklist, or narrative format.
6. One system at a time and leaning hard toward stark simplicity, change sequences and add or delete steps as necessary. Add new systems as needed. Discard the ones holding things back. Experiment. Make each of your systems perfect.

7. As a mandatory part of this system-improvement process, document each tweak you make into the working procedure for the particular system.
8. Keep the updated working procedures in play and tend to them on a regular basis, inspecting and tweaking as necessary. Remember, system-improvement is not a random, when-I-find-the-time-to-do-it approach. It's a methodology permanently imbedded within the structure of your business and your life.

YOUR PERSONAL ANALOGY

In step one above, *getting it* is mandatory. Without this deep-down grasp, steps two through eight just won't happen in your real, mechanical—and in a very real sense—unforgiving world. *The strength to take a new direction comes more from a belief lodged in the belly rather than from something learned in the head.*

To truly internalize the perspective, it is useful to create a personal system analogy that will permanently reside in your consciousness, a systems template that you find meaningful. Your analogy will illustrate systems methodology to *you*, a reminder of the characteristics that all systems share. In your day-to-day existence, you will keep this analogy in the back of your mind in order to keep your new perspective front and center. A vivid system analogy is an antidote to a too-busy day that ruthlessly attempts to divert your attention from the system enhancement process to wasteful acts of fire killing.

Your analogy must be utterly believable, its mechanical basis something you don't question. Coin one that is easy to visualize as separate from its surroundings—one that can stand on its own. You want a closed mechanism.

If you are in medicine, bodily processes offer unlimited possibilities. You can draw examples from organ function, skeletal structure, respiratory and circulatory systems, etc.

If you sell cars for a living, consider the car itself. It's a primary system made up of a multitude of subsystems. Think about how those subsystems must be monitored and maintained in order to keep the primary system—the car as a whole—at peak efficiency.

As a firefighter, think about the equipment that must operate flawlessly no matter what.

A pilot has the preflight checklist, which is a near-perfect example of examining a primary system (in this case, the aircraft) for flaws while ensuring that all submechanisms are at peak efficiency. A single flight in itself is a textbook system analogy as the aircraft automatically makes directional micro-adjustments, confirms subsystems are operational, and warns of impending dysfunction.

Your analogy will keep your energies channeled toward system management as it reminds you that a jumble of fire killing will drag you down. It will be a steady reminder that you are a project engineer who calmly creates and maintains efficient systems, not a fire killer who responds like a puppet on a string to crisis after crisis.

Your analogy will especially help you at the beginning, and later—after it's hardwired into your psyche—will be an occasional pleasant reflection of what you believe and how you see things.

As an illustration, here is the analogy I use. As you read, start to think of one that fits your own world. No, you don't have to put your analogy down on paper. If it's a good one, you will effortlessly internalize it.

THE NEW-SERVICE FACILITATOR

My personal analogy is about electricity: how it reaches people in their homes and businesses, and my past role as an electric utility project engineer.

High-voltage power line circuits exactly illustrate the mechanics of the systems mindset to me. I can easily visualize an electric distribution system as a separate, unique entity and not one on which the surrounding complexities of the world constantly infringe. It's my private and perfect illustration of the mechanics of linear systems everywhere.

When I was twenty-eight, I took a job in the engineering department of a rural electric utility in central Oregon. The utility, Central Electric Cooperative, is one of the largest Rural Electrification Administration (REA) co-ops in the United States, with thousands of miles of power lines branching throughout the central and eastern Oregon regions. The co-op serves tens of thousands of residential, commercial, and agricultural customers.

The utility's outside-operations staff face extreme geographical, meteorological, and physical challenges. On the same day, linemen can experience both mountain snowstorms and desert heat; vertical mountain pitches and long river crossings; high-density city construction and remote rural troubleshooting.

For the first half of my seven-year stint with the co-op, my job title was new-service facilitator.

As one of the co-op's four new-service facilitators, I met with contractors and landowners who were about to build homes. Or sometimes a rancher would be adding a pump. My task was to arrange for our line crews to "tap" into the nearest existing power line in order to extend new electric service to the customer's home construction or pump site. Usually the distance from the power line to the site was no more than a few hundred yards.

I assessed the new construction project, found the closest power pole, and wrote up instructions and a list of materials for the construction crews so they could get power delivered to the customer via a transformer and low voltage overhead and/or underground cable.

My job at that time had little to do with the primary electrical distribution system. My area of responsibility was outside the massive power-generating dams that created the electricity far to the north on the Columbia River, and also had little to do with the thousands of miles of high-voltage power lines and associated complex equipment that distributes the electricity in bulk throughout the region. My simple task was to establish small power line extensions to individual new customers. These subsystem extensions were simple, minor additions to my utility's massive electricity-delivering network, the primary high-voltage electricity distribution system.

I filled this position as new-service facilitator for three years and then was promoted. My new job moved me from the periphery of the massive electrical distribution system to the heart of it where I would have a much greater impact on the primary network itself and on the many customers it served.

My overall job title was now project engineer, a precise description of my new role. (And—as a business owner—with your new systems mindset it will be your new title too, so pay special attention here.) I would be responsible for designing and supervising the construction of large high-voltage distribution feeders into whole subdivisions, as well as working on other complex projects that affected thousands of customers at a time. I'd manage large transmission construction projects, too. It was also my job to keep an eye on segments of the older primary system in order to spot problems and to recommend repairs and revisions, as well as upgrades due to population and load growth. There was the necessary overall maintenance, too. System components aged and the environment changed over time, and it was my task to monitor these variables and submit designs for fixes and upgrades.

In short, my job was to analyze the main electrical distribution system, design improvements, and then pass those improvements on to our construction crews. It was here, in my role as project engineer, that I learned the concept of system-improvement. It was a term we engineers constantly used.

I put my designs and material lists down on paper using an exacting format. The goal was to be thorough yet concise; to give the line crews the information they needed—no more, no less—so they could proceed quickly through their construction work.

Note how the analogy describes my transition from handling small and isolated add-on tasks to large internal system-improvement projects. Also note there were strict design and documentation protocols.

FLIRTING WITH THE NEW SYSTEM-IMPROVEMENT PERSPECTIVE

My previous position and my new position had an important commonality. In each case, when I went to work, from the beginning of the day to the end of the day, I was focused on the co-op's electrical network. While I was on the job, the electric system stood separate from the rest of the world. Sure, I took breaks, had lunch, and made a personal phone call now and then. But overall, the electricity distribution system—the network of poles and wire—was paramount in my consciousness, standing out in my mind as its own entity, separate and distinct from the land it crossed and 100 percent detached from my children, finances, politics, or health. When I was on the job, the electricity distribution system had my focused attention as if nothing else existed. And it was not just separate in my mind. It was that way in reality, an independent mechanism inserted into the physical world, spreading its tentacles in order to fulfill its singular purpose of delivering electricity to lots of people.

At day's end as I returned home to pay attention to the other systems of my life, I changed my perspective as if a switch had been flipped. I didn't consciously notice this daily mental transition, and little did I know that I was quietly internalizing the outside and slightly elevated system-improvement perspective that would dramatically change my life many years later.

If you are like most people, you already have an unconscious tendency to dissect complexities so exposed components can be dealt with one at a time. The Work the System Method will turn this soft ephemeral proclivity into an assertive, structured quest—an everyday pilgrimage to isolate and then "work" the systems that compose your world. And if you do that, the good results—the results you actually want—will materialize spontaneously.

SYSTEM MANAGEMENT

With the promotion to project engineer, my role morphed from designing small subsystems for individual customers to improving elements of the primary electrical system that served multitudes of customers. Instead of adding to the electrical network in bits and pieces, I was managing huge segments.

I tweaked the network to keep it strong and efficient.

Notice that I was not climbing poles or stringing wire. My job was to devise revisions that would make the primary electrical system more robust and then to oversee the implementation of those improvements by other people. It was a strict protocol. As project engineer, I would create the design, but professional linemen would perform the physical work. This is a crucial point of the analogy.

My job was system management. Back then, *I was unconsciously working the system, and after my awakening many years later, this view would be per-*

manently etched into my root thinking process. Today, my former role serves me well as a template—and analogy—for how I visualize all aspects of my life. Like my position as project engineer with the electric utility years ago, today I spend my days examining, adjusting, observing, maintaining, and upgrading all the processes of my existence . . . while I avoid getting caught up in secondary add-ons or doing the work that others can perform.

I no longer major in minors. I major in majors. Your personal analogy will remind you to do the same.

MAINTENANCE AND 99.99 PERCENT RELIABILITY

Electricity originates from a generating facility and then power lines carry it to the end user. For the electricity, it's a long, hazard-wrought trip through multiple electrical subsystems and tough terrain. Weather extremes, vandalism, and the incessant ravages of time imperil the electricity's delivery. Yet interestingly, in checking official statistics at this utility where I used to work, I found that over a seven-year period, the average customer's power failed an average of just seventy-three minutes per year. Wow! Think about that. There are 525,600 minutes in a year, which means the average electric utility customer had steady electric power 99.99 percent of the time.

Does that percentage sound familiar?

In considering a power line's path through hundreds of miles of hostile environment, combined with the volatile high-voltage electricity itself, which is so anxious to escape its confining wire conductor, how does the staff of an electric utility accomplish this astonishing degree of reliability? They do it by viewing their electrical network as a closed mechanical system that must be assertively maintained, not as a conglomeration of poles, wire, and equipment that receives attention only when there are problems. The people employed by the electric company start by designing and installing a robust electrical *machine*, and then, via a corporate-wide system-improvement approach, they pander to it. Fire killing? Nope.

In any part of life, in order to avoid system failure and to ensure top efficiency, the performance of regular system maintenance is mandatory: changing the car's oil, conducting staff meetings, watering the houseplants, dinner out with one's spouse, ball games with the kids, bonuses for the best-performing employees, routine visits with customers, record-keeping, physical fitness, brushing teeth, and on and on. However, for people in the grip of chaos, these important wheel-greasing chores are the first casualties. In so many life situations that include careers, marriages, friendships, mechanical devices, play, homes, health—all of it—the necessary routine maintenance is skipped because of fire killing, simple laziness, and especially ignorance of the way linear systems execute in the real, mechanical world.

Without proper recurring attention, outside factors (yes, parasitic outside systems) will cannibalize your efficient processes and things will deteriorate. Your fine-tuned systems must be kept on track.

For me, an especially satisfying personal maintenance system is the daily half hour I spend at home working my "reorganizing system." This is perhaps my simplest personal system. It's nothing more than an allocated daily time period dedicated to a narrow purpose: thirty minutes spent cleaning things up.

It's free-form time used to create and maintain order—straighten out my office, my closet, the garage, my email inbox, and help Diana around the house. On our Kentucky property, sometimes it's going outside with the chainsaw and cleaning up the surrounding woodlot.

It's about putting my individual life facets in order and it's the antidote to insidious clutter, both physical and mental.

Another one of my free-form maintenance systems is reading (preferably a hard-copy book, not via a computer screen. No Kindle for me. Call me a Luddite.). I read daily for at least an hour, usually more. If I choose a good book, there is the entertaining/informative content, of course, but I also do it to stretch out my attention span and just to give my brain a break. It's therapy, as it removes the mental frenzy that can accumulate through the day. In the wonderfully profound movie *Joe Versus the Volcano*, the Tom Hanks character is diagnosed with a fake disease called Brain Cloud.[6] That's a good description of my mental state when I don't read for a few days.

Reading a hard-copy book daily will indeed stretch your attention span. In these days of smartphones, sound bites, and too much coffee, it's

---

6 The Farlex Free Dictionary defines Brain Cloud as "The temporary inability to think properly, or to remember something."

perfect for head maintenance. (Read these books by Nicholas Carr: *The Shallows: What the Internet Is Doing to Our Brains* and *The Glass Cage: How Our Computers Are Changing Us*.)

WATCH YOUR WORLD FROM A DISTANCE

As I visualize an electrical power network as an analogy for all the systems of my life, I am reminded to avoid being a worker and instead to be a project engineer. In your own life as you apply your analogy to your business or supervisory job, you will find yourself deflecting hands-on work to others or automating . . . or discarding useless systems altogether. Instead of doing the work you will be creating new systems, devising enhancements for existing ones, simplifying, removing clutter, and supervising the people who perform the actual work. Of course, if you are a traditional artist or other creator this will not be true. Yet whatever your life's role, there is room for significant movement in the work-the-system direction—movement that will dramatically improve your life. (I'll discuss more about job and creator aspects in Chapter 19.)

In considering your new analogy through your new posture as a project engineer, you will begin to watch your existence from a distance. The more time you spend seeing your life from this bird's-eye view, the faster you will attain your goals—and the more time you will have to spend on this outside and slightly elevated perch.

It really is this simple: *Avoid becoming caught up in the work. Instead, step outside, look down, and isolate individual systems. Then, deciding overall what you want them to accomplish, identify defects as well as outside changing situations. Then improve the systems while always documenting the revisions.* Because you have designed these system mechanisms to operate without your constant involvement, you can then back off and occasionally (but routinely) monitor and direct.

After just a short while you're going to get good at this!

I approach all my systems from a project engineer's stance: systems to stay fit, keep in touch with extended family, invest money, maintain computers, and climb mountains. This includes our dog, Justy, too. He sees the vet at least twice a year whether he likes it or not!

In the beginning of my new approach I would constantly visualize my electric system analogy and its dictate that my role be that of a project engineer. Now I don't think about my analogy too often because the systems mindset is permanently hard-wired inside my skull.

In every aspect of my life I am a project engineer.

What's *your* analogy? A car, a human body, an airplane, a ship? *See the simple beauty of your encapsulated parallel and apply it in every situation in which you find yourself.* You can do this because all systems everywhere operate across time in exactly the same 1-2-3-4-step way. This is not theory. This is mechanical reality.

Toilet Paper

This illustration borders on the nonsensical, but it cogently makes two points. First, the systems perspective is not common. Yes, second, once the logic of it is understood the perspective becomes permanently ingrained.

As an example of systems thinking, and at the risk of making an awful pun, reaching for a piece of toilet paper is the bottom line. Toilet paper is a mandatory tool. It may be the one material thing that all of us have used daily for all of our adult lives. As an illustration of a system that is ubiquitous *and* clearly separate from the surrounding world, it's perfect.

The act of loading toilet paper on a dispenser is a system—a system that proceeds in a linear fashion until the goal is accomplished. Maybe your routine is as follows. Step 1: In the bathroom, approach the sink. Step 2: Open the cabinet door underneath the sink. Step 3: Reach into the cabinet and grasp a roll of toilet paper. Step 4: Approach the toilet paper dispenser with the roll. Step 5: Install the roll in the dispenser.

Ask yourself the following question: Right now, in your own house or apartment, is the toilet paper roll loaded on the dispenser with the free end of the paper rolling off the top of the roll where it can be easily grasped? Or is the leading edge rolling off the bottom of the roll, where one must, a bit awkwardly, reach underneath the roll to retrieve it?

continued

With a couple of notable exceptions, paper flowing off the top is most convenient. It's the better way to retrieve it.

Off the top or off the bottom? For the fun of it, and as a student of human behavior, over the years I've kept an informal tally. Not counting hotels and motels where professional housecleaners have been instructed on the most efficient positioning, it is nearly a fifty-fifty split with a slight advantage going to those who chose off the top. This means most people don't think one way or the other about the insertion of the roll in the dispenser. (Or, implausibly, one-half the population is adamant that the roll be inserted one way, and the other half of the population, the other way.)

Since having the retrieving end of the paper on the top of the roll makes grasping the paper easier, why doesn't everyone load the paper that way every time? Is the task of inserting the roll one way more difficult than inserting it the other way? Not at all. So, what's up? Truth is, deciding to always do it one way or the other would require a one-time systems-thinking analysis—in this case it would take just a few seconds to establish a permanent protocol—but *most people don't go that one layer deeper. They don't spend time considering underlying processes.*

Yes, maybe this is a silly illustration, but try to get past that and see it as an analogy for the big picture. See that the mental act of deciding to load the paper one way or the other puts you outside the actual act of loading toilet paper. You are deliberately managing the process in order to produce an incrementally better result every single time the toilet paper retrieval process is executed in the future.

There is another, more visceral lesson here, and maybe it's a bit unnerving. Because you have considered this toilet paper question, it may cause you to choose to load your rolls in a more deliberate way, or the contrarian in you may consciously decide *not* to do that. Whatever your choice, my prediction is that *from now on you will think about the toilet paper system every single time you use toilet paper*. Like it or not, due to reading this illustration in this moment of time, there is a small slice of systems methodology that has been permanently embedded in your mind.

Ha! Welcome to my world!

Some time ago, I polled my management team in a staff meeting on how they load their paper at home. I got this paraphrased response from every single one of them, all in unison (and all a little bit surprised that I would even have to ask the question): "*Pleeeze! Off the top, of course! Duh!*" Even in the most mundane tasks, my Centratel employees reflexively take a posture of being outside and slightly elevated from their tasks. Because they have studied this book and dealt with my insistence on the system-improvement mentality . . . and actually worked with the logic of it, witnessing the good results, the principles are permanently ingrained in their heads. Like my staff at Centratel, the systems mindset will keep *you* ever alert to small daily-life enhancements that can easily be implemented.

In the toilet paper illustration, what are the "notable exceptions"? Toddlers and cats are amused by quickly stroking the off-the-top loaded toilet paper roll, thus creating a useless pile of paper on the bathroom floor. The system tweak for these special situations? Load the paper so it dispenses off the bottom of the roll!

It's hard to say this delicately, but what the heck: for me, using the toilet has become a powerful recurring reminder—an anchor—for the systems mindset. I'm betting that you will see it this way for yourself, too. Think about it: several times every day, the bathroom experience happens out of necessity, and what goes on in there involves several important systems in addition to the paper, including the human body, with its requirement for the elimination of waste; freshwater delivery to the house, the sewage system where waste flows away ultimately to be purified and sent back into the environment. The bathroom primary system is a critical yet underappreciated system . . . until one steps outside, becomes slightly elevated, and really thinks about it.

Yes, this is the systems mindset! It watches, thinks, appreciates, and acts, all the time and everywhere.

So, will you forever use the bathroom with a new thoughtfulness? Each time, will this primal system experience be an anchor, driving the systems mindset to the front and center of your consciousness? My bet is, yes.

CHAPTER 10

Your Strategic Objective and General Operating Principles

I don't want to be a product of my environment.
I want my environment to be a product of me.

—Frank Costello (Jack Nicholson) from the movie *The Departed* (Warner Bros. Pictures, 2006)

To review: My mini-enlightenment arrived because I was under titanic mental and physical pressure. Until that late-night revelation, my strategy had been to approach life with a bulldog, damn-the-torpedoes, pound-the-moles, I'm-so-damn-clever persona. It was a toxic brew of arrogance and ignorance—perhaps the most noxious combination of negative human traits.

The seething chaos had reared up and was about to crush me for good. Instead, it delivered a flash of insight. I dropped the bulldog routine, adopted an outside and slightly elevated perspective, and found new confidence. I knew exactly what moves to make and then I charged out of my self-imposed prison.

Boring but true: to end workplace chaos, identify the separate systems, get the system elements of each down on paper, and then make adjustments in those systems.

Work your systems one by one.

First, put together the strategic objective. It will require just a few hours to develop a workable draft and maybe another five hours total. Spread the task out over another couple of days or even weeks to get it right. Creating it is pretty much a one-time task, but allow for future minor revisions as the environment changes and new insights arrive. Limit it to one single-spaced printed page.

Second, after you create the first draft of your strategic objective, you will begin work on the general operating principles, the contents of which will be accumulated bit by bit and then refined off and on over a period of a few months.

Third, you will begin to create a collection of working procedures. Like your other two prime documents, a working procedure is in itself an archetypical system. A product of the system-improvement process, each working procedure is an exact guideline for executing the system it describes. (This third primary document will be addressed in detail in the next chapter.)

Over the long term, you and your staff will spend 99 percent of your documentation time creating new working procedures and improving existing ones. Be patient and trust me here: *first, create your strategic objective and operating principles!* They are the foundation for your working procedures. (Yes, I know you will want to immediately charge ahead with your working procedures, but don't. Believe me here, you'll save time and effort by not doing that. The sequence matters.)

At work, all three documents will remain front and center in your mind. Remember this, and trust me here, too: *Generally speaking, and averaged out, for every unit of time you expend on the three documents, the return will be at least a hundredfold. This is not an exaggeration, and in fact I am being conservative.*

CREATING YOUR STRATEGIC OBJECTIVE

As I first saw Centratel from my new outside and slightly elevated vantage point, I realized that it had no direction or objectives. Without a clear pathway, how could we reach our targets? And anyway, what precisely *were* our targets?

When I bought the ailing Girl Friday Telephone Answering Service thirty-six years ago, my goal had been to make the company the best in the industry. That objective quickly evaporated as my small staff and I coped with serial fire killing. For fifteen years we thrashed. But in year sixteen, as we began to plow through the systemization process and witnessed immediate increases in quality, my dream of Centratel being the best in the US crawled out from its hiding place. We would not just survive. Per verifiable statistics we really would become the best among the (at that time) ten thousand competitors in our TAS industry. This was our first concrete objective.

I dug in and laid out our direction, targets, and general strategy in the strategic objective, the first and most important of the three primary documents. It gives identity and direction. It prevents flailing away. With this overall guideline at the forefront we no longer squandered time and energy in efforts that didn't contribute to the overall objectives of the business.

The other two primary documents follow from it.

For Centratel, the ultimate purpose of the strategic objective is straightforward, as noted in the use of the present tense in the first line: "Statistically we are the highest-quality telephone answering service in the United States."

All large and small decisions follow from the strategic objective statement: Every ounce of energy is focused on the primary goal. *The strategic objective is not a nebulous, feel-good mission statement based on self-aggrandized hope. It is not something designed to make the board of directors feel good about themselves or intended to impress stockholders and staff. Instead, it's a blueprint in which we acknowledge the day-to-day existence of the business in a mechanized, objective way.* Without syrupy excess, it includes a brief narration of what the company does, where it's headed, and how management and staff will get there.

Keep it to one page only.

Most business owners have a cursory idea of what success would look like and an inkling of what they have to do to succeed, but because they're hamstrung with fire killing, they don't take time to sit down quietly and firmly establish objectives or to develop specific strategies. *They don't even take the very first mechanical steps necessary to sort things out.* As you garner the self-discipline to create your strategic objective, you will find new strength as you hold the single sheet of paper in your hand. You'll instantly insert yourself into an elite category: as the owner of a small business, you'll be one of the very few who has a document that outlines company identity and intention. You'll have direction!

Once you have this concise, tangible representation of who you are, what you believe, where you are going, and how you will get there, you'll find it uncanny how the physical world will align itself, how it will manifest what you've put down on paper. When you get past the words in this book and take real-world physical steps—the first of which is the creation of your strategic objective—you will know you do indeed have more than enough strength to pull yourself out of the hole. (Centratel's Strategic Objective is in Appendix A.)

CREATING YOUR GENERAL OPERATING PRINCIPLES

After I completed the first draft of the strategic objective, I began creating the second critical document, the general operating principles. Congruent with the spirit and the specifics of the strategic objective, this became a collection of foundational guidelines for making decisions. In the end, it included thirty separate operating principles, so we named it simply "Thirty Principles." You will have your own set, and of course they may number more or fewer than thirty.

I'll jump ahead a bit here: Centratel's Thirty Principles document is a working procedure in itself. (And note that in this usage, it's a *nonlinear* working procedure—a set of guideline components that are not sequentially related, but each must be considered across a wide spectrum of decision-making situations. And yes, for that matter, your strategic objective is also a nonlinear "guideline" working procedure.)

Operating principles are tried and true, sensible, and simple to understand and remember. They are not flashy, as they quietly lie beneath the events of the day. They change very little as circumstances evolve. Over time they will be slightly adjusted, but their long-term immutability will be evidence of their soundness.

Your operating principles are guidelines for decision-making. It's helpful to make up a set for your personal life, too. You will find your personal principles resemble the set you put together for your business, because they reflect your character and your preferred way of approaching the workings of the world. In whatever roles you play, these principles will remain constant.

For an illustration of how the principles can work, consider the following from Centratel's Principle #8: "Just a few services implemented in superb fashion." Twenty years ago, this tenet mandated that we stop selling cellular telephones as an add-on service. Because of the marginal quality of customer service provided by the cellular company for which we were an agent, the elimination of this service ensured that *all* of our services would be high quality. This decision also simplified our operation, helping us to better meet our objective of "just a few services." Had we not written down this principle in physical form and then abided by it, we could still be selling cell phones today at a considerable detriment to our overall operation.

Another example is Principle #30: "We strive for a social climate that is serious and quiet, yet pleasant, serene, light, and friendly." Because this principle is written down, our office is like that. Like the other 29 Principles, it's a hoop through which all decisions must pass. The openness of Centratel's physical layout, the abundance of live decorative plants, the cleanliness, the special full-spectrum lighting, and the orderliness and quietness of it all make Centratel a comfortable place to work and a nice place to be.

The general operating principles, like the elements of the strategic objective, keep us steadily moving in a focused direction, whether there's a tendency toward non-action on the one hand or a momentary burst of impetuousness on the other. We are dogmatic about following our Principles.

The strategic objective keeps us focused; the principles document guides our decision-making so we are in keeping with the strategic objective. Read that again. It's important.

Don't expect your principles document to be finished in one sitting. Because it was sometimes two minutes here and five minutes there, it took me more than a month to create the rough list, select the proper wording, and polish it. Begin by writing down several principles you already have in mind. Then take notes as additional principles pop into your head over the course of the day. Be sure to seek others' input as you compile your list. (Centratel's Thirty Principles are listed in Appendix B. Feel free to use as a template for your own set.)

Why Can't We Find Employees?

It's our greatest challenge: Centratel's pay and benefits are very good, but no matter how aggressively we advertise our positions, we don't have many job applicants. Because we have a hard time finding qualified people, we are fortunate our staff has little turnover. But the irony of simultaneous recruitment challenges and staff stability is understandable. If one digs a bit, it becomes clear why we have problems finding job applicants—and why we have high staff stability. It's our drug-testing policy, as posted in the Employee Handbook.

Before we instituted drug testing, we had plenty of job applicants, but there was high staff turnover.

A staff that uses drugs is flighty, and a flighty staff means call-handling expertise achieved through long-term experience and unhampered focus won't happen. People come and go, physically and mentally.

Our seemingly improbable conclusion is that only a limited number of service-industry job candidates are drug free, especially in Oregon where cannabis is legal and the possession of small amounts of heavier drugs is overlooked. It's a painful, almost unbelievable conclusion, but we operate on that basis because the statistics bear it out. The choice seems to be, "I'd rather smoke dope at a minimum wage/no benefits/no-future menial job than *not* smoke dope at a job where I could earn nearly double the minimum wage, receive full benefits, and have a management ladder that could be climbed." Ouch.

Many business owners understand the truth of this so they don't require drug testing. Of those who do drug-test, it's a gamble. There was a local restaurant that had to close its doors after an impromptu drug screening of all its employees. The restaurant owner had to terminate employment for nine of their twelve people. Another business located in a town near Bend, a new big-box store, selected twenty people for its automotive department. Sixteen of the twenty failed the subsequent drug testing! (Clearly management did the job-awarding/drug-testing sequence backward.)

At Centratel, did our decision to use drug screening stem from an

continued

outside and slightly elevated perspective? No question. Per our Strategic Objective we looked down on our complex answering service business and decided we couldn't reach our goals without a stable, clear-thinking workforce. We decided to trade the chaos of high staff turnover for the staid challenge of finding drug-free people who are steady, fantastic performers. There was no other choice if we were to become the best.

And our staff stability is almost scary, with employee tenures up to thirty years.

To be sure, the introduction of a drug-testing policy must be handled with care and supported by a well thought-out written policy.

CHAPTER 11

Your Working Procedures

Keep your eyes on the road, your hands upon the wheel . . .

—By permission, from the song "Roadhouse Blues," written and performed by The Doors (Elektra/Asylum, 1970)

Know that a this-will-happen-every-single-time protocol won't materialize via mind reading, a one-time conversation, or when discussed in a meeting. A system must be set in concrete if it is to be executed the same way every single time, and this means creating it in hard and/or soft copy and then ensuring it will be implemented.

I said this earlier: *The difference between a large successful business and a small struggling one? Documentation. The former has it. The latter doesn't.*

The quality of execution of a recurring non-documented system—an "organic" system—will vary with the time of day, the weather, or the mood of the individual executing the process. In the workplace, salvation lies in making these ephemeral processes as substantial as the mechanical objects that surround us.

Boring but true, we do this with documentation.

At Centratel we analyze an individual system-process and document it as it is. Then we find the cause of any inefficiencies, devise fixes for those causes, and then create a prototype written working procedure that will include the necessary steps to eliminate those causes, thus preventing the inefficiencies from returning ever again. We always test the procedure in the real world, tweaking it into a final written form that precisely explains the desired execution of the process. The new working procedure is released and Centratel employees follow it exactly as written. (Will 100 percent of staff buy into this rigid protocol? Yes, for four reasons that I will discuss further on in this chapter.)

I want to reiterate something I just said. It's about going to that deeper level I talked about in Chapter 6: *we don't just repair a less-than-ideal outcome. We also modify the causal system so the bad outcome doesn't repeat itself.*

And again, because it's critical: *a working procedure makes a system touchable—something to be seen, grasped, understood, perfected, shared, and then executed exactly the same way every time.*

As a leader, it is your ethical responsibility—not just an efficient way to operate—to provide written direction for your staff. I occasionally remind my employees that it is management's moral obligation to provide them with the tools to do their jobs. Expecting an employee to be able to read the boss's mind is not just an absurd expectation, it's unfair. I tell them that.

OVERVIEW OF CENTRATEL WORKING PROCEDURES

At Centratel, the same inefficiencies kept cropping up over and over, devouring any bottom-line profit and literally killing me physically. These recurring problems were the natural result of undocumented and therefore unmanaged organic work systems. Now, working procedures prevent serial headaches by converting uncontrolled feather-in-the-wind organic work processes into predictable mechanisms. Today, we have approximately eight hundred of them. Depending on the task, working procedures can range from the utter simplicity of three short sentences, to line after line of details that encompass a dozen pages.

Breaking down the overall operation, we isolate systems into enclosed system package units and then outline each on paper in simple linear, chronological format. (First, this happens; second, that happens; third, etc.)

We also have a small number of nonlinear working procedures that better explain themselves in a narrative, bullet-point, or checklist format.

After documenting a given protocol as it is, as a team we analyze the mechanical process and then develop a streamlined finished product with attending final working procedure tweaks.

This is important, as we begin to optimize a system: *we mentally remove ourselves from the process in order to look down from above to study the entire written working procedure.* This way, we can grasp the whole system and then, with that overall understanding, make precise adjustments in that system.

We fine-tune the working procedure to make it the best we can. Then we implement it. And as I said, everyone follows the new procedure exactly as it is written. By trial-and-error as we repeatedly use it, we tweak it to perfection over time. It's a living thing. We constantly "work it" to make it better and better.

We follow this routine over and over again, making every individual system super efficient.

Note that our working procedures sometimes appear in hard copy, but most of the time they exist solely in digital form in the software platform we've created. (Go to www.businessdocumentationsoftware.com.)

Feathers in the Wind

Remember, a working procedure must be in written form. *Instructions that are not written down are feathers in the wind.* Think of it this way: You can't represent yourself as being a college graduate unless you have the diploma. No diploma, no degree. No exceptions. You are either a college graduate or you are not. Think of your working procedures in that same way. If they are not in tangible form, they are not working procedures.

FOUR KEY POINTS FOR CREATING YOUR WORKING PROCEDURES

Key point number one: Create a formal "bottom-up" corporate expectation whereby front line staff is encouraged, and expected, to both poke holes in existing working procedures and draft preliminary new ones. They will then pass their work on up to their direct managers. And those managers will do the same with their managers and so on, right on up to the top of the particular administrative chain. *In all cases, review of a new procedure, or a recommendation for an existing procedure change, should happen* *quickly*. A fast bottom-up strategy is the key to both hyper-efficiency and staff buy-in, and yes, it's contrary to traditional cumbersome top-down corporate/governmental thinking.

Key point number two: For designing and producing working procedures, use the best solution every single time the process occurs. At Centratel, we collectively decide what works best in the majority of circumstances. We cast the procedure in concrete—in written form—and then apply it exactly as written every single time. No matter who applies the protocol, the same best solution will always be applied, and therefore best results will almost always occur.

Yes, if there are problems with the procedure along the way, adjustments in the documents are immediately made, and the revised procedure is instantly redistributed.

It's the same for special circumstances. Your people should have the latitude to make personal judgments in applying a working procedure; but they really do need to be able to point out to their manager the "why" of their deviation, and thus a tweak in the working procedure for that particular special situation may of course be in order.

Always remember: this is a numbers game, and your task is to minimize randomness. In the real world, will a working procedure provide a perfect result in every situation? Of course not. But results will be perfect *most* of the time, and that will be plenty good enough to ensure the primary system is performing with enormous overall efficiency.

Yes, there is a vast difference in the degree of perfection between how someone answers a phone in an office and the launch of a missile at Cape Canaveral.

Key point number three: Procedure documentation is not limited to just the obvious problem systems. It applies to all internal systems, no matter their perceived efficiency. Documenting a seemingly flawless system will often reveal small defects. If a subsystem is already 90 percent effective, yet it can be boosted to a level of 98 percent effectiveness, that's obviously a good thing. It will take a while to turn every system into a working procedure, but the boost in efficiency due to these multiple efforts will accumulate geometrically. What could be better for a primary business system than to spend one's time incrementally improving its subsystems?

Key point number four: Create your working procedure documents for anyone "off the street." This means that someone who doesn't even work for your organization could instantly perform the process. More on this coming up soon.

These days, little goes wrong at Centratel, and what does go wrong is fixed instantly. As fire killing has been reduced to near zero, and most processes have been automated and/or delegated, additional free time is available to make things even better. This circular protocol is why our managers seldom work more than forty hours a week, and why I hardly work at all . . . and why, in our industry, we're the best.

OUR FIRST WORKING PROCEDURE

Coming immediately after my midnight epiphany (as I described in Chapter 4), our first working procedure was the Deposit Procedure, which provided our administrative staff with exact directions for processing the scores of client payments that arrive by mail in our office each day. This process involved more than just taking the checks to the bank. It goes back to when we physically received the incoming checks, up through crediting them to clients' accounts in the receivables software, cross-checking the totals, etc. Years ago, when we created this first procedure, three management people including me were authorized to prepare and make the daily deposit. Whoever was available on any particular day did it. Sometimes it took thirty minutes, other times sixty. No written instructions existed.

We each performed the operation differently.

The reason we focused on the Deposit Procedure first was because it was a critical system and it had deep flaws. It was our most troublesome process. Without any set protocol—with each of us performing the task in our own unique way—we too often made random mistakes, seldom in Centratel's favor (and if they were in our favor, a client was shortchanged). We applied payments to the wrong accounts, and too many times deposit sums were incorrect. One time, a $3,000 bank deposit was lost by one of our managers, only to be inadvertently discovered weeks later under her car seat. (She had taken the deposit to the bank but forgot to drop it off, as she was late to pick up her son at daycare.)

Each of us had our own homegrown shortcuts and unique propensity for error, a perfect recipe for random bad results.

Of course, any wasted money was subtracted dollar-for-dollar from the bottom line. As we describe in Operating Principle #10, "The money we save or waste is not Monopoly money!"

And with all the gyrations and outright errors, the process was taking too much time, and *that* was a waste.

So, the very next day after I had had my dream-epiphany, the three of us put our heads together and agreed that this particular process was causing the most day-to-day trouble. After thoroughly interviewing my managers about how they did this task, this first working procedure took me four hours to compose. Then, to make it perfect, we tweaked it numerous times. To accomplish this, it took maybe three more hours spread over a few days.

This first Deposit Procedure contained *fifty-three* individual steps. Here's how it went:

Step 1: "Put the envelopes in a stack in front of you on the desk and open all the envelopes. (Do not yet take the contents out of the envelopes.) Leave them in a stack."

Step 2: "Open the receivables software and go to the deposit module."

Step 3: etc. progressed through the procedure, up through the last step, step 53—"Place the bank deposit receipt in the daily deposit file in the receivables file cabinet in the CFO's office."

We agreed that if any one of us saw room for improvement in this first working procedure, we would collaborate on the spot to discuss a modification. If we were convinced the change would improve the process, we would *instantly* update and "publish" the revised working procedure.

This is important: *a published procedure itself is inflexible, yet we will immediately change the construction of the procedure if the change will improve it.* This "change it immediately" parameter is exactly congruent with our do-it-now Operating Principle #14. (See Appendix B for Centratel's "Thirty Principles" document.)

We put the Deposit Procedure into play. From then on, no matter who performed it, the deposit process was executed the same way every single time. Over the years, of course we incrementally improved it and each time we improved it, the procedure became more efficient. We built double-checks into it so we knew for certain the payments were tallied correctly, and we added steps to ensure that the deposits made it to the bank.

Because we put the procedure together in a simple 1-2-3-4 format, anyone within the company could make a deposit. As a result, I didn't make deposits anymore. All these years later I recall the moment I physically handed this very first written working procedure to someone else in the office. I remember happily thinking, *I am NEVER going to have to make a deposit again!* And I also remember realizing that because of the written procedure's simple yet thorough construction, I didn't have to take time to train this staff member on how to execute the task. I just physically handed over the working procedure and walked away!

It was a profoundly memorable moment, and *that* was the precise point in time when I knew we really would document every system in the company.

Completing that first working procedure reduced my personal workload by approximately two hours each week. That's two hours per week saved over twenty-one years. Do the math: for me, that is a personal time-savings of almost exactly one year of forty-hour workweeks . . . due to just this one working procedure! Yeah, man!

I was pumped, and so were my managers.

In its own way, that first procedure was a tiny masterpiece and, as I said, through the years we've continually polished it to even greater effectiveness. Since we started using it twenty-one years ago, there have been only a couple of small, easily corrected errors. Of course, repairing those errors was cause for two more enhancements in the written procedure. Like anything else, the more practice one has in a given endeavor, the more proficient one becomes.

Teresa, our receivables manager, tells me we most recently tweaked it back in 2018. Today the deposit process is technically much more complex, yet the working procedure has been reduced to forty-nine steps because of Teresa's assertiveness in simplifying, streamlining, and economizing.

My managers are *really, really good* at this working procedure thing!

You can see the latest deposit procedure (somewhat redacted, of course) in Appendix C.

Even though we put that first procedure together so long ago, I remember this vividly: it was satisfying beyond words, not just to know I didn't have to perform the process anymore, but to know it had become rock solid, stable, and super efficient. My satisfaction has not decreased over time.

The working procedure is a mandatory element of the system-improvement process. It's not theory or feel-good fluff. Rather, a working procedure is a mechanical tool that is down-and-dirty *mandatory* in the real world of business. This reminds me of the title of a short story by Raymond Carver, one of my favorite writers: "A Small, Good Thing." That's what a working procedure is, a small, good thing. The idea is to give your business a large accumulation of these small, good things.

A Structure of Steel, Cast in Concrete

Again: yes, the working procedure is inflexible. It must be executed exactly as described. For staff or even outsiders, this intense regimentation can be off-putting at first. However, there is a critical counterbalance. *If a staff member recommends a change, and affiliated staff and direct management concur, the working procedure will be tweaked instantly.*

A WORK IN PROGRESS

What was Centratel's second working procedure? We analyzed, dissected, and set in stone the methodology the TSRs use to process incoming calls. It was complex and it took us a full month to complete and implement it.

Our TSRs have executed this "Call-Processing Working Procedure" thousands of times *every day* since we put it into place twenty-one years ago. For them, precisely following this procedure is the ticket to relaxing and enjoying their work. They know what's coming. They know where to go for information and what to do if there is an irregularity. For example, if there is a problem in delivering a message promptly, the TSR holds no blame as long as he or she followed the message-delivery protocol exactly.

The majority of errors are not their errors. Because they follow this working procedure exactly, most slipups are traced back to clients who have not informed us of changes—changes that invalidate the previous, on-record data for that client. The procedural system was at fault, not the employee. The cure is to make an immediate mechanical update in that client's relay information, not take issue with the TSR. This lack of finger-pointing contributes much to the serenity within our office.

And of course, a complex working procedure like this one is never complete. It's always alive. It's constantly being tweaked to higher and higher effectiveness.

We were jazzed. In the months after instituting the Deposit and Call-Processing Procedures, we continued to hammer hard, working our systems, analyzing and streamlining scores of other recurring systems, including how to put together the staffing schedule, how to simplify collections, and how to pay the bills. We created procedures for performing the monthly customer invoicing, ensuring various housekeeping tasks were done on a regular basis, how to answer the front-desk phone, and for making the most effective sales presentation. It went on and on and things got better and better.

In the quest, as we created working procedures for every process in the company, *we always repaired the most dysfunctional process first.*

For some undocumented processes our analysis suggested that creating a working procedure wasn't necessary, and in fact we had been wasting our time performing the process at all! Eliminating the system of storing hard-copy records of customer contacts is a good example of this purging action. In analyzing the system from the perspective of outside and slightly above, we discovered that after years of carefully storing paper evidence of every client interaction, no staff member had *ever* gone back to those files for information. *Not once!* When these obsolete systems occasionally appeared, we dumped them with a flourish, a collective grin on our faces. (Now client interactions are automatically trapped in our online client-modification interaction folder.)

In reinventing Centratel there was nothing more satisfying than discovering and then discarding useless processes.

For other less-than-efficient tasks, we found ourselves devising radically different protocols, with final versions unrecognizable from the originals. It was a cleansing process, and as we dug in even deeper, it became contagious. It was a self-sustaining, relentless "positive obsession."

Centratel became strikingly more efficient. Our focus had shifted from killing fires to improving and documenting system after system. Interestingly, there were rarely relationships among the procedures we created or revised. I'll say this again, to keep you on track as you begin: the sore spots we tackled were unrelated, but we had a simple strategy for setting priorities—*we straightened out the weightiest problems first.*

As we worked up the new procedures and released them as official, I delegated more and more tasks that had been my individual responsibility. Yes, with a smile, I simply handed a completed working procedure over to the appropriate staff member and then walked away. I was steadily creating additional time to reinvest in tackling more problem areas. It was the same situation for my managers as they delegated tasks down the chain of command.

We were no longer "at work." We were obsessively working our systems.

Through all this, the number of incoming problems and complaints plummeted.

And of course, it wasn't just the delegation of tasks that saved time. We ruthlessly automated processes whenever we could. Having a machine do the work instead of a human is the consummate act of delegation. (In Part Three, in both Chapters 15 and 19, I will talk of our system-improvement mantra: "AUTOMATE-DELEGATE-DISCARD.")

Although the original one-time heavy lifting ended years ago, we continue to assertively apply the system-improvement strategy on a moment-to-moment basis.

We now spend the preponderance of our time coddling our machinery so it produces exactly the results we want. We spend very little time coping with bad results because we just don't have any.

The Test of Time

Regarding the strategic objective and the operating principles, know that an endorsement of their viability is the test of time. If you are truly using them and they change little over the months and years, this is confirmation they are sound. On the other hand, working procedures should constantly evolve, and that evolution is evidence *they* are valid.

JUST WRITE IT DOWN

Note that the very beginning stage of documentation is where the ball can be dropped—where a massive error of omission can occur—not only because this is all new, but also because the addiction to the immediate gratification of fire killing is still gripping you, still poised to haul you back into serial mole-whacking.

And I promise you that at first it will seem you don't have the "spare time" to work through the working procedure process. Know this is wrongheaded. If you think creating procedures is a spare-time task, the process will take a backseat to the crisis du jour. *Procedure documentation must go to the top of your priority list or the effort will be derailed in a week or two.* You will fail. For your business or job, raise the importance of creating working procedures to the number one task, even above some of the fire killing of the day. Forget about finding spare time to do this work. Don't derail yourself by buying into that premise.

There is no such thing as spare time.

So although it might take an hour or two a day to write up and then institute new working procedures, do it. Time savings will begin immediately upon implementation of your first one, and when you and your staff watch this happen, you will have all the proof you need to dig in even deeper. As the same old recurring fires crop up, one by one you will douse them, each for the last time. Soon you will crave spending time on your quest to document your entire operation, and the addictive fire killing that used to provide a kind of morbid satisfaction will disappear forever.[7]

Note that maybe the best way to instill the system-improvement mindset is Work the System training and/or Certification. (Go to www.workthesystem.com for comprehensive information.)

---

7 Note: If you are a creative, visionary leader who simply can't get pen to paper, training a "Business Systems Manager" to spearhead the documentation process is a good alternative. Information about Business Systems Manager Certification can be found at workthesystem.com.

Remember, the litmus test for simplicity is that anyone from outside the company—"off the street"—would be able to perform the procedure. Of course, depending on your business or job, this simplicity might have to be more specific. For example, writing an electrical engineering procedure for an off-the-street layperson is not going to work. But writing an electrical engineering procedure for an off-the-street electrical engineer makes perfect sense.

I touched on this already as I described the creation of our very first procedure. With detailed off-the-street working procedures you will save much time in training people to full effectiveness. An employee who doesn't know the ropes of a particular task will simply read the procedure and then get the job done with little assistance. There will be no belabored, error-prone "learning by osmosis."

Important: *first-timers are a great source of new information for moving a procedure toward perfection.* Someone using the procedure for the very first time has fresh eyes and is not jaded by an insider's can't-see-the-forest-for-the-trees limited vision. Have the new staff member execute the procedure, and then ask them what can be improved to make it truly off the street. (As they perform the procedure, they should be taking notes of what is not right or what seems confusing.)

And once more, there's this: for yourself and your staff, the extra time saved is used for improving other systems even more. It's the cycle of increasing returns.

Here's another large plus: with written working procedures in place, your operation will become more upscale and professional. Your people will recognize this and raise their expectations for the company and for themselves personally. Your staff's pride and enthusiasm will shine brightly as they know your operation is in the one-in-one-hundred category.

A MACHINE TO MANAGE TASKS

Our point-of-sale internal communications had hinged on Google apps for many years, which kept us organized through its standard calendar, task list, and contact information sections. But now we've created our own

"CIA" platform, our Centratel Information Application. It integrates all of our databases and processes. It's a beautiful thing.

Of course, there are off-the-shelf organizational platforms that are going to be suitable for your operation, at least for the time being. Whatever the software tool, one key is to keep any uncompleted tasks spotlighted, and to have the manager who delegates a task be the same person who confirms the task is completed. There should always be a full-circle conclusion to the delegation process.

A PROCEDURE TO CREATE PROCEDURES

As we first began creating working procedures at Centratel, I felt compelled to do much of the documentation myself. It took me months to see this was unnecessary, and I caution you to not fall into the same trap.

There is a system for everything, so certainly there is one that will direct the creation of procedures—a Procedure for Procedures. This master working procedure lays out the format and tone you want staff to use in creating this documentation. Once it's complete, you will train your people to use it exactly. (Centratel's Procedure for Procedures is listed in Appendix F.)

Whenever I mention the Procedure for Procedures to an audience, I hear some "aha!" chuckles. This reaction is not because a "Procedure for Procedures" sounds silly. It's because it is so profoundly logical, as it illustrates in a nutshell the essence of how to make your business a self-sustaining machine, a machine that can operate itself. *Of course* one needs a Procedure for Procedures!

Consistency is key and that consistency starts at the very top.

A centerpiece of management staff training should be the Procedure for Procedures itself. And when I say train, I mean train. Consider setting aside group classes that will be uninterrupted. You will be the teacher and your managers will be the students (be sure they study this book). Note: A quiz for testing comprehension of work-the-system principles is available at www.workthesystem.com/quiz.

Having your staff create their own working procedures ensures they will buy into the approach and they will see the logic of it firsthand, from the bottom up. However, until you are confident in their proficiency, be hard-nosed in examining the procedures they create. You want to know what's happening and to keep everything going in a straight line that is in concert with your strategic objective and operating principles.

WILL STAFF BUY INTO THE RIGOR?

On this point I am adamant, so here's another repeat point: it is the staff member's first responsibility to implement a procedure exactly as written . . . or to explain to a manager why they wish to deviate. There is no latitude here. Do my staff members comply? Yes, for four bottom-up reasons, most of which I've already mentioned:

First, simple logic. Because the written procedure methodology works, they buy into it 100 percent.

Second, *they* produce the procedures so they are fully vested in them. (In fact, Centratel's employees create 99 percent of all procedures and have a heavy hand in the other 1 percent that I write on my own.)

Third, if an employee has a good idea for improving a procedure, we will make an instant modification—with no bureaucratic hang-ups. No one wades through the procedure process grumbling about how intractable it is because of bureaucratic hang-ups.

Fourth, staff appreciates that if a procedure is followed and something goes wrong, he or she is not at fault. It is the procedure that is in error.

Compare this to typical small business or governmental top-down protocol!

RUTHLESSNESS AND FLEXIBILITY

Point number three in the previous section merits further discussion. *Yes, be ruthless in insisting that your staff follow procedures exactly, but balance this strict rule with the understanding that if a procedure can be improved, it will be improved instantly*. The procedure itself is rock solid and inflexible until the moment your management people agree that changes are necessary.

At Centratel, my management staff makes the decision to modify a procedure *right now* in an ad hoc meeting any time, any place. We adjust the procedure *in that moment*, and in the next moment the revised procedure is distributed to all parties affected. The entire enhancement of the document, including its distribution, can happen literally within minutes. *Unwieldy bureaucracy is the enemy, and like a supervirus, it infects most organizations.*

If one of us witnesses slow-moving decision-making in another business, we cringe. But the classic example of bureaucratic paralysis is, of course, government, the "public sector" nonprofit organization that is literally in business to spend other people's money on other people. Bloated, incredibly inefficient government has given documentation a bad name. If there is a cultural generalization about the nightmare of paperwork and bureaucracy, one can point to the overabundance of governmental organizations that surround and engulf us. (But yes, certainly you knew that already.)

And there is this: government systems too often prey on efficient "private sector" businesses that are the foundations of any healthy society. Of course, government is necessary, but in the United States for example, empowered by the COVID-19 panic, *local, state, and federal governments now eat up over 50 percent of GDP.* It's even worse in some other Western countries. Government systems always justify their own growth by referring to themselves as benevolent entities. Truth is, government agencies too often camouflage themselves behind the screen of compassion as they voraciously devour the resources of those who truly create value.

The Centratel Staff Is Paid to Tweak

Based on their personal performance in a current month, we pay TSRs a bonus of up to 30 percent of their previous months' wages. However, in order to qualify for the bonus, each month the TSR must submit at least fifteen recommendations for improvement to the main customer information database—the same one they use to process client calls.

This database of our fifteen hundred clients is massive, and errors or less-than-perfect descriptions/instructions can occur due to the sheer immensity of information. This huge data file is constantly utilized by TSRs, therefore making them the best qualified to make recommendations for system-improvement. Their submissions may be as minor as a missing comma or as large as a recommendation for a whole new client message-relay protocol. Via our CIA information system, each suggested revision is submitted to a supervisor. The supervisor reviews the suggestion, and if it's viable, instantly makes the database revision.

This is how we keep the information system that is the heart of our operation 99.99 percent accurate: by paying our people to aggressively search out flaws and to make improvements.

YOUR COMPETITORS DON'T DO THIS

I used to be involved with answering-service trade groups. I've served as president of two national associations and was a board member for a couple of others. I became knowledgeable about the politics of my industry and enjoyed communicating with my peers.

Twenty years ago, just after my systems-mindset insight, I gave a presentation to sixty answering-service owners in Las Vegas. The topic was "Working Procedures and their Importance." At the beginning of the one-hour session, I asked the group, "How many of you have written procedures for your operation?" *No one raised a hand!* I'm still shocked to think of that moment when I realized the vast majority of small businesses operate without any written guidelines whatsoever. It was easy to believe because I had been one of those people just one year earlier.

Too many business owners are looking for answers to their chaos problems in the wrong places because they have not gone through the dissection process that thorough documentation demands. They don't see the internal inefficiencies of their systems so they seek spur-of-the-moment global solutions: some quick fix—a magic pill—that in one fell swoop will make everything better.

Often the magic pill they seek is a God-like new manager—a mind reader and a fortune-teller—an extraordinary human being who will flawlessly oversee the business with little guidance and take it to its deserved success. Of course, no such people exist.

Here's what most small business owners don't get: terrific employees *are* out there, but in a nondocumented business, none can function anywhere near their potential, no matter how advanced their IQ or educational pedigree.

At the risk of audacity, I ask, is it any wonder that Centratel can advertise itself as the highest-quality telephone answering service in the United States? Our people know exactly what to do and exactly how to do it. Errors seldom occur because we unremittingly tweak internal mechanisms to perfection. *It's what we do with our time. We endlessly work our systems.* And when there is an error, that "red flag for improvement" spurs us to devise an even better mechanical process so that particular glitch never happens again. (See Operating Principle #7 in Appendix B.)

One more time: *We don't spend our time coping with random bad results that are the products of neglected systems. We're down in the basement, working our systems so random bad results won't happen upstairs!*

It's simple mechanics: *if each component of an organization is flawless, the organization as a whole will be flawless*, as evidenced by profitability, net worth, customer satisfaction, client longevity, staff longevity, reputation, and so on.

It all adds up to supreme satisfaction for your on-the-ground people, super-high quality for customers, and solid profits. Measurable evidence of the efficiency of Centratel lies in our TSR quality statistics for the twelve months of 2019. Our TSRs averaged one client-reported error for every 7,629 messages processed, orders of magnitude better than industry standards.

Centratel's seven managers are tenacious in applying the work-the-system strategy. They assertively search for inefficiencies, revel in devising enhancements, and enthusiastically create or adjust working procedures to make those more efficient systems permanently efficient. Their individual rewards include reasonable-length workweeks, personal freedom with lots of room for creativity, and intense pride in what they do and where they work. Also, they are very highly paid.

Systems, systems, systems!

Our service rates? Depending on the type of account, they are sometimes higher than the competition's—but even then, not by much—because our systems methodology has eliminated waste and therefore generates tremendous cost-savings, which is passed on to our customers. And our customers? Successful in their own businesses, they are happy with the arrangement with Centratel as illustrated by our average client tenure, which approaches seven years. (Keep in mind that the average small business has an 80 percent chance of failing in its first five years.)

How about your own business? Attain the systems-perspective epiphany and then buckle down to start the documentation. The day you begin you will be in select company, way out in front of 98 percent of your competitors (or, if you work in a business owned by someone else, your coworkers).

Written working procedures are not often necessary for your personal life. Why? First (and please applaud me for my firm grasp of the obvious), it's just silly to write down how you will maintain the car, work on the intimate details of your marriage, stay in good physical shape, or relate to your friends. With your systems mindset ingrained deep in your belly, you'll naturally handle these processes efficiently. No need for documentation.

Second, a primary reason for creating working procedures is to make sure the people you supervise are handling details in the most efficient way. Since you are the only one operating your own life (I hope!), it is good enough to mentally internalize your personal working procedures. No written documentation necessary. The exceptions? Travel itineraries, shopping and to-do lists, and intricate technical instructions, perhaps for complex in-home electronic devices, for travel related check-off lists (e.g., so Diana and I don't miss any details as we move between our two homes). You can find a number of Centratel's working procedures in Appendix C.

I'll reiterate this here: You are not documenting processes and then filing them away. In real time, you are creating and modifying exact step-by-step instructions for completing everyday tasks. The word "working" in the term "working procedures" denotes movement. Constantly keep your documentation in the middle of things—on the front burner!

A Summary of Procedure Documentation

1. At work, every recurring process requires a working procedure. The procedure will precisely define the best way to execute the process, handle the situation, or answer the question.

2. A problem is a good thing—a "red flag for improvement"—when your staff takes it as a cue for the creation or enhancement of a working procedure.

3. Do not create an unwieldy bureaucracy by writing up procedures to handle problems that are random or seldom occurring—problems that have little chance of resurfacing. There is the danger of being inundated with a massive conglomeration of rarely used procedures, thus creating complexity due to the sheer volume. Solving infrequent problems requires just a bit of common sense based on the guidelines provided by the strategic objective and general operating principles documents.

4. Be sure your staff is involved in the creation, revision, and/or review of working procedures. In fact, relentlessly delegate and even reward. It's bottom-up!

5. By making procedures identical in presentation, their individual instructions will come through loud and clear without becoming confused by various style, tone, or typeface variations. This is especially where you as the leader come in. It's up to you to keep affairs simple and consistent. (Create a Procedure for Procedures, Appendix F, and see Business Documentation Software, Appendix H.)

6. Without exception, test every new procedure. Before releasing it, give it to a staff member who will carefully go through the steps to spot glitches. Take this stance: *in a new or revamped procedure, glitches will always appear.*

7. As the leader, sign off on major procedures. Make sure they are congruent with your overall vision. Always keep your operation in line with your strategic objective and operating principles. That's your job. And . . . your people will be watching you.

One more thing: Yes, links, photos, and videos can be incorporated into working procedures. We like video-based Camtasia. And for still shots, there's Snagit.

I've kept this chapter simple in order to better explain things, but once you understand the principles of what is necessary for effective working procedures, I encourage you to create them to fit your personal desired format. (In his consulting business, one-on-one with the client, my associate Josh Fonger goes deep into this particular customization. See Appendix D.)

Frank Zappa's System-Improvement Strategy

Frank Zappa (1940–1993) was perhaps the most ground-breaking and prolific rock artist of the 1960s, '70s, and '80s. An iconoclast, he scored each note of every song and required 100 percent performance accuracy from his band members. After a concert, when most of his contemporaries would likely be living it up at a post-performance party, Frank would be conducting a mandatory-attendance postmortem with his backup band.

During these performance autopsies, individual players were assessed a $50 fine for each and every note missed. New band members were quick to challenge Zappa's recollection of their individual performances. More experienced members knew better. Frank's perfect recall of the performance was easy enough to verify. The evening's audio recordings would confirm what Frank already knew, and the fines would stand. Band members who were penalized were not likely to forget to more thoroughly rehearse their parts before the next performance. Frank set the bar high, and his innovative success is rock music history.

Does this attention to detail seem persnickety? If so, prepare to change your viewpoint. Your challenge is to embrace this level of attention rather than be repelled by it. The end result? Less work. More time. More money.

By the way, Frank Zappa never used drugs and was quite the family man.

PART THREE

SO SAY WE ALL

CHAPTER 12

Good Enough

A good plan violently executed right now is far better than a perfect plan executed next week.

—George S. Patton

To preface this discussion, understand we're talking about work, not about relaxing or some combination of the two. If you own a business, your mission is to work hard but not long—reducing your workweek significantly—and to earn more money than you require. If you have a job, the goal is to use your forty-hour workweek to produce large quantities of superior output in order to quickly ascend the corporate ladder so you earn serious money and can call your own shots.

This needs to be said, and it's a good time to say it: if you are going to work, then work! Kill the Facebook/Instagram routine, get your feet off the desk, stop the pointless babbling with coworkers, and put your head down.

Get in, do the work, and get out.

If you're a "smell the flowers" person, sniff the flowers later when you can give them proper attention. Combining working and relaxing will result in frustration in both areas: in your work, long hours spent in a mishmash of unsatisfying mediocrity, and in your leisure, an unsettled persona.

LESS-THAN-PERFECT PERFORMANCE IS OK

Here's my definition of "perfect," as noted in the work-the-system glossary at the end of the Introduction: *In the business world, 98 percent accuracy*

IS perfect because trying to achieve that additional 2 percent demands too much additional effort. It's the law of diminishing returns in action and it's a catch-22. Unlike brain surgery, Olympic competition, and world-class chess, in the vast majority of situations, the extra energy required for this tiny 2 percent betterment is in itself imperfection because that energy could have been put to much better use elsewhere.

So, here it is, for most instances: getting a process too perfect is shortsighted and counterproductive. The following story illustrates that more-than-good-enough can be a horrible waste of time and money.

When I was twenty-four years old and studying land surveying in technical school, the instructor told our class a story at the beginning of the term to prep us for the curriculum lessons that would follow. The story setting was the early 1950s, when the typical survey crew consisted of a party chief, who was responsible for supervising the actual in-the-field survey work, and three crew members.

The party chief was given a project and it was up to him (in those days, it was almost always a "him") to take the crew into the field, do the job of marking the property properly, and report back to the owner of the surveying company with accurate and usable notes so a map of the surveyed land could be created. With the notes and the map, the landowner's questions of property size, boundary lines, and future development possibilities could be answered.

A land survey project is a linear, encapsulated process—yes, a system with a well-defined beginning and end—and a project starts when the survey-company owner tells the party chief, in not so many words, "Here's the job. I presume you can handle it. Be quick and accurate according to the specifications I give you, then come back and give me your field notes so our draftsman can make a map of the property. Then I can get paid by the landowner."

BEN AND JOHN

This scenario is about a land survey company and the two survey crews it employs. The two party chiefs and their respective crews are to measure the boundaries of two adjacent parcels of land. The landowner wants the surveys performed in order to get a general feel for where the property lines and property corners are located.

The owner of the survey firm assigns the first parcel to one crew, with Ben as the party chief, and the second (similar-sized) parcel to the other crew, with John as the party chief.

The survey company owner provides Ben and John with concise verbal instructions about what is required. As in any land survey project, the crews must measure the distances and angles of the property boundaries quickly and with suitable accuracy. The degree of accuracy depends on the reason for the survey, and of course higher degrees of accuracy require more crew time and therefore are costlier. In actual land survey work it's a balancing act between speed and accuracy as a crew moves along, physically marking property corners and providing distance and angle statistics to the party chief who takes notes.

Time is always of the essence to the survey company owner because he pays his crews by the hour but receives a flat fee from the landowner. In this story, time is even more critical because the property owner has a deadline to meet. The crews must get to work immediately and finish the two surveys promptly.

The surveys will be challenging. Each parcel is wooded, undulating, and steep. They are each several miles in circumference. Based on the survey company owner's verbal briefing, each party chief makes a determination of how much accuracy is required to survey his particular parcel.

The next day the two crews separately gather the necessary materials and equipment and head off to their assigned projects. Both crews go to work.

Ben decides his survey requires measurement to the nearest one hundredth of a foot—a high level of accuracy. Using a transit (a sophisticated tripod-mounted instrument for measuring precise angles), and a steel tape measure for calculating near-exact distances, his crew slowly and yes, systematically, works through their parcel, carefully marking the physical property corners, exactly measuring distances and angles, checking and double-checking their work. Ben takes careful notes in his field book. The four are focused and fastidious, their work exact.

It takes the crew four days to complete the survey at a total cost of

$800 to their boss, the owner of the survey company. Their work is superlative: the submitted survey notes are neat and concise and super accurate, especially because Ben took an additional half-day to review them.

In the meantime, John determined that his crew would survey their parcel with less accuracy, measuring only to the nearest whole foot, thus allowing his crew to finish the job quickly. Using much less sophisticated equipment to measure angles, a staff-compass instead of a transit, the crew moves at full tilt. They mark approximate property corners while rapidly taking their angle and distance measurements. Yes, they do take their measurements twice, avoiding any gross errors. John takes quick notes, double-checking his work as he goes. The crew moves quickly.

They complete the survey in just one day. John immediately submits his work, telling the survey-company owner that the measured distances are accurate to the nearest foot, and angles are not precise, but in his mind, close enough. The submitted notes are smudged and wrinkled, evidence of a fast-moving crew that is not concerned with appearances. The total crew cost for John's one-day survey is $200.

The owner of the survey company reviews the notes of each party chief and . . . *fires Ben!*

The party chief who took so much care and produced such accurate work is fired? *Why?*

In land surveyor parlance, Ben committed a "blunder." The survey didn't require measurements to one-hundredth of a foot, so the additional time expended to provide that level of accuracy was an utter waste. In his original briefing to each party chief, the survey company owner had explained that the landowner wanted only a general idea of where the property boundaries were located. Ben had not listened carefully, self-enamored with his ability to produce tremendous accuracy. In his zeal for precision he wasted three days and $600 by providing a colossal amount of super accurate but useless information.

It was narrow-minded and a little bit arrogant. The delivery of unnecessary precision is often just that.

98 PERCENT PERFECTION IS PERFECT

Time and money wasted is time and money gone forever. And a waste of time and money means some other positive things that could have happened, didn't.

The Good Enough rule is especially applicable to working procedures. A 100 percent accurate document that took forever to create carries imperfection because the extra time spent creating the masterpiece is lost forever. The finished product has an embedded taint and it can never be called "perfect."

Yes, this principle also apples to calculating moon shots, writing computer code, and performing complex medical procedures; albeit in these cases 99.999 percent accuracy may be the necessary level of "good enough."

So, make your working procedures detailed but don't make them *too* detailed. They should be good enough so the desired results are consistently produced and so someone "off the street" can execute them, but no more. See it this way: in putting your procedures together accurately enough, you are actually attaining a kind of perfection—the perfection of a useful product created without waste.

Throughout this book, I have asserted that you must tweak your procedures to perfection. Now you better understand why my definition of perfection is, figuratively speaking, 98 percent, not 100 percent.

Regarding the work-the-system methodology, are there exceptions to the rule? Yes, there are two. Both your strategic objective and general operating principles documents should be as close to 100 percent flawless as possible despite the additional time it takes to get there. These documents are your guiding lights for today and tomorrow. They are short and you and your people will read them repeatedly. Imperfections will stand out and overshadow and, to some degree, invalidate the overall message. The strategic objective and the operating principles documents are the brief summations of everything you are and how you will proceed, so yes, spend good time on them.

Beware Useless Information and Whining

Guard your consciousness and your focus. Don't waste time on useless information or complain about what you can't influence. With the people and events around you, be militant about relegating unimportant media- and advertisement-driven trivia to the mental trash pile. Don't let zero-relevance details poison what is important to your life, no matter how dogged the encroachment.

This Is Not a (Expletive) Clock

Back in the early '90s, I was a power line construction superintendent working with crews that build overhead electric power transmission lines. Following written construction designs, the crews use massive crane trucks to insert gigantic seventy- to eighty-foot wood poles in the ground. Then they go back to string heavy-gauge conductor (wire) between the poles. It's tough, dirty, and dangerous work.

In those days, the crews were exclusively male.

The men on these crews are weather-beaten, hard-living, all-American linemen. Straight out of the union hall, they have the surly countenance of loggers and roughnecks and do not suffer fools gladly. These guys do not practice yoga, burn incense, drive electric smart cars, or smoke weed. They drive Ford pickups. They drink Jack Daniels.

It was deep summertime and I was managing such a crew in the torrid, windswept backcountry of eastern Oregon when I found fault with the work they had just completed. In sighting down a half mile-long stretch of six poles, one pole in the middle of the series was clearly set wrong, three feet out of alignment with the others.

I pointed out the problem to the crusty foreman. To correct the error, he would have to order his men to go back with their heavy equipment, carefully remove the poorly placed pole from the ground, fill in the old hole, drill a new hole, and then reset the pole in the proper alignment. My foreman was not pleased. Nobody likes to do the same hot and dirty job twice, especially when there is a degree of humiliation attached.

continued

I will never forget his grizzled scowl and clear disdain for college-boy bosses like me. He spit on the ground, glared at me, and growled, “We’re building a f’ing power line, not a f’ing *clock*!”

Well, the pole *was* out of alignment, and his crew did go back to reset it properly, but his power line/clock analogy has stuck with me through the years. That cut-to-the-bone comment, however off-target in that particular circumstance, remains an enduring reminder that the quality of work must not exceed the required result.

CHAPTER 13

Errors of Omission

We do not so much look at things as overlook them.

—Zen proverb

It's an interesting exercise to look back and ask, "In descending order of impact, what have been the top five mistakes of my life?" When I propose this question to friends, they chide me about dwelling on the past and focusing on the negative. Yes, I understand all that, but if one spends some time summarizing, a commonality will surface, one that can be useful for future decision-making.

It's important to approach the task with an objective and detached persona. Take time to think it out carefully from different angles and then get your list down on paper, and my bet is it will stand the test of time. That's how it's been for me. My top-five list has remained pretty much unchanged for thirty years.

On my list—and I'll bet yours, too—the largest errors were not the result of overt mistakes. They were the outcome of failing to take steps that should have been taken. These are errors of omission. The large errors of omission are bad enough, but numerous small ones will add up to an equally dire end.

Is there a primary cause for errors of omission? Yes. Too often it's procrastination, or what I call a lack of quiet courage. (I'll discuss quiet courage in the next chapter.) And lately, in this age of smartphones and way too much electronic media and entertainment input, it also occurs because we're distracted and not paying enough attention to the details that actually matter.

CHRONIC, COVERT, AND INSIDIOUS

The list of your life's five largest mistakes might include not finishing college, not heeding that stop sign just before the traffic accident, or not starting that savings account way back in the teen years. What about not keeping one's mouth shut at a crucial moment, or not doing the little things that could have saved a marriage? Maybe you should not have physically whacked that guy back in your youth even though he damn well deserved it. Maybe some other time, pride stopped you from apologizing when it was the proper and courageous thing to do. Other errors of omission: failing to get enough sleep, forgetting to lock the door of the car, not submitting tax payments on time, or leaving the airplane without a split-second look-back to see the smartphone was left on your seat. I'm guessing you've already anticipated this possible future omission: not taking the time to establish direction and to define the systems of your business or job.

One could say that not taking action is the physical manifestation of an error of omission.

WHAT HAVEN'T YOU DONE?

The errors-of-omission principle is a simple enough concept, but it lies buried beneath the jumble of life's demands. As with most problems, recognition is 90 percent of the solution and, good news, the ability to take action is heightened once the systems mindset takes hold. And just as the outside and slightly elevated perspective provides a better vantage point for observation of life's hard and cold mechanics, internalizing the errors-of-omission principle gives you a better foundational stance to cover details which would otherwise be overlooked.

Here are more errors of omission. Think of your own examples. Failure to . . .

- exercise leads to a lethargic energy level and an unhealthy mind/body
- recognize birthdays, anniversaries, and holidays contributes to the transformation of a friendship into an acquaintance

- pay a bill leads to late charges
- drink sensibly leads to a less-than-productive next several days
- make the phone call, close the sale, smooth out the misunderstanding, or ask for help contributes to less-than-desirable outcomes
- clean the house contributes to an underlying sense of confusion
- admit a stupid mistake from the past leads to the end of a great romantic relationship

The errors-of-omission principle works hand in hand with the axiom, "What you say or think is irrelevant. It's what you *do* that counts." Nike's simple "Just Do It" credo, which is as metaphysical and profound as a dictum can be (and is perhaps the most recognizable three-word sequence in the English language), confirms Ockham's admonition for "parsimony in scientific explanation."

INACTION IS ACTION

In any context, an omission is something left out, something not done. Here's the rub: it's a *choice* not to do something that should be done. Laziness and procrastination are choices, therefore *not taking action is a choice!* No matter what we do or don't do, like it or not, we are always making choices.

Sitting on a couch and not moving a muscle is a choice. And when we do nothing we continue to have an impact on our environment. At a minimum, we take up physical space, absorb energy, and create waste, so it makes sense to get off the couch, take that body that is already using up resources, and do something constructive with it.

And there's this, the thirteenth-century credo, "Time waits for no man."

It boils down to simple, flat-out logic. Since you are making choices all the time anyway, focus on making more active choices and fewer inactive choices.

Does your body—the physical mechanism that carries you around—need attention? Mentally disassemble it into easily understandable subsystems and then take first steps toward improving them one by one.

Does your disorganized home-system require attention? Acknowledge the disarray and begin to organize, one room at a time.

Don't just sit there!

WHAT AM I *NOT* DOING RIGHT NOW?

How can you, minute by minute, apply this action principle to your daily life? Stand apart and watch the events of your day; as they occur, ask, "What am I *not* doing right now that is holding me back?" Should I stop and buy a small gift for my lover? Should I find a way to exercise for an hour? Should I have a chat with a certain employee who seems disconsolate lately? Shall I start, right this minute, to read that book I bought two months ago? And of course, today will I begin to get a grip on things by writing a first draft of my strategic objective?

Of course, you already know this approach is in exact alignment with the systems mindset. Your new life will be on the offense, not the defense.

The Power Is Out

Late in the afternoon on July 3, 2006, the electricity in most of Bend, Oregon, failed. A lightning strike had disabled a main transformer at the power company substation on the edge of town. I was 160 miles to the north, in Portland, when Andi called to say that half of Bend was without electricity, including Centratel. As a private 911 emergency message processing operation, losing power is not an option for a variety of reasons, not the least of which is that we promise our clients ceaseless fail-safe service. Our clients have emergency situations and so they literally count on that promise.

This particular power outage did not present an immediate problem because Centratel's internal battery backup mechanism automatically took over, keeping all telephone answering service computers operational.

But the backup system had only a three-hour capacity, so while the electricity was out we held our collective breaths hoping the power company line crew would fix the problem quickly. They did, replacing a substation transformer in just over two hours. Andi phoned me with the good news.

Over the years, it had been our experience that the infrequent power outages had been brief, and in this case, although the outage lasted longer than usual, our backup system yet again covered it. Without a hitch, our TSRs continued to process incoming emergency calls from all over the United States during the power outage.

But because of an aspect of our system-improvement methodology, this was not the end of the story. Principle #7 of our Thirty Principles document says "Problems are gifts that inspire us to action. They are 'red flags for improvement.'" In other words, a problem assertively prompts us to create or improve a system or procedure. We don't want setbacks or scary moments, but when they occasionally occur we think, *Thank you for this wake-up call*, and take assertive system-improvement action to prevent the setback from happening again.

Yes, our internal backup mechanism worked flawlessly, but per Principle #7 we didn't just breathe a sigh of relief and move on. Instead, we asked this question, "If we have only three hours of battery backup, what would happen in a worst-case scenario? What if the electricity was out for more than that, maybe an entire day, or longer?" That extreme power outage condition had not occurred in central Oregon in more than forty years because devastating storms are rare in our region. But nonetheless, what if this outside system—the power company that is not under our control—experiences a catastrophic long-term failure?

We concluded that the possibility of an extended outage was real enough, and for the welfare of our clients and the viability of the company itself, we had to consider that worst-case scenario. So, we took the incident as a warning-shot and decided we could no longer rely 100 percent on the electric company and our internal battery-backup system.

For long periods of time, we had to be able to process calls without externally supplied electricity.

The system solution? We purchased an on-site generator. The installation was a long, drawn-out and expensive process with numer-

continued

ous complications, including structural challenges, permits from city government, and finding the right people to do the work. But the new on-site generator, which operates on either natural gas or propane, ensures that should a catastrophic power outage occur, we will be able to continue to process calls indefinitely. (Power outages don't typically cause telephone service to fail because telephone companies have their own backup generators.)

Per a recurring working procedure task, our technical people test the generator once a month and then do a complete power-outage test every three months. With off-the-street simplicity we have documented every single step of the generator activation process in that working procedure, and we always follow that exact documentation in our monthly testing.

Here's a recent system-improvement that we made in the process itself. To do our major quarterly testing, from the generator we were lugging a hundred-foot one-inch cable through the operations department in order to reach our backup battery system. The cord was heavy, long, and a tripping hazard, so we had electricians come in and install a permanent internal cable from the generator to the battery system. With this, should there be a long-term outage, no one will be having a physical accident.

It's interesting that, over the first few years especially, with each monthly test there were incremental revisions made in the lengthy procedure. The Power Outage Working Procedure is a living thing, adjusting to a changing environment, advances in technology, and the tester's additional ideas for making the process better.

And how does this generator installation conform to work-the-system dictates? Perfectly. We got outside and slightly elevated from our operation and looked down to see the potential power-outage problem. Then we inserted a generator between the outside electric grid and our operation, creating an alternative power source should we need it. No longer must we rely on a critical system that is outside our circle of influence.

Have we since had a long-term power outage and had to use the new generator system? No. Not yet. But for sure we're ready, almost waiting with anticipation for that event to occur.

CHAPTER 14

Quiet Courage

People with courage and character always seem sinister to the rest.

—Hermann Hesse

The dogs bark but the caravan moves on.

—Old Arabic proverb

Your task is to lead the caravan and leave the barking dogs behind.

Although there are many possible technical excuses for failure, it is a lack of what I call "quiet courage" that often precedes sudden downfalls or long-term failures.

Quiet courage is unadorned action and is the opposite of procrastination. A lack of quiet courage incites an error of omission. Quiet courage resides deep inside and causes one to buck up to do what needs to be done, whether one wants to or not. Founded on internal fortitude, it is made real by self-discipline.

Yes, for certain it's there inside you, but sometimes it might go into hiding.

No surprise, understanding the quiet courage concept is just a matter of digging a little deeper. Here are some demonstrations of it:

- As a parent, facing the misbehaving child in the evening with the same patience, fairness, and respect that was given to the child in the morning when the parent was rested and fresh

- Going to work on a day when one just doesn't want to go to work
- Finally facing up to a dead-end situation and taking action to address it once and for all
- Exercising on a regular basis
- Apologizing
- Taking on a long-term project and finding it more draining and frustrating than expected, but carrying on to finish anyway
- Living up to an agreement when it is way more convenient not to live up to it
- Taking extra time to train an employee when the day is busy
- Making a necessary organizational change when doing nothing would be more acceptable to everyone around you
- You knew this was coming: taking the time to create a strategic objective and a set of general operating principles, not to mention starting to put together a collection of working procedures

The quiet-courage scenarios that escape notice are in contrast to the occasional overt gallant acts that earn instant recognition, such as challenging the boss with a delicate subject, overtly walking away from an argument with someone who is unreasonable, approaching a neighbor with a legitimate but potentially inflammatory complaint, or removing the delinquent young adult from the house.

Never underestimate the damage caused by timorous avoidance.

Buck up. Steady doses of quiet courage combined with your system-improvement strategy will take you where you want to go.

ONE CAN'T MEASURE THE BAD EVENTS THAT NEVER OCCUR

Problems that will never happen can't sap your time and energy. They can't hold you back. Therefore, problems that will never occur have tangible value. But how can we measure these future problems that won't happen—problems we prevent before they become reality? The answer is, we can't.

Measurement and stark objectivity are important, but an inability to measure should not stymie efforts to invest resources.

This is where one must summon common sense as well as courage.

Here is an example of action based on—and in spite of—something that was unmeasurable. At Centratel, our staff wage scale is much higher than industry averages. How do we measure whether this elevated pay scale is a smart thing to do? That's an easy question to address: we don't measure it because we can't measure it. Too many variables and too much subjectivity preclude objective analysis. Instead, we pay high wages because we have enough quiet courage to believe the extra cost is a good investment and not a waste of money.

At the beginning, it was tough to take this expensive, subjective stance when a hard, objective statistic—the total payroll dollars we paid out every two weeks—repeatedly screamed that we should hold the line on individual wages. An escalating payroll is easy to measure, but the benefits of an additional expenditure are impossible to pin down in hard numbers.

For instance, our high wages engender low staff turnover, which means less hiring and training. In dollars and cents, how does one measure the savings of the hiring and training costs that don't happen? And, because of our superior-quality staff, some quantity of error won't ever occur. How do we measure the benefit of complaints that never happen?

And further, how do we gauge the value of customers *not* lost due to the poor quality of service that didn't happen? How many customers remain with us today who otherwise would have gone elsewhere? Impossible to say, but we're guessing it's substantial.

So we invest time and money to prevent unmeasurable negative events that won't happen and to foster equally unmeasurable positive events that will happen. This is quiet courage.

Yes, when it is possible and appropriate, of course we should quantify.

PROCRASTINATION IS THE EVIL ONE

At Centratel, maintaining the quiet courage posture is easy for us because it aligns with the rest of the work-the-system methodology. It's a learned habit, ingrained by simple Pavlovian positive reinforcement. It works, so we do it.

When Centratel was just moments away from collapse back in 1999, finding the wherewithal to summon up quiet and not-so-quiet courage was not a problem because there was a gun to my head. The loss of everything was a real probability thrust right in front of my face, and I exhibited the same visceral reaction I would display if someone were to physically push me toward the edge of a cliff. Dismayed, I thought, *If I don't do something, right now, my business is finished . . . so what have I got to lose?*

As Henry Ford put it, "The greatest inspiration is often born of desperation."

But without the presence of a gun-to-the-head motivator and when making excuses is enticing, quiet courage's number one nemesis, procrastination, is always there, ready to quietly insert itself. A sweeping antidote is the point-of-sale action posture. We'll talk about that in the next chapter.

In the meantime, here are two immediate cognitive strategies for fighting back when paralysis is at hand.

The first tactic is to visualize laziness as an object, something physical that is outside of you and perched on your shoulder like a small rodent. Once the mechanical laziness is observed—most often it is temporary indolence cloaked by some convenient excuse such as "I'm too busy right now" or "I'm too tired"—just throw off the external seduction and get moving without a second thought. Get outside and slightly elevated, and then jump ahead without hesitation. Knock that rodent to the ground and move on.

As the excuses line themselves up, the second approach is to ask, "Why am I being cowardly in this moment? Why am I being a *wimp*?" It's a bit of twisted psychology that rattles the cage and invokes passionate reaction. Of all human failures, cowardice is perhaps the most abhorred.

Procrastination—that is, the lack of quiet courage—will ruin your life if you let it. Be strong and fight back. In the moment, don't be a scaredy-cat.

Here's something else to think about as it relates to making decisions and procrastination. Paraphrasing WTS Consulting associate/licensee, Josh: *The mark of a successful CEO lies in the ability to take diverse and sparse empirical evidence and rapidly make cold, hard decisions.* The effective leader doesn't dilly-dally, mired in analysis, statistics, and what-ifs. Decisions are sometimes made from the hip, but decisions are made. For these special people, procrastination just doesn't happen.

This ability to move ahead through a battalion of question marks is the heart of courageous entrepreneurism.

You Will Begin Now

Here is a real-time, outside, and slightly elevated exercise. It's about what is happening *right now.*

Here, you are the story.

Anyone can read a book, but it's a gutsy act to actually shift in a new direction. Clearly, because you have read this far, implementing the Work the System Method is a new life-trajectory you are considering.

How do you get to the point of actually beginning the process without relegating it to some future date when spare time *might* become available?

Here's how: After finishing this particular paragraph—physically put this book down. (Or if you're driving and listening to the audio version, get ready to shut off the audio and pull over at your next opportunity. Reading online? Get ready to walk away from your device.)

Now, find a blank piece of paper and write "Strategic Objective" at the top.

Just do it.

You've started! Now, place the paper in a location where you will easily find it later so it will serve as a reminder for you to get on the computer and actually finish it up. Now that you've started, the rest of it will flow more easily than you think . . .

Putting your strategic objective together won't take much time—it's just one page long—and I promise you'll be happy with yourself.

Congratulations! You took the first step! With this seemingly small action, your pilgrimage is well under way!

CHAPTER 15

Point-of-Sale Thinking

Why? Because I'm the mommy and I said so.

—Anonymous mommy

Do it now and let's get on with whatever is next!

Carefully prioritizing, get the proper wheels spinning NOW and—via automation and delegation—keep them spinning at full speed. It's a machine that you are building. Once built, it's going to be your ongoing task to supervise its operation.

Point-of-sale is a phrase taken from the cash register industry. It describes action where (and when) the purchase takes place.

Consider the cash register. Before the customer walks away from the till, payment is confirmed, a receipt for the customer is generated, a replacement for the purchased item has been ordered for inventory, internal accounting is completed, and the sales commission is tallied. The concept is spelled out in our operating principles document, Principle #14: "Do it NOW. All actions build on 'point-of-sale' theory. We don't delay an action if it can be executed immediately. Just like any major retail outlet, we 'update inventories and databases at the exact time the transaction takes place.'"

At Centratel, there is no paperwork floating around the office after a transaction. We ask, "*How can we complete the task NOW so we don't have to deal with lingering details later*?" Bam! We completely finish a task *NOW*, take care of the background adjustments *NOW*, and then get on with whatever is next . . . *NOW!*

The aim of point-of-sale processing is to gobble up details as they arise. It's the converse of fire killing.

Point-of-sale means being on the offense, eyes open and ready to handle whatever comes up, instead of procrastinating and/or burning up precious time sorting through old details. You will be in an assertive posture, better prepared to handle the inevitable body slams that are part of living a life.

Like quiet courage, the point-of-sale positioning is the opposite of procrastination.

Keep a clear horizon. You'll not only be ready for whatever future challenges arise . . . it's good for the head.

New project? Get the wheels rolling *this* minute! Finish it up ASAP!

For both your business and your personal life, the point-of-sale posture allows you to focus on the path ahead while your other systems strategies prevent problems from sneaking up from behind. Wear the point-of-sale banner on your sleeve and you will experience robust confidence, the opposite of overwhelm. The excuses "I don't have enough time" and "I've been too busy" will disappear from your life.

Here are two point-of-sale strategies that will help make your life simple and clean. The first is to altogether reject procrastination and *make it your moment-to-moment quest to knock off tasks as they appear*. Get tasks out of the way *now* by immediately doing them, delegating them, or discarding them. Be seriously aggressive about it.

The second strategy is to automate a task and thus altogether eliminate the requirement for human action. By doing this, the do-it-now goal is achieved without any effort at all. And you know this by now: the outright deletion of a not-so-valuable protocol is always a great thing.

The point-of-sale chant? AUTOMATE-DELEGATE-DISCARD.

Your Conga-Line-Dance Leadership

Embracing the point-of-sale stance makes you the first person in the systems-mindset conga line. *You* are the one determining the line's direction and speed. The dozens of followers shadow your movements. The conga line goes where you want it to go, despite the disparity in shape,

> size, and finesse of the dancers who follow behind. You are the leader. You forge the path ahead while those gyrating behind sort themselves out on their own. (The simple systematic task for those following? They must only keep their hands on the hips of the preceding dancer, and stay in step.)

IT'S JUST THE WAY WE DO THINGS AROUND HERE

When the "Shall I do it now or later?" question comes up for a new Centratel staff member, their not-yet-disciplined internal dialogue may go something like this: "What's the difference if I do this task now or later? I just don't feel like doing it right now. I'll do it later because my guess is I will feel more like doing it then." A variation is: "I function better under pressure. I need an imminent deadline to force me to take action, so I'll take care of this next week when that deadline arrives . . . or maybe the task will somehow disappear by then." Sound familiar?

We ask the new employee to change that internal self-talk to, "I'll do it now because that is how things are done at Centratel."

Our veteran managers embrace the do-it-now tenet not just because it's our policy, but also because in their experience it has been so potently effective. The refrain is, "Do it now and then get on with the day!"

This because-I-said-so dictate may grate a bit, especially in the milieu of independence and freedom we Westerners demand. We don't like arbitrary rules imposed by others, but in a business setting an employee has the freedom to quit if the rules don't seem reasonable. In the free world, anyone can leave a job to go to work for someone else, start a new business, or sit on the couch at home and uselessly take up space.

But for the new Centratel employee, once he or she tests a concept and its workability is proven, it's a no-brainer. The logic? *Consistently superior end-results are justification for a cast-in-concrete Operating Principle.*

Of course, the point-of-sale concept also spills over into personal decision-making. Here's somewhat of an oversimplification that captures the point: "I'm shopping for clothes. Since I'm out, should I make one more stop to buy groceries for tomorrow?" The answer of course is, "Yes!"

Multitasking Is for Machines

An important goal of the point-of-sale strategy is to foster super efficient primary systems. However, it's important to remember that in a point-of-sale cash register, the *all-at-the-same-time tasks are automated*. Multitasking—many systems executing at the same time—is a perfect application for a computer, not for a human being. Let your systems do the multitasking. In fact, a tenet of Centratel's operating philosophy is that our staff members do *not* multitask. Rather, they "give full attention . . . to the task at hand" (See Appendix B, Operating Principle #27).

This means proceeding in a single sequential, linear format.

THE WORKWEEK IS FORTY HOURS LONG

The systems-mindset approach naturally produces strategies that save time, so there is no question that point-of-sale thinking has much to do with keeping our salaried staff's workweek to a reasonable length. I say to my employees, *"Here's the deal: if you give us 100 percent, we will compensate you well."* Yes, it's a generalized promise, but nonetheless it is our guarantee to staff that when they work hard and produce, we will provide them a healthy wage, great benefits, generous bonuses, and a workweek of reasonable length.

Because of our efficient procedure-driven point-of-sale methodology, our people do not see the fifty-to-sixty-hour (or more) workweeks that are common in service businesses like ours. Also, I prefer that employees work no more than forty hours a week. I *want* them to have a life outside of Centratel. And there is this: when they have time to unwind, they are fresh and spunky when they return to work, able to give the required 100 percent that is their "part of the deal."

COMMUNICATIONS AND POINT-OF-SALE

Point-of-sale methodology is at the heart of our communications strategy, too. Fine ideas have a way of passing quickly through the thought process without being captured. One might be driving, talking to a colleague, or lying awake in bed when a great idea arrives out of nowhere, only to depart in the next instant. Fleeting as they are, great ideas are too valuable to lose only because there is no mechanical way to instantly capture them. That's why I rely on the digital voice recorder in my smartphone. If a great idea pops up out of nowhere, I immediately record it and then email it to myself. (We call this an EVM message. See below.) And I sometimes use the voice-to-text application.

With my thoughts recorded, my uncluttered mind can then chug along to whatever mental gyration is next. The new insight will be waiting for me later.

Communication with my management staff is rarely via a regular one-on-one conversation. Using mobile phone voice apps, a large percentage of our internal management back-and-forth is via "EVM" (electronic voice mail). It's a very simple thing: day or night, and no matter how tied-up the intended recipient might be, via email, Andi and Marcello and Josh and I frequently send these voice messages to each other and to our staff. On my iPhone, I like both the native voice app and the Say It and Mail It app. (Oh, you use a droid? Try Tape-a-Talk.)

We have also configured our office voice-mail system so EVM voice messages can be easily emailed to the entire staff or to various subgroups. Yes, in our communications protocol we include simple email, group email, and instant messaging, but for many issues a voice message explains a situation faster and with more nuanced subtlety. (See Appendix G for an overview of Centratel's communication strategy.)

Ruthlessly Unsubscribe

"Unsubscribing" is not just about keeping your email inbox clean. Elsewhere—in your business, job, or personal life—how much of what you deal with really matters? This is not a loaded question. It's one of important pragmatic consideration. Be relentless in eliminating life-spam: the thoughts, data, and preoccupations that have no value. Also look hard at the information that is of *some* value. See if it serves *enough* value to make its existence worthwhile. If any information you receive is not used, or is of marginal use, categorize it for what it is—a waste of time and energy—and then, with a big grin, dismiss it from your life.

Ruthlessly unsubscribe!

What will you do with the time and energy you save? You'll expend these precious resources on things that matter.

STRENGTHENING THE HABIT

Procrastination most often appears during the low times, the times when willpower is weak because of stress, fatigue, problems, distractions, and/or inexplicable lack of motivation (for whatever reason). Failing to carry through with the point-of-sale mandate is often the first casualty. You think, *Yes, point-of-sale is a good concept, but this afternoon I'm tired, and there is always tomorrow.*

You're right, of course. There is always tomorrow: more often than not, a task *can* happen tomorrow. The danger is that *when you compromise a habit, the habit becomes weaker.* But when an excuse to put something off arrives and you do it anyway, the do-it-now habit becomes incrementally stronger, deep inside. There is value in strengthening your own willpower. Take any opportunity to do that.

Point-of-sale actions are about self-discipline and the willingness to stretch into uncomfortable territory. Just do it!

Is Your Tail Wagging Your Dog?

Which is it? I mentioned this earlier: as you read this book, shake off any hard-and-cold business, personal relationship, or political beliefs you hold. Don't reject them. Just set them aside for a while, especially for the areas of your life that haven't been working to your satisfaction. *The fact that you're struggling in a particular facet of your life could very well indicate that your tail is wagging your dog, rather than the opposite.* And believe me: if you're the dog, YOU want to be wagging your tail!

Here's another way to look at this. Is your life's "operating menu" determining how you deal with reality? Or, is reality the basis of your operating menu?

You want the latter . . .

And in this vein, here's another equally-potent question to ask yourself: *have you been confusing what you want reality to be with what reality actually is?* Painful as it might be to accept, it's possible you've been working with a conjured-up world. One that doesn't exist . . . in reality.

Politics, relationships, personal health—all of it—begin with what IS, whether you like that "IS" or not . . .

SLOW IS SMOOTH—AND SMOOTH IS FAST

Too many people live in chaos because they fail to slow down enough to set goals and determine sensible strategies to reach those goals. Too often, mindless rushing prevails when one should instead be calmly making system adjustments.

Yes, the key is to *slow down* and—let me guess—slowing down is what you are struggling with right now as you work your way through this book. Am I right? If so, take a deep breath and . . . *just slow down!* If slowing down doesn't feel right at first, that's normal.

Be patient and slow down anyway . . .

Breathe . . .

I had my first clue to this quietly potent mindset on my high school alpine ski team while training for slalom, a discipline that requires forethought, fast reflexes, strength, and balance. I used to slam through the slalom gates with reckless abandon, powering down the course off balance, my arms and legs flailing. I was giving it everything, but my race results were mediocre and too often I crashed and didn't finish the course at all. On my own, I couldn't see that the multiple errors and inefficiencies were generated by my brute-force, hell-bent approach. Stupid, really.

My aggressiveness generated my inefficiency.

Then one day, Otto Frei, my coach, told me to relax, to think "slow and smooth" instead of "mindlessly thrashing." At first it was frustrating because it seemed to me I was not trying hard enough. *It just didn't feel right.* But as Otto suggested—no, actually he insisted—*I forced myself to hold back*, to hard-focus on skiing smoothly and calmly. My results instantly and dramatically improved. From then on, including two years on a college team, I never failed to finish a race and consistently ranked in the top five in fields of over one hundred competitors. But that lesson at sixteen years of age was just a lone clue to a more effective way of handling things, and at the time it affected only my skiing. It would be decades before I smartened up and let this slow-down-and-be-smooth lesson spill over into the rest of my life.

Measure Your Body

I mentioned this earlier, but I want to go into more detail here. Back in the depths of my workplace chaos, I was also dealing with a sick body and an exhausted mind. I was delirious during the day and couldn't sleep at night. My doctor had me on antidepressants, then Ritalin. He was convinced my problems stemmed from depression—my hundred-hour workweeks notwithstanding!

But as a result of my mini-enlightenment regarding the systems of my business, I knew that my body was likewise a collection of systems. I asked myself, "What is my physical body made of?" It was obvious. The human body is composed of chemicals. Armed with this realization, I asked my doctor to give me a wide range of blood tests. Convinced that my depression was at fault and not just a symptom, he at first balked at the idea. But then he conceded.

The blood analysis showed that my two adrenal glands had shut down and so the "master hormone," DHEA, was not in evidence. The stress hormone cortisol was in the stratosphere, two other important hormones were deficient, and I was chronically dehydrated.

My task was to work on the dysfunctional subsystems individually and one by one bring each back to normalcy. Once I got all five flawed systems back to proper functioning, I would have a balanced, holistic body and an alert mind. How could it be otherwise?

For the next two years, I took blood tests repeatedly while I faithfully

continued

took supplements. I doubled my fluid intake and modified my lifestyle, bringing my problematic chemical systems back into balance. At the end of that two years my blood was back to normal and I was physically strong, my thinking clear.

Was it that simple? Yes and no. On the one hand, the road to recovery was obvious—*what* I had to do was clear. On the other hand, it was sometimes a struggle to be self-disciplined enough to do what needed to be done. I stumbled once in a while, but I succeeded enough to enormously improve my physical being. Do I still stumble? Yes!

How about you? Are you sure the chemicals that compose your body are OK? If they aren't, could this be negatively affecting your physical and mental performance—your happiness? Consider taking your health into your own hands by directing your doctor to authorize full-screen blood tests. Then again, your solution may not require a doctor. Maybe you just need to get regular exercise, eat better, and go to bed earlier.

System-improvement!

A final thought about measuring your body. If you are addicted to a substance, however benign, an imbalance exists. Any foreign substance throws your systems off, so a good starting point is to quit those substances and face the world cold-turkey. It may not be easy, but if you can pull it off you'll be in select company.

There is no better place than one's body to start getting matters straightened out. Using systems strategy to analyze and then repair the physical chassis—the vehicle that holds and transports your consciousness—is the most dramatic outside and slightly elevated effort you can make.

CHAPTER 16

Extraordinary Systems Operated by Great People

Start with good people, lay out the rules, communicate with your employees, motivate them and reward them. If you do all those things effectively, you can't miss.

—Lee Iacocca

I haven't yet sufficiently addressed an essential aspect of the business machine you will create: design it to be operated by regular people like you and me, people who don't have superpowers.

Acquaintances have said to me, "I'm sure you are successful because you've been lucky enough to find very good people to work for you." Translation: "Obviously you just stumbled into finding employees who respect you, know your every thought, and willingly perform your every wish . . . and who work their tails off. You lucky guy!"

Examining the notion that one must "find the right people" reveals an almost universal misconception. It's not that the statement isn't true. It's that the inference is backward. At Centratel, we *do* have an extraordinary staff, but that is not because of my skill as a personnel recruiter, or just dumb luck. It's because *we attract and keep quality employees due to the great work situation we offer. The great situation attracts the great employees. We just need to have enough sense to recognize them when they walk in the front door and then, once hired, treat them like the adults they are.*

Plenty of disciplined, hardworking, honest potential employees are out there, quietly looking for a fair shake so they can put themselves on the line to show what they can do. And when they perform well they want to be financially rewarded. All you have to do is find these people and then give them respect, black-and-white instruction, good pay, and the promise of a bright future. As always, it's just simple mechanics.

Seeking the consummate employee who will solve all problems—a from-the-top-down quick fix—is not systems thinking. In the work-the-system business, your job as a leader is to provide an exceptional business machine that will cultivate a hardworking, loyal, and long-term staff—a bottom-up solution.

So, these great people *become* great employees. You make it possible for them to shine by providing an open playing field on which they can display their innate skills and high motivation. You listen attentively to their recommendations. You give them opportunity and then you turn them loose.

Assertively Apply the Guidelines

Help your staff avoid the danger of becoming bogged down in the pros and cons of a decision. Do this by encouraging them to assertively apply the guidelines of the three primary documents (See Part Two, Chapters 10 and 11) without always double-checking with you first. Tell them it's better to make mistakes than to hem and haw or wait for approval.

At Centratel, I like it very much when a manager mentions that he or she is taking a certain action simply because it's congruent with a guideline within the strategic objective, the operating principles document, or a particular working procedure. I like it even more when they have a recommendation to improve one of these documents.

TO THESE PEOPLE YOU OWE YOUR BEST

You want smart, honest, clean-living, and enthusiastic employees who will believe in what you have created—individuals who become intrigued with your vision and who will want to continue into the future with you, at least for a while. These good people are the bedrock of your future. To them you owe the best, and the best's centerpiece is the carefully constructed system-based business machine you provide. Then, if you teach them well and they grow with your company, it will be a compliment to you if someday they go out and start their own businesses. On the other hand, it will be the supreme personal tribute if they choose to stay with you over the long term.

Is the Focus on the Product or the System?

It seems logical that the business leader should hyper-focus on producing the product or service and finding customers. But this is the problem! Exclusively concentrating on these vital missions without an overall strategy of system-improvement of the product or service—and the delivery—ultimately leads to dysfunction.

Failure to adopt an outside and slightly elevated perspective over the entire operation is a primary reason only one new business out of one hundred will survive fifteen years.

Here's good news: the bulk of those one-out-of-one-hundred survivors are doing very well indeed. Albeit grim, here's some good news for you personally: the vast majority of your new competitors are doomed.

Understand what all large successful businesses have in common. *The leader's largest time-expenditure is not in coordinating big deals. Instead, the leader is spending most of his or her time supervising improvements in the system mechanisms that produce and sell the product or service.*

GETTING YOUR STAFF TO BUY INTO THE METHOD

There are staff-empowering subtleties that must be built into your new machine. For instance, as already mentioned, employees should not just be encouraged to create new working procedures, they also ought to make suggestions about improving existing ones. (This is a key element in our Business Documentation Software, see Appendix H.) Also, as previously discussed, a staff member's suggestion should be considered and decided upon as quickly as possible (see Part Two, Chapter 11, "Your Working Procedures").

There will be other important nuances regarding staff action and interaction that will naturally evolve out of your strategic objective and operating principles. And be sure to look hard at finding ways to reward employees for great individual performance (see Part Two, Chapter 11 for the explanation of how Centratel employees are "paid to tweak"). A salient point is that you won't be turning your business into a democracy. You are the leader and that's OK! Being a strong leader is what you want and it's what your employees want.

The ultimate key to empowering your employees lies in your own internalizing of the systems mindset. Once that happens, the subtleties of management and guidance will come to you naturally. And know that once staff members are invited to be an integral decision-making part of your silky-smooth operation, you won't have the attitude problems that plague so many businesses. It's an amazing transformation to witness, but it's logical: *treat your employees as adults and as the critical part of the business they are, and they will want to climb on board in building your business the way you want it built.*

EVALUATING PEOPLE

Your team must see the operation in the same way you do. If you are going to be in control, you are going to have to be in charge of your staff, and that means you will have to remove people who can't or won't deal with your vision. (Sorry about that.) You will replace them with new people who share your systems mindset.

In our search for system-oriented personalities to work at Centratel, here are the primary "hoops" job applicants must jump through. Note that clear-headedness and self-discipline are the common threads. Did the applicant:

1. show up for the interview on time?
2. achieve the minimum required score on the aptitude test?
3. know about the business? Did he check out the website before applying for the position? Are there questions about what goes on in your business or is the applicant just looking for *any* job? Is advancement important?

4. smile? Seem happy? Generally, did she seem to be self-disciplined?

5. listen to you, or were your words sliding by unheard as she waited for the next opportunity to pitch her expertise?

6. carry on a reasonable conversation; look you in the eye?

7. appear literate? How does the resume and any written work performed as part of the interview process look? How did the applicant talk? Too many yeahs, likes, I means, and ya knows? Are they up-talking? Vocal frying?

8. convey that they take care of themselves? If not, the raw truth is that in most cases of personal neglect, there is a lack of self-discipline.

9. have a stable work history; not bounce from job to job?

10. pass the drug test? (As cannabis becomes legal in many states and drug testing itself comes under scrutiny, is there a source of drug- and alcohol-free people? Indeed. See https://www.workthesystem.com/clean.)

11. pass the criminal background check?

12. have solid references?

By breaking down the subjective interview process into bite-size component parts, we transform it into an objective black-and-white pass/fail test. Yes, intuition can be important, but it should never override your guidelines. Don't confuse feelings with logic, the subjective with the objective. However compassionate, hiring someone because of a "this person needs a break" gut feeling is usually a mistake. *Use gut feelings to disqualify rather than to qualify people.* (That's a useful guideline to follow elsewhere in life, too.)

At Centratel, it is critical the job applicant passes through *all* of the aforementioned hoops. If he or she fails just one, we won't offer the position because that one negative indicator points to a problem that can't be neutralized even with all the other positive attributes added together. We are hard-hearted about this and don't make exceptions.

College education? We don't worry too much about that, although a college degree might indicate someone who can stick through long-term challenges to reach a goal and who has learned to mentally focus. Unfortunately, these days, too often a college degree is not a reliable barometer of literate capability or of a reasonable mindset. Only two of our seven top managers have four-year college degrees (and in fact, both of those degrees are, oddly enough, in political science).

You know this already. Hiring and then firing someone is not just a bad investment for the company, it's an intense personal blow to the employee. For the job prospect, it's infinitely less painful to not get the job in the first place. Be compassionate by creating a thoughtful (and of course, documented) hiring protocol.

KILL THE MOLES, COMMAND THE FLEET

And what about the attributes of the leader of a large, successful company? Most times, these people are not innately superstars. Beyond an adequate degree of intelligence and their willingness to work hard, their leg up is that they naturally operate from a systems perspective—while the huge majority of people do not. These leaders are heavyweights because they understand that moles must be eliminated, not repeatedly whacked.

Yes, the systems perspective is permanently ingrained in those who direct large, successful organizations, but despite the fact that it is such a simple precept, many of the leaders who execute that systems perspective can't describe it, much less pinpoint it as the critical factor of their success.

Via managers who understand the system-improvement process, the successful leader is focused on perfecting processes and then keeping them that way, constantly making efficiency adjustments while simultaneously making modifications for trends and market permutations. It must be the same for you if you are to climb out of the confused, unmanaged tangle within which most people struggle.

For your business, you must find and keep employees and suppliers, supervise the creation and sale of your product or service, make payroll, pay taxes, and steer the whole enterprise toward a profit. If you are to leap ahead, what you sell must be consistently superior, and that can't happen if your people don't hyper-focus on the underlying machinery.

In the short term, you must concentrate on creating extraordinary, well-defined systems. In the long term, you and your staff must relentlessly improve and maintain them. The by-product will be an exceptional product or service that people want.

All the ships in your fleet must be traveling at full speed, so you will want to ensure that *all* your people are on board. One slow boat will hold back the entire flotilla. You'll want everyone in your organization working at peak capacity, creating, adjusting, and repairing. The fleet must move forward full steam and be precisely aimed toward your goals. It's your job as a great leader to make that happen.

If you hold a job and you want to advance, you have equal personal challenges. To win in the long term you must be more efficient than your peers and you can't accomplish that by winging it, depending on good looks, magnetic charm, college degree, or by endlessly playing Whac-A-Mole like everyone else around you.

A Super Supermarket

A by-product of the systems mindset is the ability to instantly distinguish the efficient from the inefficient.

In Southern California there is a certain grocery store chain that passionately ensures that all of its stores are precisely organized, uncluttered, and customer-centered. The shelves of goods are full. Everything is clean and polished. Yes, the people who work there are clean and polished too! Walk the aisles and catch the eye of a clerk. You can feel the pride.

Each store is assertively systematic. I don't personally know the top management people, but it's obvious that here is an impeccable model of thought-out and documented systems strategy, directed from the top of the organization down to the customer-contact level.

continued

Of course, other businesses just like this one exist everywhere. They are not common, but you will find them. When you do, spend time there and think about the system protocols that are behind the efficiencies. Watch and learn.

It's easy to find floundering businesses. You can't help stumbling across them because they are everywhere. In visiting such businesses there is also much to absorb. Note the lack of pride, the fire-killing/in-the-nick-of-time comportment of the employees, the lack of detail oversight. Feel the chaos. This is the antithesis of what you want for your work and your life. Watch here too, and learn.

CHAPTER 17

Consistency and Cold Coffee

My goal in sailing isn't to be brilliant or flashy in individual races, just to be consistent over the long run.

—Dennis Conner

In the Pacific Northwest, the coffee kiosk is pervasive. Unlike the much more substantial bricks-and-mortar coffee shops that abound, kiosks are often smaller than a hundred square feet in size. These tiny portable buildings inhabit parking lots adjacent to busy intersections and high-traffic streets. Most often operated by young, perky, bright-eyed baristas, they are convenient for the drive-up-on-a-whim coffee drinker. The concoctions they serve run the gauntlet of complexity.

Yet, although the kiosks are everywhere, I don't often use them. When I drink coffee on the run, I go out of my way to buy it at an established coffee shop. There's a single reason for this.

A long time ago, in the midst of my eighty-hour workweeks, I experimented with patronizing a new kiosk near my home. Early one morning, in a way-too-little-sleep daze, I was on the way to the Centratel office. I pulled over to a kiosk, desperate for a cup of strong, hot black coffee.

The barista reached down to my car window and served my coffee in a paper cup. I set the cup in the cup holder, negotiated my car back onto the busy street, and was again on my way to the office. I was *so* ready for that first sip and . . . *Yeck!* It was tepid, thin, and tasteless. *Arrggghhh!* I instantly ratcheted to ten on the frustration level—and have always remembered the intensity of my annoyance with that particular cup of coffee . . . and this happened thirty years ago!

Going out of my way, I drove downtown to one of my standby shops and with a ceremonial flourish, dumped the still-full kiosk cup in the trash bin outside. I stepped inside and bought another cup.

As was usual for this shop, the coffee was hot and strong. And to this day I remember my gratification with *that* particular cup.

Here's the aftermath that still surprises me: I shy away from buying coffee at a kiosk. Why? Am I being too critical, too unforgiving? Neither. It's more self-serving than that. It's because I don't want to deal with the inconvenience again, and especially because I don't want to feel like a fool for making the same mistake twice in one lifetime.

Yes, I know this sounds stupendously nitpicky, but it's real.

So, after all these years my first impulse is to avoid patronizing a kiosk if one of my regular coffee shops is relatively close. And for similar reasons I also have this same aversion to a number of other local establishments, including half a dozen restaurants, as many retail stores, and more than one gas station. To be sure, my gut-level judgments are not completely fair or entirely rational, but as I said, they are real.

How about you? Have you had the same kind of experience and knee-jerk reaction?

Centratel is a pure service operation, so judging quality of service is my natural focus everywhere I go. When out and about I find myself evaluating the service quality of sandwich shops, retail stores, movie theaters, public transportation services, government officials, etc. It's an unconscious analysis until there is especially poor service . . . or super-great service, at which point I instantly become aware.

On the spot, I have offered jobs to upbeat servers or cashiers who can't keep smiles off their faces, who carefully listen, and who seem truly happy that I am there. Then there are the other times when someone with a lousy attitude forever alienates me from that business.

Outside of work, Centratel managers naturally do these evaluations, too. Once the systems mindset takes hold, it's impossible to ignore the terrific *or* the terrible. There's no going back!

In fairness to kiosk operators, a number of years ago we elected to have Centratel's "Latte Monday" drinks (we buy coffee or cocoa drinks for everyone on busy Monday mornings) be provided by a kiosk operation, not one of the local shops, as had been our tradition. The kiosk drinks were consistently great. Could it be this particular kiosk had something special going on? Could it be it was being operated differently than the cold-cup kiosk of so many years ago? The answers to those questions are obviously yes and yes.

(As an update, a couple of years ago when that kiosk operator retired, we installed our own coffee-drink equipment, giving us ultimate control over this small—but important—process.)

Why was the coffee so poor at the cold-cup kiosk? The proprietor clearly had no procedures installed to ensure consistent quality. Disorganized, she had no inkling that one has to consciously manage systems in order to keep customers. And further, she had no idea of the enormous negative impact of one bad cup of coffee. I'm sure she winged it every day, hoping for the best, hitting and missing, a victim of her emotions, the attitude of her customers, or even the weather. The result? That particular kiosk went out of business soon after I was served that horrible cup.

THE LEADER'S PRIMARY OBJECTIVE

Objectively observing my reaction to that single cup of cold coffee, I learned that the success of a business depends on *consistent* high quality.

What if one works for someone else? That's easy and the rule of thumb is, "My boss is my primary customer. At work, my number one task is to never let my boss down." (Of course, if the boss is impossible or the position is dead-end, exiting the situation is probably a better strategy.)

In our culture and despite the universe's hunger for efficiency, service quality is too often poor, mostly because of the human tendency to neglect the systems that produce the results. But the good news is that it's easy to provide terrific service if the focus of the business operator is on creating and maintaining organizational processes that will ensure consistent quality.

Here it is yet again: *the creation, maintenance, and enhancement of internal systems must be the leader's primary objective.*

The following example is not so tongue-in-cheek. You don't want a customer treated badly by an employee who has a hangover. What you want is a protocol that will cover the bases for someone who is having a bad day (presuming this someone is not a chronic problem employee). You can't stop the person's headache but you can create solid, fluid, and sensible procedures that will get them through the shift without alienating customers or coworkers. Not providing guidance and leaving affairs totally up to your not-doing-so-well-today employee is a losing bet—the numbers do not bode well for you, the business owner or the department manager.

It's a powerful human idiosyncrasy, this willingness to make snap yet irreversible bad decisions based on a moment's bad mood.

And what if *you* have a hangover? If you've sufficiently worked your systems so they carry themselves, sit back for a day or two and stay out of the way. Don't gum up the works with your sour disposition. Disappear and let your systems carry the load.

So, know that when customers are disappointed in your service they will have a predilection to go elsewhere next time, never to return. Your best bet is to not fail them in the first place.

The Tip System

Consider this anecdote about tipping as it relates to our discussion of refining a process. Serving customers is a recurring protocol that can be shaped into a fluidity that will produce huge tips. Or not.

My female companion and I sit down for a meal in a local restaurant. At this point, even before saying a word, the waitperson, in this case a female, has earned a 25 percent tip. It can be downhill from this point forward. If she greets us with "How are you *guys* today?" there is an immediate 5 percent reduction in the future tip for offhandedly yet confidently referring to my date as a male. Now the tip can be no more than 20 percent. If the waitperson delivers the food and walks away with a semi-pretentious airheaded "enjoy," there is another 5 percent deduction. If she delivers the check along with the food (workingman's diners excepted), there's another 5 percent off the top. If she checks in to see how we are doing at midmeal and blatantly interrupts one of us in midsentence, yes, there is another 5 percent markdown. Now we're approaching no tip at all.

Although I don't sit there consciously tallying a waitperson's performance, and seldom does one go without being tipped, the essence of my thinking process is in this formula. It is systems thinking both at its best and at its most ridiculous. (And for the record, I am a generous tipper.)

How does this compute? If I were the owner of a restaurant, understanding that my business is a collection of repeating processes, I would monitor my own reactions while watching my own people and while dining at other restaurants. I'd take notes. Working closely with my waitstaff, I'd produce lists of "prohibited phrases and actions" and "recommended phraseology" and then make sure every single one of my servers knew those documents by heart. The lists would be part of the "Server Performance Working Procedure." (Yes, really. That is exactly what I would call it.) As the restaurant owner, this working procedure would be my personal obsession and my staff's center of attention. We would continuously update it. Only a few pages in length, it would be *alive,* always evolving. It would be the centerpiece of discussion by old hands and new hires. Over time we would relentlessly work this documented system to higher and higher potency.

I would post this working procedure prominently in the kitchen, in my back office, and the lounge. I might even frame it and hang it near the front door where customers could see it.

Staff buy-in? No problem, because staff helped create it.

For the restaurant owner, how much effort does this entail? A simple working procedure like this could quickly take service quality from mediocre to five-star, an incredible payback for a relatively tiny investment of time and effort.

WE WATCH AND LEARN

At Centratel we watch and learn and then we use that new information in the future. We try hard to avoid foul-ups, but when we do commit an error, we're obsessive about fixing it. We bombard the unhappy customer with tender loving care to the point where he or she is happier after the error than before it. (Via our Complaint Procedure, we call the customer back afterward a minimum of two times at prescribed intervals of one day and then three days after the complaint, to make sure the error has not repeated itself.) Also, we have two customer service people whose sole purpose is to call customers on a regular basis to see if everything is OK and to update account information.

What if you don't operate a business? If you are someone's employee and your position has potential, apply these principles and watch your rapid ascent up the corporate ladder.

TWEAKING AND MAINTAINING

Again: a primary commonality among successful businesses is the concerted effort to maintain consistency in product and service quality. This means that in a prosperous enterprise the leader spends most of his or her time supervising the adjustment and maintenance of subsystems. The more successful a business is in gaining and retaining customers, the more one can be sure that whoever runs the business is focusing on documenting protocols for quality assurance and customer service. And yes, for the employee aiming to climb the corporate ladder, this system-improvement thought process is also the center of attention (although confined to one's area of responsibility rather than to the entire company).

Just how hard can I beat this concept to death?

It's all about perfecting systems and then maintaining that perfection!

What about your personal life? It's what your mom told you: Say thank you. Don't tell lies. Be a good listener. Smile. For loved ones, systematically celebrate holidays and birthdays. If you promise something, make sure you do it—no matter how trivial. If you foul up, apologize.

Consistently do these simple things and people will trust you. They'll know you're dependable and will want to maintain a relationship with you.

A PLACE FOR EVERYTHING AND EVERYTHING IN ITS PLACE

You must develop the habit of consistency, the child of character and self-discipline. Consistency is not a hand tool one picks up to use only when needed; it's a trait to pack around everywhere, a permanent part of your being.

To cultivate this habit, the largest challenge is to fight the old habits of laziness and procrastination. By paying attention and being moment-to-moment proactive, good results will come quickly. And with those good results you'll soon find that consistency becomes effortless.

It is no good to set up a highly tuned organization at work and then return home to chaos. It doesn't pay to exercise a few days of the month, be nice to your spouse most of the time, or to apply the work-the-system principles sporadically. If life is to be efficient, staying steady and dependable is a full-time job.

Sixty-two years ago, I stood beside my grandfather in our garage, next to his workbench. Grandpa was a quiet and gentle man, and as we contemplated some small repair to my bicycle, I was taken by the perfect assortment of tools hanging on the wall and nestled in his great big toolbox. It all seemed so orderly and I couldn't understand why he made such an effort to keep things so thoughtfully sorted out. I asked him about that and I can still remember his exact words, uttered slowly and carefully: "Sam, there is a place for everything, and everything in its place." I was eight years old then, and in not so many words I wondered aloud how he knew his favorite saying was true and why he seemed so caught up in the idea.

Was there proof this was a good idea?

His simple response was *it's just true that being organized is worthwhile*. At first, if you must, take it on faith that being organized is something good. Then find time tomorrow to straighten out that top drawer in your desk, and this weekend go out to the garage and start the cleanup. Do some organizing every day, even if it's just for fifteen minutes each time. Work on the old clutter as you avoid creating new clutter.

Accomplish a particular cleanup and then step back and ask yourself how you feel. There will be satisfaction, and you'll find this satisfaction becomes addictive. You'll want to feel it again and again. Keep at the cleanup and soon disorder will bother you. You'll become a devotee of system-improvement as you watch your world become smooth and efficient.

And more than ever before you'll notice disorganization in the people and places around you—disorganization you can't fix—and you will shake your head as you understand the waste of it.

Will your new orderliness make you an uptight control freak? No.

On the contrary, you'll find yourself loosened up and relaxed. You'll be a smooth operator with time and energy to spare.

Breaking the Rules and Job Security

The following narrative is not about employee discipline or conflict resolution. Simply, it has to do with thorough documentation and staff buy-in that will circumvent most of those grim management entanglements.

With clear-cut rules for your people, no gray areas exist to cause uncertainty, argument, and/or anxiety.

Twelve years ago we had simultaneous problems with two Centratel employees. The first one's work was very good, but he failed a random drug test. The second one's work-quality was also good, but she violated our computer privacy policy. Both instances were serious breaches of the company's written guidelines.

What to do? It crossed our minds that we could sweep these major offenses under the carpet in order to spare unpleasantness and eliminate the time-consuming search for replacements. But we had to ask: If we allow employees to violate policy, wouldn't this render our policies impotent?

The system solution? We concisely spell out rules, regulations, and guidelines in our Employee Handbook, viewing this collection of policies as a primary system in itself—a giant working procedure. All employees are required to understand the company's policies and to sign a statement showing that they accept them as a condition of employment.

Per the handbook, the serious violations mentioned above are cause for job termination. And that's what happened. On the spot, we ended the employment of both. There was no arbitrary corporate judgment call. We simply followed the established, printed guidelines.

Our Employee Handbook allows leadership to be objective, circumventing any emotional temptation to manipulate. It exactly spells out our policies as it explains the ramifications of not following them (albeit most violations don't result in employment termination). These two employees knew they were gambling. They lost their respective gambles and their departures were simple and clean. Parties on both sides—and our remaining staff—understood why these terminations occurred.

Because we follow our policies exactly, Centratel employees know that an overt act of crossing the line will not be met with wishy-washy "don't let it happen again" platitudes or interminable second chances. After a serious violation, do employees deserve a second chance? Well actually, as a matter of policy they don't. But because of this intractable position, policy violations seldom occur, and we are almost never faced with disciplining an employee.

Employees want rules to be consistent and fair.

In contrast to some conventional corporate wisdom, my managers and I believe that when we let someone go for assertively violating clear-cut policy, our remaining staff members feel *more* secure in their jobs, not less. Yes, we lost two valuable people in the instances described here, but the losses were far outweighed by the positive message to the remaining rule-abiding staff who always understand where things stand and that management is fair and decisive.

Your human resources manager will love you for this!

There is an important subtlety here. Did we terminate the employment of these two individuals to set an example? No. We fired them because "that's the deal." If an example was set, it was a by-product of the action.

CHAPTER 18

Hyper-Communications: Grease for the Wheels

The quality of your communication equals the quality of your life.

—Anthony Robbins

It seems sensible that a discussion of communication would parallel other work-the-system protocols, protocols that dictate that quality supersedes quantity. However, in considering communications, I pointedly disagree.

The sense I have developed over the years is that *the quantity of communication is a direct determinant of the quality of communication.* I am referring here to sensible discourse between two parties. (Of course, it's no good if one person spews endless gobs of useless information while ignoring what the other person has to say.)

Simply looking at global affairs confirms that between nations, the degree of synergism is in direct proportion to the *amount* of two-way communication that occurs. Paranoia naturally ensues if exchange is limited.

Quantity of communication connects directly to any success or failure. It's this way everywhere. More communication leads to better efficiency, stronger cooperation, and deeper trust. Between two nations—or between two people—if silence reigns, problems will arise in the relationship or there will be no relationship at all. And of course, if one party is crazy, communicating can become worse than a waste of time. It can be destructive.

Clicking Communications?

Are there situations where it seems communications don't click? For instance, have you ever been going back and forth with someone who insists on clipping you off just as you are finishing your sentences (and so you know for sure they weren't listening to you in the first place)? Another annoyance: How does it feel to be repeatedly interrupted when you are deeply involved in a focused process such as a phone conversation, reading a book, watching a movie, or immersed in some complex detail of your work? In cases like these, the solution could be to diplomatically communicate your frustration to the other party, asking them to please knock it off. Or maybe it's cleaner to relocate yourself.

And of course, as you shield your own self from intrusion, avoid interrupting others. As always, observe yourself from an outside and slightly elevated perspective.

Bottom line? If lots of communication occurs, the quality will take care of itself.

Because our regular back-and-forth communication at Centratel is point-of-sale and frequent via our simple protocols and special communication tools, I am sometimes at a loss for agenda topics for our occasional in-person, top-management staff meetings. Nevertheless, we meet now and then even if it's just to chat about an upcoming wedding or someone's birthday. It keeps us in touch and we feel like a team. We laugh, and that alone is worth it. In any case, we keep the meetings short because we have work to do.

As the leader who has lately been spending a lot of time in our second home in eastern Kentucky, I have periodic get-togethers—by phone or Google Meet—with my CEO, Andi, who has a deep understanding of the company's overall systems strategy. These meetings quickly get to the root of things. Discussions are fluid and concise and in a few minutes we cover a variety of issues.

Andi handles her communications with her management staff in the same way.

It's the same with Marcello, our IT chief based in Italy. Also with WTS Consulting business associate/licensee, Josh, who resides in Arizona.

There's a caveat (it seems there's always a caveat) to the idea that quantity trumps quality: communicating with oneself—one's own self-talk. In Western culture, excessive internal communication is a problem. We examine, reexamine, dissect, and massage our thoughts, endlessly wondering, what is the problem? Is she angry with me? Did I say something wrong? Did I do enough? Do I need medication? Counseling? Am I a good person? Arrrgghhhhhh!

We would do well to communicate with others more and self-ruminate less.

Do What You Say You Will Do

Keeping promises is a system in itself, a habit that bolsters one's personal self-respect as it propagates solid relationships.

Don't distinguish between large promises and small promises. Keep them all. Keep them to everybody you make them to, including yourself. Keeping promises will set you apart from the crowd as it increases your own self-esteem. Think about it. In your experience, how many times have people failed to do what they said they would do, especially relating to the classic end-of-conversation assurances "I'll call you tomorrow," and "I'll take care of that"?

What if you become 100 percent reliable among your friends, family, and work associates? What if you dogmatically keep the promises you make, rather than using them as manipulations intended to change the topic or exit the conversation? What if people don't have to prod you into action? What if you do what you say you will do exactly as promised, and quickly? The short answer is that the people around you will hold you in high esteem as someone with integrity, someone who can be trusted.

COMMUNICATION MECHANICS

Discussing communication mechanics can be a monstrous proposition, so let's boil it down into separate pieces. This is basic stuff:

- Point-of-sale is paramount. Respond as quickly as possible if someone needs something from you. Keep those wheels spinning.
- If there is a problem with someone, have a meeting immediately. Talk it out one-on-one. If silence is encroaching, be assertive in promoting dialogue. But be careful. If emotions are running high, put point-of-sale aside and wait for things to calm down.
- Be accessible. Give people an opportunity to leave a private message if you are not available. Can the people who are important to you reach you readily or are there mechanical, bureaucratic, and/or psychological barriers? Promote fluid discourse by making a wide range of communication tools available to your staff.
- Use communication tools that keep you in touch but are not promoting interruptions all day long (e.g., train your people to use texting for urgencies only).
- Be open. Can your staff, clients, and potential clients find out more about you through a website and social media? Do you talk about yourself to the people around you or do you stay on the sidelines? Mysterious people typically don't do well in relationships.
- Yes, it's important to keep lines of communication open, but are you going back and forth with a person who routinely works against you? Are the other party's intentions systematically contrarian, malevolent, or manipulative with an ulterior motive? This could be with an employee or client, or with a family member or friend. *Is the person crazy?* It's irrational for you to continue to communicate with people like this unless, God forbid, you *have* to. End the relationship if you can. You are not in the business of wasting time, defending yourself, or being coerced. Do you have a close family member who is on the attack or is a crazy-maker? If so, I sympathize. That's a tough one.
- Get to the point. Unless you are at a barbecue on a Saturday afternoon, cut yourself and those around you some slack by getting on with things.

- Be cordial and friendly but don't overdo it.
- Never bash others behind their backs. It's low-class and any employee, client, or relative who has any degree of social sophistication will consciously or subconsciously devalue *you*.
- Talk up to people if that is the context. Your client, who is paying you, wants the bottom line—your personal friendship or clever witticisms are not part of the deal. Likewise, with your boss. While you take direction and provide information, stick to the topic. Know when to minimize the small talk.
- Put yourself in the shoes of the people you employ. As the leader, what they want most from you is concise direction, respect, and paychecks that arrive on time. Everything else is secondary.
- At home, be the adult/parent your son or daughter requires. You aren't pals with your child. You're the parent. Don't try to be some neighborhood playmate . . . or Santa Claus. It's unnerving to see a father down on all fours, goo-gooing with an infant; on the other hand, it's equally unsettling to see a father reasoning and explaining to his four-year-old as if the child were twenty.

In perfecting the communication mechanism at Centratel, we didn't limit ourselves to subsystem devices, tools, documented protocols, and policies. Our physical office is also part of our communications strategy. Burning up time looking for each other is utterly wasteful, so we provide a physical subsystem to prevent it: each administrative office has big glass windows on three sides so we can always see one another. To determine the availability of another manager, all we do is raise our heads to see whether that person is actually in their office, and if they are, whether they are busy talking to another staff member or on the phone. There is no need to call or walk down a hallway to knock on an office door in order to investigate availability for a one-on-one chat.

Our administrative headquarters/operations department is an energizing space. Open and bright, with lots of windows to the outside, it promotes positive group chemistry as each one of us sees the rest of the team quietly hammering away. *We're all in this together!*

The TAS operations department itself—the heart of the answering service we provide—is in the center of our office space, with the previously described administrative offices surrounding it, around the periphery of the large room. It's a psychological reminder for everyone that the main purpose of our business is to take and deliver messages. But, mentioned previously, because of the COVID-19 fiasco that erupted last spring, today, most of our TSRs handle call-processing off-site, in their home offices. Now, perhaps 10 percent of our answering staff reports to work at our HQ offices. Why? For training and because some of our people just prefer working in an office. (At the end of Chapter 20 you will find an essay I wrote about how we, via the work-the-system methodology, were able to survive and thrive through this economic fire-storm that instantly destroyed a number of our answering service competitors.)

I do my part of management without having to show up. I don't even have an office in our HQ building. Of course, not unique in this day and age, in-office capabilities are available anywhere I travel because there is online access to all files and I can videoconference with any number of devices. Also, financial, sales, and operational reports come to me automatically at very specific times during the month. With no fuss, team members from Centratel, Pathway One, Kashmir Family Aid, and WTS Consultants—located in Oregon, Idaho, Kentucky, Tennessee, Florida, Arizona, Italy, Romania, and Azad Kashmir—connect with me for quick one-on-one chats or for occasional planning and R&D meetings. We keep things simple by using Zoom, Google Meet, EVM, etc.

We don't wing it with our communications. *Intense management of communications systems delivers freedom.* (See Appendix G for Centratel's Communication System.)

CENTRATEL INFORMATION APPLICATION (CIA)

Automate-delegate-discard is our mantra and, with that, we're constantly refining our operation to save time, get more accurate real-time data, and eliminate wasteful bureaucracy.

Centratel's infrastructure is a collection of specialized and diverse IT and application systems: telephony, billing, human resources, the infrastructure itself, customer service, sales, and communication, etc. We created CIA to manage the data from those systems. It's a web-based platform that gathers and then processes data from on-site and cloud data sources, automating many of our day-to-day activities.

One of our largest needs was to have those independent systems seamlessly communicate with each other. Any information entering the system would have to be instantly processed by the specialized application and then instantly communicated to the other involved systems.

Based on those considerations, we decided to develop this custom-made platform from scratch, exactly tailored to our real-time, inter-systems communication requirements.

Acting as a "man-in-the-middle," CIA allows us to control exactly which kind of information is intercepted and exchanged, as well as to react to problem patterns and opportunities for improvement. In accomplishing this we have significantly reduced each manager's inbox traffic, and we've ensured our data is 100 percent real-time accurate.

For example, CIA handles the quality call-review process, which is integral to overall Centratel service quality. Every week, for each TSR, CIA connects to our voice recording database and extracts ten random voice clips for each TSR, based on a set of criteria that provides our desired call-profile (for example minimum call length, customer complexity, etc.).

These calls are presented to the quality reviewer via a dedicated web-based interface so he or she can listen to the specific call, grade each quality point, and leave time-annotated notes along with suggestions for improvement to the TSR.

At review completion, CIA instantly notifies the TSR of the results of the review and provides direct access back to the reviewer. The TSR then can leave a note to the reviewer or even schedule a time to go over the call one on one. During this process, CIA collects all the information and stores it to be used at the end of the month for the overall employee evaluation and bonus calculation. (For TSRs, Centratel provides up to a 30 percent performance bonus of the previous month's wages, based on call-review results.)

Bottom line, CIA automation saves a massive amount of human time, not just in the call review process as described above, but throughout the various departments.

(Centratel's CIA platform is proprietary and not for purchase.)

Gone Missing

Fifteen years ago, I had my home remodeled. Immediately after, I "flipped" another house. In both cases, numerous subcontractors, both experienced and inexperienced, did the work.

In this world of framers, plumbers, electricians, roofers, and concrete professionals, there is an interesting commonality among the inexperienced: it is difficult to communicate with them. Phones go unanswered, messages are left with no return calls forthcoming, and/or voice-mail boxes are full. The subcontractor has gone missing.

One has to wonder how these people stay in business (and I know for sure that most of them don't).

The dysfunctional communication system is a reflection of the new subcontractor's chaotic business methodology in which he or she is so wrapped up in doing the work and reactionary fire killing, that insidious inefficiency goes undetected as it quietly devours profits. It's a profound error of omission in which potential and paying customers are relegated to the bottom of the priority list.

But then again, when Diana and I had our second home built in rural southeastern Kentucky three years ago, the well-established local contractor, Ronnie Bryant, was stunningly efficient and always reachable, a master of his art. Building that house—working with Ronnie—was downright fun.

CHAPTER 19

Prime Time

It has been my observation that most people get ahead during the time that others waste time.

—Henry Ford

The Prime Time approach is about executing the most potent actions when brainpower is at peak capacity. Here's how to exert tight governance over the most powerful primary system at your disposal—yourself.

There are two components. The first has to do with your most effective time of day due to biological makeup. Let's call it biological prime time, or BPT. The other component has to do with *what* you do with your time. This is mechanical prime time, or MPT.

The prime-time concept is mind-numbingly elementary and has everything to do with Ockham's foundational premise that the simplest explanation is invariably the correct explanation. Like all systems-mindset fundamentals, the unadorned logic makes it easy to understand.

THE EPHEMERAL NATURE OF BIOLOGICAL PRIME TIME

First, let's talk about biological prime time. I'm robust but an older guy, and I function at maximum effectiveness for just seven or eight hours within a twenty-four-hour day. If you're younger, your BPT could very well be twice that amount.

Pay careful attention to this fascinating facet of human performance. To illustrate, I am a morning person, and over a period of two years, six days a week, I wrote 95 percent of the first edition of this book between the hours of 4:00 a.m. and noon. That's still my brain-work pattern. I write at this time of day because my energy level is at a peak and my thinking is sharp. But again, that's me. Your BPT could occur later in the day.

Like most early risers, I wake in a flash. Then, because my BPT quality and speed are at peak until late morning, I avoid expending any of this time on television news, exercise, or reading. I spend it only on my most important projects—the projects that promote freedom and peace. I hammer. By noon, my critical thinking ability has begun to decline. A fatigue wave soon engulfs me. My energy slumps hard.

If any one of us frivols away our daily allotment of BPT, that's a full day's peak creative allotment wasted.

I'm blessed to have an early-morning BPT because most of it occurs while the rest of the world is sleeping or just trying to get started. I can focus without incoming interruptions.

In the early- to midafternoon I tend to nonessential or less mind-intensive activities. I humbly accept my afternoon downturn because it's just a mechanical phenomenon—a low point in the sine wave, a decreased performance period in my bio-structure that has nothing to do with my overall intelligence or strength.

Because my car is out of gas does not mean it needs repair.

If a peak performance is required during my low-ebb period, I exercise or find some other way (hopefully nonchemical) to stay in gear. In any case, I get a second wind at about 4:00 p.m. It lasts a few hours but is not as potent as my early-morning hammerfest.

My ebbs and flows are certainly genetic. Both my mother and my father shared the same pattern.

But for most, BPT comes later. These people are most effective from 9:00 a.m. onward. Talk to someone with this more "normal" BPT, and they'll tell you they are zombie-like if they must rise at 4:00 a.m. They often awake after 8:00 a.m., and need some gentle time to get into gear. Their second wind comes in the evening. For a couple living together, conflicting BPT schedules provides an interesting challenge. As the highs and lows overlay each other, it is both amusing and problematic.

WHEN IS YOUR BPT?

Analyzing the *why* of BPT is not important because it just is what it is. What is vital to know is *when* it occurs.

If you are a night person, as I said, you'll cruise gently into the day and gradually work up your head of steam. If this is you, zealously protect these midday and evening BPT hours because, unlike people whose BPT is in the early morning, you will be much more challenged by the world's demands and distractions. Events of the day will be in your face, making it a chore for you to concentrate unless you take preemptive defensive steps. Turn the mobile phone off and shut the office door or disappear into a library or obscure coffee shop. Protect yourself.

So, what is your BPT? Stand outside yourself and very deliberately observe your energy levels over the course of a week or so. Note when you are most motivated, positive, and energized—and when you do little more than stumble around. The start of a downturn is the easiest to pinpoint. It hits like a hammer.

You'll figure it out with no problem unless you are a habitual user of mood adjusters, such as caffeine, alcohol, antidepressants, or other state-of-mind modifiers. For instance, morning coffee thoroughly masks the BPT energy cycle. If you are addicted to caffeine and wish to stop drinking it in order to pinpoint your BPT—you know this already—expect mental depression and a lack of motivation . . . for weeks.

My experience with caffeine is that it is a sixteen-hour top-to-bottom drug. People who are mildly addicted need it in the morning to counteract the withdrawal symptoms of the previous day's indulgence, but after their morning dose they can get through the afternoon and evening without it. Removing 90 percent of the withdrawal effects of mild addiction takes at least a month of total abstinence. If you are a heavy caffeine drinker—you drink it all day—my condolences, because quitting is going to be onerous. Here's a great book on caffeine: *Caffeinated* by Murray Carpenter. (No relation.) You can find a great podcast interview with Carpenter on the Art of Manliness website. (You'll find an interview with me on that site too. Go to www.artofmanliness.com and do a search by my name.)

There is another benefit to getting through the day without dependence on a state-of-mind adjuster: personal pride in facing the world cold turkey. In my life, am I completely clean? No. With Diana, I enjoy an espresso most mornings, and during my long-haul trips overseas to our offices in Italy and Romania, from Oregon, a jet-lag body slam of nine and ten time zones, small doses of melatonin help me with jet lag.

MANAGING YOUR BPT

During your BPT is when you should create your strategic objective, general operating principles, and working procedures. It's also the best time to sit with your staff to explain your new strategy.

Of course, there are other aspects of your day besides work in which you need to be sharp, and BPT will be there for whatever requires focus. You will learn to cherish these golden hours as a commodity to be carefully parsed, never squandered. When you can, shift your schedule around so important thinking and critical meetings can happen during your peak.

After your peak, remaining non-BPT hours are available for taking care of less-demanding activities and for recharging the biological, psychological, and social batteries. These are the hours for napping, periodicals, movies, yard work, exercise, and time with friends. *The lo-fi non-prime-time hours are a reward for the prime-time hours that were well spent. Both periods are equally gratifying.*

Day-Chunks of Life

If you are going to break complexity into workable components, try consolidating time into one-day manageable chunks. *It's easier to master one day at a time.* Plan each day carefully, pay attention to your linear system sequences, and watch the hours quickly pass as you work toward your goals, riding the ebbs and flows of your energy cycle. At the end of the day, look back and evaluate your accomplishments. Take what you learned, good or bad, and apply it in your next day-chunk.

IS THIS YOU?

For too many, this is the twenty-four-hour cycle: upon waking, external demands of work and family kick in. A way-too-big dose of caffeine generates an artificial morning prime time no matter the natural BPT cycle. The day's fray begins and the fire killing takes over. There aren't enough hours in the day to do what must be done. The hours are spent whacking moles, and any plans for making things better remain amorphous and ill defined. There is so much to do and so little time to do it!

By evening, the caffeine buzz has transmuted into nervousness and alcohol is ingested to forcibly calm down. That night, deep sleep suffers because of the lingering effects of the day's mood adjusters. (This is a serious consideration because every night a minimum quantity of deep "delta" sleep is necessary for solid mental and physical functioning the next day. As time goes on, sleep debt increases and until it is paid back, performance and mood suffer.)

The next morning the repercussions of long-term sleep deprivation, combined with alcohol and caffeine withdrawal, begin anew and another caffeine pick-me-up is mandatory, just to crawl out of the hole. It goes on and on, day after day, and . . . whew! The result is a nervous and exhausted treadmill human being. Just another rat in the rat race.

It is understandable why so many Western adults take yet another step, trying to find peace in antidepressants, with estimates indicating real-time usage by one of every nine adults. And here is where things can get seriously shaky. Notwithstanding sleep deprivation, how can anyone be cutting-edge effective, much less at peace, with caffeine, alcohol, and antidepressants circulating in the body?

Within this chemically driven mood-adjustment cycle, is there any hope for an unadulterated BPT focus each day? Not without some serious effort. Thus for most people, the magical BPT hours remain a mystery, muddled by mood-altering substances, unpredictable external demands, and exhaustion.

If this is you, and you truly don't want it to be this way, you can clean things up. Discover when your BPT occurs and then discipline yourself to use it judiciously. Never waste your biological prime time!

UNIVERSAL UPS AND DOWNS

For the population as a whole, a general surge of energy occurs during two periods of the day. The first is in the morning around 8:00 a.m. and extends six to eight hours. The early- to midafternoon hours are low key (which is the reason much of the world takes a nap after lunch). Around 7:00 p.m., energy picks up again and a secondary surge begins that can last several hours. At around 10:00 p.m., mental sharpness steeply declines and it's time to get ready for bed. This universal cycle is part of human biology; and whether you are a morning person or a night person, your individual sine-wave peaks and lows will intermingle with that universal pattern.

MECHANICAL PRIME TIME AND THE REAL BUSINESS

Mechanical prime time (MPT) has to do with *what* you do with your time. It's the time spent building primary systems such as a business or a career and, with some notable exceptions that I will discuss, it is not the time spent working at a job for money or mechanically producing the product or service.

If your goal is freedom and prosperity, maximizing your MPT is critical. Create as much of it as you can. Unlike BPT, which happens automatically whether we are ready to take advantage of it or not, MPT exists only if we generate it.

Many people never experience MPT because they are too busy killing fires to spend any time there. Most just steer into it occasionally, either because they have a gun to their heads or because they are riding a wave of temporary fervor.

Your task is to identify exactly what MPT is for you, and then spend as much of your day there as possible.

Let's define MPT through the back door by discussing my rather strict definition of a real business. This interpretation presumes there are but two positions in an enterprise. Either one is the boss or one isn't the boss. One either owns the enterprise or one works for the enterprise. The obligatory caveat: Can a person be both? Yes, but it can be seriously messy unless one is very careful. We'll get to that.

In a real business, the owner is not the one physically generating the product or service. This can be a bitter pill, but it is difficult to dispute that if you are the one creating and/or delivering the actual product or service, you own a job more than you own a business. Yes, even with attendant high income and prestige, doctors, attorneys, consultants, celebrities, and professional athletes have jobs, not businesses. (Don't get me wrong here. A job is not a bad thing, and offers some real advantages over my rigid definition of a business. We'll get to that soon, too.)

The key indicator of a "job" is that one has to show up. Not so with a true business. A real business operates with cursory supervision from the owner, churning out profits as its own primary money-making machine—its own organism, self-sufficient and independent. Think this pleasant thought: "Money keeps materializing in my bank account while I'm elsewhere."

This is no small thing: MPT is the time spent building a business in order to achieve the above. It is not the time spent working *in* the business producing the product or service, or dealing with everyday recurring business affairs.

If you are a professional and have other professionals working *for* you—and without your direct moment-to-moment input they are accomplishing goals you have set out for them—this portion of your life is a business, and the time you spend dealing with it is MPT. In contrast, the ongoing time you spend with patients or clients is production work, so that part of what you do is a job, not MPT. If you must trot out into left field as a New York Yankee, or are the star of a feature film, or a brain surgeon in the operating room, you have a job—albeit a very good one!

Here's an illustration of a job versus a real business: real estate sales. If the real estate professional is selling property and living on the income, that time is spent working a job. However, if some time is expended allocating commissions into personal investments in rental properties, lots, or bare land, that is definitely a business. Here, MPT is the time spent doing the legwork of acquiring and managing a personal property portfolio, not the time spent showing up to list or sell someone else's property.

What Matters Most?

As you analyze your actions know it is the moment-to-moment mindset that matters most. During the workday look at each action you take and ask yourself if it is contributing to making more and working less. The day you *get it* and switch your focus to the blow-by-blow mechanics of building a business for yourself, while leaving aside theory and wishful thinking, freedom and wealth will begin to materialize. You've attained the systems mindset.

IT'S YOUR JOB *AND* YOUR BUSINESS

If you are a creative person making a living in art or performing—for example, a professional athlete, a writer, an artist, or an independent consultant—or the centerpiece of some endeavor or another—yes, you have a job, but you also have a business. *You* are the business and you carry your business everywhere. Yours is a unique skill that is a blessing—you are a creator—but as you create, you must deal with the showing-up challenges of managing the day-to-day gyrations of the enterprise.

You not only must do what you do as the creator, you have to preside over accounting, purchasing, accounts receivable, advertising, customer service, public relations, and so on. And if you make your living as a celebrity there is the additional notoriety baggage that comes along with the package. This is the reason why, in an enterprise where the creator is doing the production *and* managing the associated mechanical details, life can be exhausting at the least and nightmarish at the worst. Use the MPT mindset to find ways to minimize the day-to-day administrative burdens so focus can remain on creative efforts.

Mental Positioning

If you are a charter boat captain taking fishermen out on the ocean every day, while every night you must hunker down to do the books, return phone calls, and prepare for the next day's outing, recognize that you have a job. And if this job makes you unhappy because you feel a lack of freedom, then only by taking an outside and slightly elevated vantage point will you be able to devise a future in which others are piloting the boat, doing the books, handling the calls, and preparing for the next day. Your new systems-mindset posture will drive you to visualize the assembly of the pieces of your endeavor in a way that will remove you from the production and deliver the peace and prosperity you wanted in the first place.

THE BEAUTY OF HOLDING A TRADITIONAL JOB

Most people have jobs and as of this writing there is not a general revolt against the concept! A job is a revered calling in any society as it carries a certain "it's a good feeling to be part of the team" camaraderie. It's understood in democratic and socialist states alike that the people who are out there working jobs are the bedrock of the society. They keep the wheels turning.

For you, having a traditional job is ideal if any one or more of the following are of the highest importance:

- It is a relief to be able to leave the job location at the end of the day and not have a single work-related worry on your mind.
- You are put off by the idea of managing the extra degree of financial risk, uncertainty, and headaches that can come with owning a business.
- You are doing what you love and feel a high sense of self-esteem.
- You are building something of value and the future looks bright.
- You are making more money than you require and creating a future of freedom just from the assets you are stashing away today.
- It is the only way you can obtain the necessary resources to do the things you truly love (flying a jet, participating in politics, fighting for your country, etc.).
- You value the social aspect of being surrounded by peer employees.
- For the moment, you must survive as you prepare for independence down the line.

- Because of your physical location, or for whatever reason, there is no opportunity elsewhere.
- You crave the security of a steady paycheck, health insurance, retirement fund, savings plan, etc.

If you enjoy your job and don't want to be on your own, know that the MPT mindset is a tremendous asset. It will provide you with a better understanding of the big picture of the organization, and with this clear vision of where things are headed you can make a potent contribution. If advancement is your goal and there is a ladder to climb, the MPT approach will propel the ascent.

BEWARE FALLING OFF THE ROOF

Presume you are the sole proprietor of a roofing company and every day you climb up on a different roof. This makes you an integral component of the roofing business system. You're the employer and the employee, and I've got bad news: you're gambling with the future because when you least expect it you may fall off one of those roofs and be seriously injured. Since you are the employee, who will perform the production work when you are physically out of commission? Your time on the roof is not MPT. Your time up there is a job, and a dangerous job at that.

MPT is the time you spend finding other people to climb up there (and making sure *they* don't fall off the roof). It's the time you spend taking action to find a way to extricate yourself from your roofing company mechanism so you're not risking everything, making sure you have the necessary time to build that mechanism to make it self-sufficient and large.

A SELF-CONTAINED ENTITY OF WORTH

Here's the great thing about owning a real business: someday it can be sold as a packaged entity, a self-contained primary system.

The capacity for a business to generate income without the owner doing the actual production or sales work is what endows a business with enduring value beyond everyday cash flow. If you are a critical mechanical element in the generation and/or the selling of the product or service, the need for your presence is going to be a problem when you want to sell what you've built. If you are a service provider who has been doing the actual work and are ready to retire and have just a customer list to sell as an asset, how much is *that* worth? Unquestionably, it will be worth much less than you want it to be.

But *if other people are doing the sales and production work, and the organization cranks out solid profits without moment-to-moment input from you, your business will have tangible worth*. It will be a money-machine for you while you own it—and for someone else who will give you a big chunk of money for it so they can own it themselves.

The ability to churn out a black-ink bottom line without the owner's presence means the entity is, essentially, an ATM.

No, this doesn't mean you will create a business that won't need you. From outside, you will have to keep it pointed in the right direction and continuously muster its growth.

Here's the essence of MPT: *the leader spends the majority of his or her time focused on driving the business to self-sufficiency, protecting it, and making it grow.* The charter boat captain or the roofer *can* turn eighty-hour workweeks into two-hour workweeks. Application of MPT gets one out of the boat—or off the roof—and turns a job into a real business, a stand-alone money machine with intrinsic value.

Remember this: *executing production is a distraction from what must be done to ultimately achieve freedom and control.*

To maintain MPT throughout the day, ask the following questions repeatedly: "For the processes required to create my product/service, or do my job, how can I automate or delegate those processes so they are still executed with maximum efficiency?" And, of course, "Can I discard useless processes?"

MANAGING YOUR BPT AND MPT

With my several businesses, I simply steer the ships from afar. There is great income and the asset base of each grows steadily. My BPT is carefully allocated to the actions that are most important for long-term gain—MPT tasks—which include reviewing and suggesting refinements, and occasional meetings with managers to provide whatever guidance or input they need to advance their own projects.

Of the brief time I spend on business, virtually all of it is MPT. (Unless I go down to the office to just hang out.)

When you are not in BPT, it's certainly OK to focus on MPT tasks—the tasks that have to do with improving and growing your business and your life. High energy or low energy, keep your work activities pointed toward primary business-building or career-advancing activities per your critical documents. In your day, stay in MPT as long as possible but remember that you must be balanced in order to avoid burnout. To have maximum positive effect on your business, you must have a life outside your work.

When you begin to see a reduction in time demands at work, you of course will be inspired to use BPT and MPT in your personal life. Maybe it will be your choice to write a book, really get into martial arts, finally clean up that woodlot, or get that easel out and paint again. You will have lots of time to do those kinds of things.

In This Moment, Be Wary

Once there is some progress there will be no going back to the old ways. You will see that you are in charge; you are building something good. Never again will you be the victim of unpredictable circumstance!

Nevertheless, in this moment be wary. You have not yet developed the powerful new habits you will need over the long term, and you are still prone to those old addictive habits. If the "my life is composed of systems!" lightning bolt hasn't struck yet, all you have right now is feel-good theory. If this is the case, maybe go back and read the chapters in Part One again, particularly Chapters 4 and 5. And, you can quickly and permanently ingrain the mindset by using the services of Work the System Enterprises (see Appendices D and E).

But even after the aha! strikes, you may have to muscle your way through the initial documentation. It takes maybe eight weeks to form a new habit, so give yourself time and be patient with yourself. But then again, positive results will probably come sooner than you think, and then your motivation will be powered by plain common sense, the most powerful motivator there is.

CHOP WOOD, CARRY WATER.

I sit here writing these particular words on a Tuesday in July. It's nearly 2:00 p.m., and I have been on task for nine hours and I'm still at maximum throttle. It's one of those rare and exquisite maximum-BPT/MPT days (perhaps because that is my topic today). I will work for a while more and then plug into some music and rake the yard because that is both relaxing and satisfying.

After that I will go for a walk in the neighborhood with our coonhound, Justy. Maybe Diana will come along. Then, there will be dinner out and after that, maybe a movie. Justy will hold the fort here at the house.

There is a Zen proverb: "Before enlightenment, chop wood, carry water. After enlightenment, chop wood, carry water." That's perfect, really, as I immerse myself in the simple mechanics of what needs to be done *right now*: creating, adjusting, and maintaining systems. Diana is no different. In her various endeavors, this is how her days go too . . .

Chop wood, carry water.

Sometimes I think, "This is *IT!*" I'm reminding myself that *this* is the existence I've envisioned and there is no need to pine for anything different. For you and me, life is as tangible as it can be when we just acknowledge it in the moment and see that it is good. No matter where you and I are, or what we're doing, this instant in time—this *right now*—is IT! Any other time is not real, either memory or conjecture.

Try this: for brief moments in the middle of working your systems, withdraw a bit in order to look down and celebrate the only true reality there is—this right now—and be grateful.

PTO and POINT OF SALE

In the system-improvement I will discuss here, we completely eliminated a complex system (as always, a delightful event) and replaced it with an automatic point-of-sale mechanism.

We went back to a premise: paid time off (PTO) is an employee benefit intended to help keep staff satisfied and happy, but most of all it's a perk that will encourage them to continue working for Centratel—and working means showing up for work!

There was a problem with our paid-by-the-hour staff's PTO arrangement. In theory, it sounded great when we first offered the benefit, but in the real-world application it was problematic.

First, PTO was a pain to calculate and administer. Did our managers do their weekly job of tallying all eligible employee PTO hours and then submit those hours to bookkeeping? Did a TSR report her absence yesterday as PTO time, and beyond that, just how many hours are still available for her to use? Did the books begin to accumulate a new TSR's PTO after his ninety-day probation was finished? In every case, our PTO system consumed too much administrative and record-keeping time, and there was error.

Second, our people used PTO hours in ways we did not intend. We had designed it for employees to get away from work once or twice a year in a way we could plan and schedule around. And our intent was that it would also be available to use for occasional sick days or appointments. But for many of our hourly-paid staff, PTO was used as soon as it was accumulated and with short notice—a few hours here, a few hours there.

Many times, it was an excuse to be absent from work under the pretense of "I don't feel good today and I think I have accumulated enough PTO to take the day off, so I am going to call in sick." Too often it turned out that the staff member did *not* have enough PTO accumulated to take a full day off and so did not work the usual weekly forty hours. For the employee, this resulted in a smaller paycheck than expected. And no small thing, Centratel was understaffed.

continued

Third, errors in the complex administrative processing invariably led to the granting of too much paid PTO, and over the years this had been a substantial loss to the company.

What should we do?

We dropped the old manually intense PTO process altogether, adopting another, much simpler one. Our point-of-sale principle was key in developing the new policy. We stopped the long-term accumulation of PTO; instead, on each paycheck we pay it as it is earned.

Based on the number of hours worked in a given pay period, our accounting system automatically determines the paycheck's PTO amount and includes it as a line-item disbursement. There is no more manual record-keeping, and the employee knows where he or she stands at all times.

Can employees take vacations? Yes, they can take time off as they wish, but they know the time off has been paid in advance and there will be no money earned while they are gone.

Now, since employees earn their pay only when they work, unwarranted absenteeism has been reduced by literally 90 percent, manual administrative paperwork has been eliminated, and there is no confusion.

An outside and slightly elevated solution? Absolutely.

(Postscript: Due to changes in Oregon Employment Law, we recently had to transition back to a form of our original PTO protocol. However, with changes in technology combined with our IT team's innovative efforts, we've been able to implement a super efficient protocol in which PTO time can continue to be tracked and issued automatically, in real-time, and in which our people always know how much time off they've accumulated.)

CHAPTER 20

The Traffic Circles of Pakistan

Confusion is a word we have invented for an order which is not yet understood.

—Henry Miller

In Lahore, Pakistan, the traffic circle is the epicenter of the driving experience. Like traffic circles everywhere, the Pakistani version absorbs vehicles from various points and then spews them out at other points. However, these circles differentiate themselves from the more refined circles of the West, with each Pakistani driver's unspoken proclamation, "Enter here but beware! I do not care what you want. Your existence is an obstacle to me! May the best man win and know that man is me!"

The driving is primal, instinctual.

The circles are beautiful, really. Raw, closed, no-nonsense hell-bent-for-leather systems in which an observer can generalize about how a host of other third-world social mechanisms operate. My favorite circle is near downtown Lahore, with five concentric circles of traffic, each with vehicles wildly careening around and around the potholed pavement.

A DEARTH OF GUIDELINES

In the Pakistani traffic circle there are three rules: go clockwise, go as fast as possible, and don't collide with other vehicles. That's it. It really is every man for himself (in Pakistan, for cultural subtleties, seldom is a woman behind the wheel), with the mayhem propelled by an invisible frenzy of mocking desperation.

A Westerner standing on the sidelines understands that for every driver it's clearly a measure of courage and personal manly pride. And, it's a game. Each driver must reach his destination just a bit sooner than is humanly possible. Within the seething circle—indeed, a living organism—there is no rule for which vehicle has the right of way, unless one considers intimidation a rule.

It's amazing. There is no agreement on protocol beyond the rudimentary rules previously noted, and in fact, it's the opposite of what a Westerner might expect. For example, more often than not, the vehicles entering the circle have the right of way over the cars already within.

The traffic rages, with all participants frustrated that the general vehicle velocity isn't faster than it is. Competing for space are fragile donkey carts, massive ornately decorated trucks, tiny Chinese cars, cantankerous bicycles, and swarms of darting, weaving motorcycles. When a truck breaks down, the driver simply stops his vehicle in the middle of things without any attempt to pull over to get out of the way. He nonchalantly lies down on his back under the disabled vehicle and attempts to make repairs. Nobody cares or pays attention to the driver, who escapes being crushed through no effort of his own.

The drivers revel in the pact that few organizing guidelines shall interfere. It is similar to most third-world gatherings of people: queuing into a single-file line just doesn't happen because everyone silently agrees that survival of the fittest is the single rule for securing whatever is to be had. In the Pakistani traffic circle, no one is insulted or irritated by the hyper-assertive jostling and the line-crashing and the horn-blowing. It's the nature of the game, and within the circle you will cut me off while leaning hard on your horn—and that's OK!

Within the circle there is no cooperation or consideration, and everyone agrees that's great.

COOPERATE OR CHALLENGE?

Comparing the traffic circles of Pakistan to those in the West provides a stunning contrast.

To level the playing field for my forthcoming theory, I am presuming all drivers everywhere share the same desire—to travel without physical damage from point A to point B in the minimum amount of time.

Here's the question: to get what one wants—in this case, traveling from one place to another as unscathed and as rapidly as possible—shall it be Pakistani-style, via independent, single-minded challenges to one another (a rudimentary free-for-all system) or shall it be by group cooperation (an intricate and formal system)?

In Bend, Oregon, it's the latter. One follows many rules of the road. If not, there will be problems. For instance, the cars already within the traffic circle unquestionably have the right of way. Incoming drivers rarely violate this rule, but if they do, a physical altercation could ensue, with the vehicles pulled over and the drivers making fools of themselves. But that doesn't happen because right-of-way rules in the Western traffic circle are ironclad, and 99.9 percent of drivers follow them exactly. Of course, there are also other Western rules that have to do with speed and signaling. No one would ever dream of changing a tire anywhere near a traffic circle, and horns are rarely heard as they would be considered an in-your-face affront. Drivers work hard to not impede traffic or to challenge one another. The mindset is on the rights of the other drivers.

This oh-so-sensitive driver persona isn't happening in Lahore, where the agreed-upon rules of the road do not consider the welfare of the other drivers. Charging into the fray without forethought is the protocol. I call it street-fight driving.

At the risk of appearing culturally judgmental, it's my contention that in getting from point A to point B, cooperation is more efficient than a competitive free-for-all. My guess is that despite the Pakistani hyper-frenzy, more traffic flows through the staid Bend traffic circle than flows through the equal-sized Lahore traffic circle. It's also my bet that there are fewer accidents in the West.

So—at the risk of making a bellicose East-West judgment—it is obvious to me that if the goal is to move large volumes of traffic from point A to point B, the social agreement of a cooperative rigid-rule traffic circle beats the chaos of a no-holds-barred, uncooperative circle. The West's higher-capacity circle illustrates the importance of mutual consideration, as well as the potency of efficiency-enhancing rules that participants understand and agree upon. And away from the traffic circles, in societal processes, it is simply more productive for each participant to consider the welfare of other participants and to carefully follow simple rules that deal with common contingencies. For traffic and for the culture as a whole, it just works better. It's a matter of mechanical efficiency.

But there is more to this than efficiency. Ignoring the mechanical aspect, which traffic circle is the more creative and fun? The more innovative and free-form? Clearly, it's the Pakistani circle. The flair and competitiveness in Pakistani streets is a remarkable thing, with a colorful, good-natured jostling that is fascinating to watch. For a Westerner on the periphery looking in, it's a spectator sport in direct contrast to the uptight, boring military orderliness of the streets of the West. These guys are ALIVE!

When I'm in Lahore, I just stand there on the edge of the madness, spellbound. It makes ME feel alive!

These drivers are not just going somewhere. They're free-form artists, creating and surviving and having a hell of a good time doing it. They're living moment to moment. We Westerners could learn something from that.

FROM THIS RIGID FRAMEWORK, TAKE YOUR RISKS

The drivers in Lahore, Pakistan, and Bend, Oregon, almost always arrive at their respective destinations. Like any business or any life—with individual comportment and social expectation being major influences—strategies for making those journeys range from vainglorious self-interest to pedantic rule-following.

The two cultures' traffic circles beautifully illustrate the extremes of how one can go about getting what one wants. But is there a middle ground? In life beyond traffic circles, could it be that an unexciting, rules-based conservative foundation is the perfect launching pad for surges of wild-eyed innovation and leaps of faith?

Think about traffic circles as you make your plans for getting your business off the mark. And consider the circles as you contemplate creating a thoughtful, planned framework—a system-improvement-based foundation that is safe harbor for new, off-the-wall notions that will thrust you into the life you want.

Today, slow down and create order and structure. Later, from this framework, take your risks.

Centratel and the COVID-19 Fiasco

For many years, we had been asking ourselves how our business could survive an evacuation of our headquarters building. As it stood, the building in downtown Bend could be completely cleared of personnel for any number of reasons, including bomb threats, street-gang civil unrest, fire, and so on. We would not be able to process calls—and within a short time we would literally be out of business. We had started seriously discussing various options in January 2018 when IT and telephony technology had developed enough to make handling calls at "remote" locations a practical consideration. But other matters took precedence and the project got put on the back burner. Then, in August 2019 we had had a bomb scare two blocks away at the county courthouse, and authorities stopped just short of emptying our building. (We were lucky. We fell just outside the radius of evacuation. For several hours, everyone between us and the courthouse had to flee their offices.)

No matter the reason for evacuating, we can't just turn our operation off, because so many of our accounts—all across the United States—depend on us to process their emergency calls. As I mentioned previously, it's our promise to customers to always be available. In fact, for the last thirty-six years Centratel has never been off-line for more than an hour . . . and the last time that happened was thirty-one years ago.

So, seeing this bomb scare as a red flag for improvement, our operations and IT staff instantly delved back into what it would take to survive a complete office evacuation. We found that it would be possible to have TSRs process calls from another ad-hoc central location or from their homes, but not without some seriously high-level IT infrastructure, telephony, and other very specific protocol modifications. We needed to

continued

develop new software and engineer some innovative, groundbreaking IoT ("Internet of Things") devices.

With a significant portion of our customers being medical professionals, the entire initiative had to comply with recent strict HIPAA (The Health Insurance Portability and Accountability Act) requirements that demanded high standards in terms of end-to-end cryptography and ePHI (Electronic Protected Health Information) data protection strategies.

So, based on our Strategic Objective and Operating Principles, it was a no-brainer to move ahead, and in September 2019 we shuffled our priorities and actually started the engineering process. We wholly relied on our IT engineers based in Italy and Romania, Marcello and Manu, as well as our Bend-based senior IT technician, Jason.

We had targeted June 1, 2020, to complete the testing, at which point we would be able to instantly "flip a switch" so the entire company could seamlessly function from anywhere outside our HQ building. In the meantime, we held our collective breaths.

All was proceeding well enough, but then the national COVID-19 lockdown began in the first week of March, about the time we were scheduled to start testing. Andi, our CEO, took assertive action, insisting we get the project done NOW! Dropping all other long- and short-term engineering system-improvement projects, we focused on finishing the evacuation-survival project ASAP, understanding that within a few weeks there was a good chance we would no longer be able to process calls from inside our office. If we weren't prepared, that shut-down scenario would literally end Centratel as a business, as our clients rushed to other still-operational answering services to cover their emergency calls.

To add to the challenge, during this crunch time our European team of five was quarantined within their homes and apartments for fourteen straight weeks. And I mean *quarantined*. They could not leave their buildings without special written government permission. (If they did leave and were caught, they would be fined and/or jailed.)

For Centratel, this was the mother of all challenges. For thirty-six years we had been processing virtually all of our incoming calls, 24/7/365, out of our Bend, Oregon, headquarters building.

Although the project was actually ready to be deployed in early March, right about the time when the emergency began, our IT team knew we would have bugs in the system that would take weeks if not months to iron out. We would need to test. Another obstacle was going to be making this a smooth transition for our TSRs who would work from home offices, ensuring they had high-speed internet, the proper computer equipment, and a quiet place to work. We accelerated the testing, purchased more backup equipment, and began retraining our people.

We *had* to make it happen *fast*. We pushed hard and by the end of March, 95 percent of our TSRs were operating from their home offices, just in time for the Oregon COVID-19 "lockdown."

Thank you, Marcello, Manu, Jason, Andi, and team!

Never did we think a virus would cause us to have to evacuate our headquarters! In avoiding disaster, we were of course lucky to some degree, but mostly *we were prepared to act.* As I mentioned in Chapter 2, many of our answering service competitors didn't make it, even after multiple decades of operation. Those businesses are gone forever.

If I had to point to the most important work-the-system principles that saved us, what would they be? I'd say it was in having the quiet courage, the innovative mindset, the communication tools, and an awesome staff that allowed us to meet and survive the unexpected earthquake.

CHAPTER 21

System-Improvement as a Way of Life

Follow your heart but take your brain along.

—Alfred Adler

Gain a more accurate understanding of the mechanics of how this material world functions and then apply this understanding in every instance. "Get it," and the systems mindset will be so embedded that it will modify even the smallest decision of the day. It will be part of you.

For a given primary system, to ensure desired results occur over and over again, the task is to adjust its subsystems so the correct components are being used and they are sequenced properly.

It's about preparation. If you pay close attention to the mechanical details of your world and make proper manipulations to the key systems that compose it, you will construct a life that is unencumbered with fire killing and seldom dictated by urgency. Flexible, strong, and resilient, it's a life of calm days, days that have lots of room for thinking and planning, for building and creating, for friends and family, and for just being yourself. It's a life that often encounters tremors but seldom earthquakes.

No longer will the tail be wagging the dog.

Whatever your station in life, if your days are frustrating, crammed to the max, and you're not getting ahead, *know that things can be fixed quickly if you really, truly see the deeper reality of how things work—that the world is a collection of systems—and then focus on step-by-step system-improvement.*

YOUR WORK-THE-SYSTEM METHODOLOGY: STEP BY STEP

Let's review the protocol one more time, from yet another different angle.

1. It starts with your change in perspective, the aha insight that has arrived in a moment of time. Now, deep down, you have permanently internalized your new vision. You see each life event as the product of the mechanism that engendered it—the 1-2-3-4 process that preceded it—not as an isolated happening, a product of luck, fate, God's justice, karma, the stars, or the benevolence or wrath of someone else. Because the insight is embedded, the next mechanical moves you will take are obvious.
2. You have established your goals and strategy through the creation of your strategic objective and general operating principles. You did this to establish firm direction and so there is continuity.
3. You examine the mechanics of the subsystems that make up your business, job, health, and relationships. You analyze them one by one, looking for opportunities for enhancement.
4. You make revisions, moving each subsystem to peak efficiency. For permanence you carefully create working procedures to describe the protocols. You create this documentation from scratch. Then, when you're done, you and your team intensively coddle your systems and their documentation, always tweaking to perfection. From now on you and your people will spend the majority of time in system-improvement.
5. Your calm and positive comportment has evolved naturally because you developed solid faith in the reliability of the systems that are at work everywhere. You're dealing with the laws of physics, the laws of nature. *It's comforting.* You are powerful and relaxed because you have successfully harnessed your systems, directing them to do what you want them to do. With subsystems isolated, perfected, and then combined together again, you preside over stunningly efficient primary processes—your business, job, relationships, . . . *you.* At the gut level, without putting your head in the sand regarding the many conditions in this world that are not so great, you grasp the indisputable truth that 99.99 percent of everything works just fine.

SUMMARIZING THE RULES OF THE GAME

Forget about making mighty homerun swings that will win the game. The numbers are more than a little against you and your too-powerful swings will be a distraction and a waste of energy. Instead, hunker down, enhance what you have, and go for the surefire incremental system-improvement advances: the singles and doubles. Be smooth. Be patient. Relish the small yet permanent betterments that will add up to something big down the line.

Small perfections add up.

Focus on the mechanical systems that produce the results and never doubt that a superb collection of subsystems will produce a superb primary system.

Maintain a positive regard for those around you and do what you say you will do. Produce quality and do it consistently. Keep your goals in mind every minute and relentlessly work toward them through thick and thin. Don't try to fool or manipulate yourself or others around you. Start and finish tasks on time. Don't complain.

Your life will get better sooner than you think.

Truth is, most people look for better results without considering the mechanisms that would produce those better results. They don't know about the system-improvement concept. In thinking locally, this gives you a great advantage. Thinking globally, you know there are a whole lot of people out there not getting what they want.

Remember that your body and mind compose the primary system that is your life. Fortunately, these two key components are the ones you can most easily adjust. Improve your personal systems at every opportunity. Maintain them always. Keep them strong. Be disciplined.

In everything you do, always focus on the pragmatic details. Perform the tiniest basics well. Keep things simple but be cautious of shortcuts.

With finesse, take life as it comes.

The largest problem with trying to hammer out a home run every time is that all that hammering will cause you to strike out too often. And all those strikeouts added together will make life a struggle or take you down altogether.

Instead, slow down and focus 100 percent on each separate pitch.

Relax, keep your eye on the ball, and make smooth contact. Your steady swing will send the ball over the fence more often than you would think.

See that each swing is a closed entity unto itself. That each has the singular goal of making contact with the ball. When you miss, and of course you sometimes will, calmly accept it as a natural outcome in this numbers-game of life, and then, undistracted, give 100 percent focus to the next swing.

Don't multitask.

Keep talking.

Every day has its flavor; its tone. Work with your individual day-chunks. Savor them as they slide by.

Stay off the circular track. Know it's the climbing you want.

Understand that most people wake up in the morning with only a vague sense of an ultimate, primary goal. Events quickly peel back layers of control and the day becomes a Whac-A-Mole epic that dictates stumbling reaction to bad results while disallowing efforts at system-improvement. Most people don't know about the machinery down in the basement.

Most people don't know the tail is wagging the dog.

In contrast, *you* carve through the hours as you direct subsystems with confidence and precision, constructing the primary systems you desire. You remember that control is a good thing, and your job is to secure it.

You see the machinery. You work that machinery so it produces the exact results you desire. No longer will invisible systems produce random bad results. You never forget that systems are executing, real time, *this minute*, whether managed or not.

By filling your days with accomplishment, the negatives that previously dragged you down will no longer factor into who you are and what you do. They will just annoy you occasionally.

Will you become blind to the imperfections around you? Not a chance. In fact, in your abundance you'll be eager to do something about dysfunction as it comes within your ever-expanding circle of influence.

One last time I remind you that *the mandatory adjustment is in your moment-to-moment perception of the world's unfolding.* All your actions stem from this new, outside, and slightly elevated vision. Your life is composed of separate systems that function flawlessly 99.99 percent of the time.

All you need to do is get this and then climb on board!

The work-the-system mindset is organized, focused, and deliberate. It's about action, not reaction.

A VISION TO CULTIVATE

Most of us have at least one endeavor in which we excel. For you, what is it and why are you good at it?

It's probable that when you are in the midst of performing this process you experience a delicious taste of precision and confidence. You bask in the flow of it. What you do well is your passion and you take every opportunity to repeat it. It's a positive obsession.

You ask: For this thing that I do well, do I love doing it because I am good at it, or am I good at it because I love doing it? The black-or-white answer is elusive, so why not consider a third possibility? Do the two go together without distinction?

Or, maybe it doesn't really matter . . .

Again, what do you do well? What stirs you inside? Leaving aside the chicken-or-the-egg question, and while continuing to hone your particular passion, extend that fire to the improvement of the other mechanical workings of your existence.

Get visceral about it. Wallow in it.

Be outside the events of your day and treat those events as elements of your overall game, a game that you will perfect with proper engineering. This game, of course, is your life.

Your existence has a limited time span. Treasure your life-gift.

Few people understand the magnificence of the systems around them—but now you do. You reject escapism as you appreciate the here and now for the miracle it is—the miracle that was always right there in front of you.

Now you are in command because you understand the mechanisms that determine the events of your life.

You will never go back.

EPILOGUE

Your Business: Is This the End or Just the Start?

By Josh Fonger[8]

By now, you know for sure this book *is* different. And here you are, finished reading—or listening—to it.

My guess is that you feel good about what you've absorbed.

But, what's next? Will you file *Work the System* away only as a good memory, hoping some future influence will somehow get your business and your personal life to finally become what you've always wanted them to be?

Or will you be bold and turn things around starting *this* moment?

The essential information and inspiration to finally break free is now in your hands—and in your head—but you're still facing the mechanically challenging part: implementation. As you know already, the vast majority of business owners *work more and make less* than if they were in the corporate world. (And in fact, shutting a business down is the most common future end point.)

So why not use this moment to surge ahead? Why not get the wheels rolling and actually implement Sam's Work the System Method?

---

8 Note from Sam Carpenter: As I mentioned in the Preface, in 2018 I sold exclusive licensing rights for my coaching and consulting operation to Josh. It was a one-time transaction and by design, I receive no ongoing compensation from his organization, Work the System Enterprises, LLC.

Thousands of others just like you have done it, and with very nearly universal positive results . . . results that came fast.

Consider reading a book written about how to summit Mt. Everest. In that book is everything you need to know to make it to the top, along with inspiring stories of others who have done it before. Upon finishing the book, would you feel prepared enough to buy a ticket to Lukla airport and attempt a solo summit the following week?

Of course not. You would find a guide who has done the climb many times before. (Note: Only 29 percent of those attempting to summit Mt. Everest actually succeed, but these are still much better odds than you have right now in business! The business success rate over the first five years is 20 percent, and it keeps going down after that!)

I am *the* official Work the System guide. For a decade, I've worked closely with Sam to lead struggling business owners from working "in the business," to working "on the business," to thoroughly enjoying "owning the business."

Making this transformation requires the implementation of six key pillars.

Here they are:

1. Mindset. The systems mindset—getting outside and slightly elevated—is essential to objectively *see* the internal workings of your business and the separate systems that compose it. *"Get it," and your leadership and influence will quickly mature, and wise decisions will naturally follow.* If right now you're consumed with killing fires, the systems mindset is the quick and permanent cure. (See Part One, Chapter 7: Getting It.)

2. Documented strategy. Do you know where your business is ultimately going and how it's going to get there? Is this strategy written down? If it *is* written down, *is it correct*? Does your team know it and follow it? Do you? (See Part Two, Chapter 10: Your Strategic Objective and General Operating Principles.)

3. Documented operating principles. Undocumented or documented, every decision made in your business has had underlying operating principles that influenced it. If those operating prin-

ciples are not documented and then carefully channeled, every person in your business will be relying on their *own* principles to guide them . . . and too often—even within a single staff member—they will fluctuate and sometimes oppose one another. *Trying to grow a business without a definitive set of guiding principles ("guidelines for decision-making") is a recipe for failure.* (See Part Two, Chapter 10: Your Strategic Objective and General Operating Principles.)

4. Documented working procedures. The systems of your business are executing *right now*, but if they are not standardized, they are "organic." This means they are each unseen, inefficient, and . . . not under control. They fluctuate. They have lives of their own. *If the spinning wheels of your business systems are not documented and agreed-upon, then plan for chaos, confusion, friction, frustration, and even failure.* Your written working procedures will provide you the stability and efficiency necessary for your business to grow and for you to achieve the wealth and personal freedom you've always wanted. (See Part Two, Chapter 11: Your Working Procedures.)

5. Team. Your people are the most vital, variable, and volatile "systems" in your business. The processes of recruiting, hiring, onboarding, training, managing, and developing your people must be systematic: carefully defined and managed. Yet, regarding your people, you must learn to "set them free" to do their jobs without micro-management. *Good employees equipped with the proper tools and protocol become great employees, a mandatory requisite for building a great business.* (See Part Three, Chapter 16: Extraordinary Systems Operated by Great People.)

6. Investment. The irony is that to "make more and work less," your business will temporarily require an investment of more of your time. You say, "*But Josh, I'm already working seven days a week and my cash flow is on the edge!*" No surprise: you're like everyone else I've helped who was sick and tired of just surviving day to day! Acknowledge your unacceptable yet fixable current state, visualize the amazing future that awaits—trust that things will get

way better, fast—and then dig deep for just a short time to invest in the future you've always dreamed about. *The money and time will show up quickly if you make managing the machinery of your business your #1 priority*. (See Part One, Chapter 4: Gun-to-the-Head Enlightenment.)

There are your six essential pillars. Now think back to the Mt. Everest analogy. Are you going to go for the gung-ho solo-summit attempt, or will you enlist a guide and thoughtfully apply the proper strategy? If you chose the latter, get back to me and let's chat. And join the WTS community. Whether you need templates, checklists, examples, coaching, tools, training, consulting, or simply a fellow business owner to cheer you on, go to www.workthesystem.com. Take a look around, subscribe . . . and then email or call me.

There is nothing I enjoy more than supporting a courageous business owner who is *done* with their treading-water status quo, and who is serious about building a great business! So, meet me at base camp! The weather is just right. The opportunity is *right now*. You're ready to climb! Let's get you to the top, and let's get you there fast!

—Josh Fonger
November 2020

ACKNOWLEDGMENTS

So much gratitude to my father, Tom Carpenter, deceased. He was a junior high English teacher who so long ago insisted I become proficient with the written word despite my strident resistance. And I am grateful to my author-mother Nancy Fox, also deceased, for her gangbuster inspiration that had everything to do with me becoming a writer.

Thank you to Andi Freeman, Centratel CEO, for your faith in me and our systems—you really get it as you never fail to watch my back; to Pattie Castner, for enduring the hard times and for making our Quality Department sing; Lannie Dell, one of our longest-term full-time employees, recently retired, for sticking it out with me for thirty years; Sandra Packard, our other thirty-year veteran, for your insistence on perfection and for weathering those many, many storms with me, back in the day; Linda Morgan, for your dependability and calm demeanor; Carla Hoekstra, for always being there to do what must be done. Each of you has been with me for twenty-five years. And gratitude to Sam Kirkaldie, my business partner for over twenty years now, for your calm strength and friendship.

And to the rest of our Centratel crew: How to thank you enough for your utterly incredible performance, day after day, year after year? I am profoundly grateful.

A long time ago, Lindsay Stevens gave me my first inkling that a business should be directed, not indulged. Reese Shepard insisted there be a plan. Roger Shields, retired banker, smacked me in the head with his air bat when I needed it most. Robert Killen, formerly of Columbia River Bank, gave me a break when everyone else equivocated, and "RC" Roger Christensen, former president of that bank, cut me some slack when the two of us were at the low rungs of our respective career ladders.

Way back in the '70s, the NYS Ranger School faculty taught me about common sense and hard work. And there was Lane Powell, my mentor at Central Electric Cooperative in Redmond, Oregon. There is much of Lane in this book.

Special appreciation to the Greenleaf Book Group gang. You've taught me much and I always appreciate your patience. My nitpicking must make you crazy. And to my copyeditor, Elizabeth Brown: thank you for your patience, light-heartedness, and expertise.

And recognition to Jack Cornelius for your "Giant Machine" story as well as for your personal recollection of Frank Zappa's system-improvement-based countenance.

Bobbi Swanson, I appreciate your thoughtful and masterful indexing.

Thank you, audio engineer Tim Underwood of Underwood Productions, for your patient and insightful input as we've recorded yet another audio version of *Work* with this fourth edition.

Thanks to Josh Fonger, my previous long-term Work the System employee and now independent worldwide WTS licensee, for never missing a beat, encouraging me when I needed it the most, making the coaching/consulting business a phenomenal success, and of course for your contribution to this newest iteration of the book.

And to Marcello Scacchetti of Mirandola, Italy, my business partner in Pathway One and CIO for Centratel, for your world-class online technical and marketing contributions to all of our business entities. Marcello manages our IT and online marketing staff of seven, located in Italy, Romania, and the US.

Fabio Bertoli: Great job on the house illustrations. You intuitively got it perfect, with very little guidance from me.

You're a good man, brother Steve. You can put the abstract in a nutshell and do it with humor (and thanks much for your contribution to the space shuttle illustration).

And special thanks to my wife, Diana, who is not just an awesome editor, but even more importantly, reminds me, when I get too caught up in contemplating the individual trees, that there is indeed a forest.

This book is about personal freedom, but the freedom to succeed depends entirely on the freedom of the society. For this reason, to the men and women of our military, as well as to all of our stateside first responders (particularly here in late 2020, our incessantly harangued police), know that there are a whole lot of us out here—the majority—who will never stop appreciating your sacrifice and your courage.

You've kept us safe and free.

—Sam Carpenter, October 2020

APPENDIX A

Centratel's Strategic Objective

NOTE TO STAFF: *The Centratel Strategic Objective is the basis for all corporate and individual decision-making.*

Clichéd mission statements that declare, "We want to be the best and we want our customers to be happy" don't provide meaningful direction and do little more than make company stockholders feel good for the moment. And voluminous multiyear work plans can't account for the day-by-day changes in our industry.

Instead, the Centratel Strategic Objective precisely describes our market and direction, as well as who we are and how we function. It reminds us of what is most important and it gives us an overview of general strategy.

By following its guidelines, growth and success will take care of themselves. In the spirit of simplicity, we limit the length of our Strategic Objective to one page. We've modified it through the years, but the fundamentals have never changed.

Statistically we are the highest-quality telephone answering service in the United States.

We understand that every result is preceded by a 1-2-3-4-step process. It is within these processes that we spend our time, as we relentlessly "work" the systems of the business to perfection.

Our guiding documents are this Strategic Objective, the Centratel Thirty Principles and Working Procedures.

Centratel's primary offering is 24/7/365 telephone answering service for business and professional offices throughout the United States. Peripheral services are voice mail and paging for the central Oregon region only.

Through intense commitment to our employees, we will contribute to the success of our clients. The consequence of having loyal, smart, hardworking, long-term, and well-compensated staff is unmatchable quality service to customers.

Our business is complex, with many human, mechanical, and computer systems in simultaneous motion. Success depends on refined communication and organizational processes, dedicated staff, documented point-of-sale procedures, first-class office space and equipment, rigorous quality assurance with continuous measurement, assertive innovation, intense planned maintenance/system-improvement, aggressive and measured marketing, and relentless attention to detail in every nook and cranny.

Competitive advantages include a near-flawless level of message processing accuracy, products designed around the unique needs of the customer, thoughtful customer service that is immediate and consistent, the latest high-tech equipment, and personal/corporate integrity. We use extraordinarily efficient communication tools and protocols. We constantly refine and improve all internal systems and mechanisms.

To grow, we proceed with an "if we build it, they will come" philosophy, juxtaposed with assertive marketing efforts.

Although we tightly direct Centratel's operation through guiding documentation, we will modify that documentation immediately if an enhancement can be made: "Our operational framework is rigid, but that framework can be modified instantly."

We segment responsibilities into specialized "expert compartments" with appropriate cross-training among departments. We have backup personnel for all positions.

Primary vertical markets include medical, veterinary, home health/hospice, funeral home, HVAC, property management, hi-tech, 24/7 on-call, front office/virtual receptionist, and utility.

(For help with your strategic objective, go to www.businessdocumentationsoftware.com.)

APPENDIX B

Centratel's Thirty Principles

1. Company decisions conform to the Strategic Objective, Thirty Principles, and Working Procedure documents.

2. We are the highest-quality answering service in the United States. We do whatever it takes to ensure the quality of service to our clients, employees, and vendors is impeccable.

3. We draw solid lines, thus providing an exact status of where things stand. Documented procedures are the main defense against gray-area problems.

4. "Get the job done." Can the employee do his or her job, or is there always a complication of one kind or another? This ability to "get the job done quickly and accurately without excuses or complications" is the most valuable trait an employee can possess.

5. Employees come first. We employ people who have an innate desire to perform at 100 percent. We reward them accordingly. The natural outcome is we serve our clients well.

6. We are not fire killers. We are fire prevention specialists. We don't manage problems; we work on system enhancement and system maintenance in order to prevent problems from happening in the first place.

7. Problems are gifts that inspire us to action. They are "red flags for improvement." A problem prompts the act of creating or improving a system or procedure. We don't want setbacks, but when

one occurs we think, "Thank you for this wake-up call," and take assertive system-improvement action to prevent the setback from happening again.

8. We focus on just a few manageable services. Although we watch for new opportunities, in the end we provide "just a few services implemented in superb fashion," rather than a complex array of average-quality offerings.

9. We find the simplest solution. Ockham's Law, also called the Law of Economy, states, "Entities are not to be multiplied beyond necessity. . . . The simplest solution is invariably the correct solution."

10. The money we save or waste is not Monopoly money! We are careful not to devalue the worth of a dollar just because it has to do with the business.

11. We operate the company via documented procedures and systems. "Any recurring problem can be solved with a system." We take the necessary time to create and implement systems and procedures, and in the end, it is well worth it. If there is a recurring problem, a written procedure is created in order to prevent the problem from happening again. On the other hand, we don't bog down the organization with processes and procedures targeting situations that occur only once in a while. Sometimes we elect to not create a procedure.

12. "Just don't do it." Eliminate the unnecessary. Many times, elimination of a system, protocol, or potential project is a very good thing. Think simplicity. Automate. Refine to the smallest number of steps or discard altogether. Would a simple "no" save time, energy, and/or money?

13. Our documented systems, procedures, and functions are "off the street." This means anyone with normal intelligence can perform procedures unassisted. The real-world evidence of this is we can hire an individual off the street who has good typing

skills and have him or her processing calls by the second day. For this result, protocols have to be efficient, simple, and thoroughly documented. (Before we implemented our systemized training protocol, it would take six weeks to train a TSR.)

14. Do it NOW. All actions build on "point-of-sale" theory. We don't delay an action if it can be done immediately. Just like any major retail outlet, we "update inventories and databases at the exact time the transaction takes place." There is no paperwork floating around the office after a physical transaction. We ask, "How can we perform the task NOW without creating lingering details that we must clean up later?"

15. We glean the Centratel mindset from Stephen Covey's books, including *The 7 Habits of Highly Effective People*, *First Things First*, and *The 8th Habit*. As well, we consider *Good to Great* by Jim Collins; *The E-Myth Revisited* by Michael Gerber; and *Awaken the Giant Within* by Anthony Robbins.

16. We pattern individual organization upon Franklin-Covey theory. We use organizing mechanisms that are always at hand. We prioritize, schedule, and document. The system is always up-to-date and we use it all the time. (For Centratel, this is Microsoft Outlook.)

17. Sequence and priority are critical. We work on the most important tasks first. We spend maximum time on "non-urgent/important" tasks via Stephen Covey's time-matrix philosophy.

18. We double-check everything before release. If a penchant for double-checking is not an innate personal habit, then it must be cultivated. Double-checking is a conscious step in every task, performed either by the individual managing the task or someone else.

19. Our environment is spotless: clean and ordered, simple, efficient, functional. No "rats' nests," literally or figuratively.

20. Employee training is structured, scheduled, and thorough. Assertive client contact is also structured, scheduled, and thorough.

21. We are obsessed with deadlines. If someone in the organization says they will be finished with a task or project by a certain date and time, then he or she commits to finishing by that deadline (or, if legitimate delays intrude, advise coworkers well in advance that the deadline is impossible).

22. We maintain equipment and keep it 100 percent functional at all times. If something is not working as it should, fix it now—fix it now even if it's not necessary to fix it now. It's a matter of good housekeeping and of maintaining good habits. This is just the way we do things.

23. Mastery of the English language is critical. We are aware of how we sound and what we write. We do whatever we can to improve. We are patient as a coworker corrects us.

24. We study to increase our skills. A steady diet of reading and contemplation is vital to personal development. It is a matter of self-discipline.

25. As opposed to "doing the work," the department manager's job is to create, monitor, and document systems (which consist of people, equipment, procedures, and maintenance schedules).

26. The COO (Chief Operating Officer) oversees department heads and overall systems. It is the COO's job to direct, coordinate, and monitor managers.

27. We avoid multitasking activities. When communicating with someone else, we are 100 percent present. We give full attention to the person in front of us (or to the task at hand). We focus on listening and understanding. Read the classic *Treating Type A Behavior and Your Heart* by Meyer Friedman. "Mindfulness" is paying complete attention to one thing at a time: read *Full Catastrophe Living* by Jon Kabat-Zinn.

28. When in the office, we work hard on Centratel business. We keep our heads down and we focus, and in turn the company pays very well. That's "the deal." The workweek rarely exceeds forty hours.

29. Complete means "complete." Almost or tomorrow is not "complete." In particular, this is germane to administration staff's use of task functions.

30. We strive for a social climate that is serious and quiet yet pleasant, serene, light, and friendly. Centratel is a nice place to work.

APPENDIX C

Sample Working Procedures

HERE ARE SAMPLE working procedures from Centratel, exactly as we use them as of the date of this printing.

The format of all working procedures should be the same, so it is important to establish a set template for all to use. We've created a software platform that has set templates for all three primary documents, ensuring consistency, privacy, and protection of all documents. (See Appendix H.)

> Note to reader: The following Daily Deposit Procedure was reduced to twenty-three steps for a number of years, but in 2011 we added a check reader so our receivables manager would no longer have to physically deliver checks to the bank. This latest system improvement also adds up the checks into a total amount, saving even more time. With this additional subsystem, the procedure is now at forty-two steps (eight of the forty-two steps are to cover the rare times the "batch totals" don't match due to an input error). So, with this system improvement, there are more steps in the working procedure but lots of saved time for our AR manager Teresa (at least three hours per week). Also, there is less liability as there is no longer any street time involved in making the deposit. It took a total of four hours to install and debug the check-reader system and tweak the working procedure. Yeah!

DAILY DEPOSIT

6/7/18

This explains how we process payments into TBS for any account as well as the instructions for depositing the checks into the Centratel bank account. Generally you will process deposits on a daily basis. If we didn't receive many checks in the mail you can hold them until the next day.

1. In TBS, under Activities menu, select "Maintain customers."
2. Click on Tab 8—Billing history. (During deposit this is helpful to see running ledger of the client to verify amounts, credits, check numbers.)
3. Click on Activities menu, select "Enter Payments."
4. Select "Direct Entry."
5. Select the hand to the left of the "Cust Ref" box, and toggle until you find "Account."
6. For each separate payment, enter the 4-digit account number, and the account will automatically be pulled up.
7. Enter the amount of the check in the "Payment Amount" box, using the decimal point. (Verify that the amount is paying the account balance or most aged invoice balance. If not, keep track of those accounts, so they may be reviewed later for discrepancies.)
8. Tab once to the "Check Number" field, and type in the check number. (If there is an excessively long check number, only enter the last five digits.)
9. In the "Payment Type" field, select appropriate payment method. If it is a money order, enter "M.O." Note: If payment is in the form of cash, type the word "CASH" in the Check Number field.
10. Click the "Post" box to apply the payment. Once posted, it will clear the screen, so the next payment can be entered.
11. Continue until all payments have been entered.
12. Double-check each check has not been postdated and has a signature.

13. When all payments have been entered, select "Payment Register." This will show all payments entered on this deposit transaction.
14. Click bank icon to pull up Web Capture login screen.
15. Use credentials assigned.
16. main deposit screen will come up, Click on "Deposit Capture" located at top left tab.

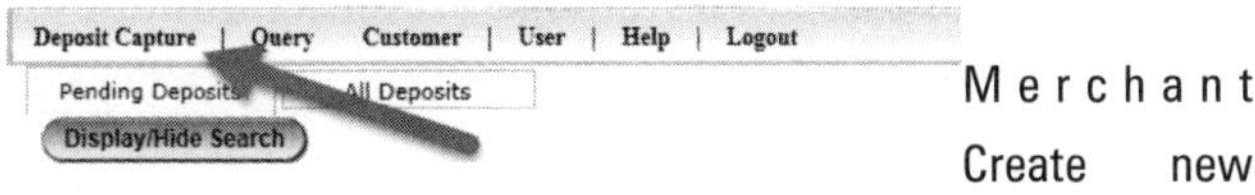

Merchant Create new deposit screen: leave work type as it appears.

18. Enter deposit amount from batch total in TBS.
19. Select account field: pick Centratel Check from drop down menu and click "OK."
20. Click "Create."
21. Place checks in scanner furthest track with checks facing the wall. If large batch (over 75), scan in groups until finished.
22. Click scan.
23. Once checks are all scanned a User Actions box will appear and click "Capture Complete."
24. Next the screen will look like example below:

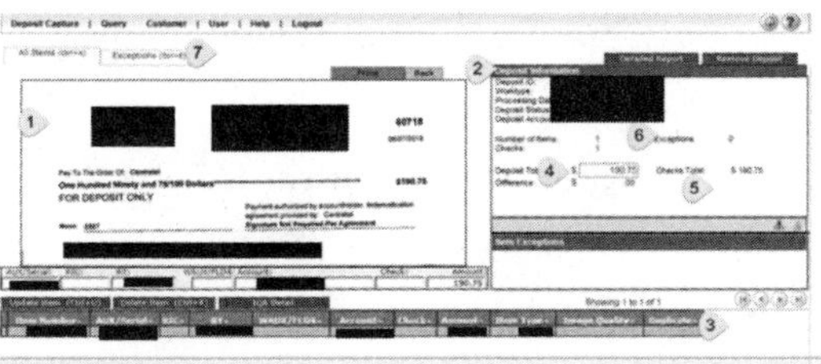

1) Image of last check scanned.
2) Deposit information box.
3) Check list status.
4) Deposit amount you entered when creating batch.

5) Total amount from check scanner.

6) Exceptions: Checks that have errors, missing amount, routing, and account numbers missing.

7) Exception tab.

25. If any exceptions, click on tab and make changes needed.
26. If Deposit and Checks total and exceptions are completed, submit deposit.
27. Back on the main screen, click on Summary report, and generate PDF report.
28. Print this report, and attach to batch report in TBS.
29. Log out of program.
30. In TBS under "Payment Register," select "Bank Deposit."
31. Verify the deposit date in the window. Click the green check mark. A window will open. For the Title, type in "Deposit" and the deposit "date" (6/7/18).
32. PRINT THIS DOCUMENT!! This is the best print of this document. *However, if you don't print it for any reason, you can print any day's deposit record, although you need to print two reports—one gives you the detail per customer and one gives you the total—the two should match. To print those reports—in TBS under "Miscellaneous—Payment Register Summary." (Click detail for account names.)*
33. After printing the document, close the window. It will ask "O.K. to deposit this payment batch?" Select "Yes."
34. Attach both printed reports together.
35. In the bottom left-hand drawer are slips of paper. Write date and attach to the checks.
36. File the batch in the front of the box.
37. Enter the amount of deposit in "Daily Receivables Journal." I:\Daily Receivables (password is "cash").
38. File the report in the appropriate folder for the month and year of

the day's deposit, file cabinet is in the Office Manager's office and in the top drawer.

*If you need tech support for the scanner, call bank for assistance [redacted]

Steps to Finish Deposit manually:

1. Run an adding-machine tape of all payments entered. (Checks, cash, money orders, etc.) *Be sure the adding machine tape and the total in "Payment Register" match.*
2. Complete a deposit slip for [redacted] for all payments. The deposit book is located in the left middle drawer of the Office Manager's desk. (Checks, cash, money orders, etc.)
3. Stamp all checks with "Centratel" [redacted] deposit stamp on the back in the endorsement space provided. The stamp is located in left middle drawer of the Office Manager's desk.
4. In TBS under "Payment Register," select "Bank Deposit."
5. Verify the deposit date in the window. Click the green check mark. A window will open. For the Title, type in "DEPOSIT" and the deposit "date." PRINT THIS DOCUMENT!
6. After printing the document, close the window. It will ask "OK to deposit this payment batch?" Select "Yes."
7. Have another management staff member verify that the adding tape and the printed deposit report amounts match. He or she should initial by the total deposit amount on the deposit report.
8. Enter the amount of deposit in "Daily Receivables Journal." I:\ Daily Receivables (password is "cash").
9. Deliver the deposit to the bank, complete with all payments (checks, cash, money orders, etc.). The bank clerk will provide you with a receipt of that transaction. SAVE THIS!
10. Attach the deposit Payment Register from TBS to the deposit receipt from the bank.
11. File the initialed report in the appropriate folder for the month and

year of the day's deposit. File cabinet is in the Office Manager's office and in the top drawer.

E-mail Signature Procedure

6/12/13

Your signature on your e-mails should conform to the following standards. Use 10- or 12-point type in your choice of Arial, Times New Roman, Verdana, Tahoma, or Garamond typefaces. You may do it in black or dark blue. List your information as follows:

1. Your name
2. Your title
3. Centratel
4. Telephone numbers
5. Fax numbers
6. Web site address

    Example:

    Jim Jones

    Telephone Service Representative

    Centratel

    Tel: 541-385-2616 or 888-482-4393

    Fax: 541-388-2351 or 800-330-7303

    centratel.com

To create your e-mail signature in Outlook*:

1. Open Microsoft Outlook
2. Click on "Tools"
3. Click on "Options"
4. Click on the "Mail Format" tab
5. Click the "Signatures" button
6. To create a new signature click "New," or to edit an existing signature click "Edit"
7. Enter the information as listed above

8. Click "OK"
9. Click "OK"
10. Click "Apply"

*I've added this procedure for those who use Outlook.

TSRs: Bidding on Shift Blocks

3/3/14

This is the protocol for filling an empty shift block. Also, it is an opportunity for any TSR to indicate a preferred schedule block, even if their desired block is currently filled.

1. A new shift block opening will be announced by e-mail to all TSRs. If a TSR is on vacation, management will make every attempt to reach the TSR, informing them of the new shift block availability.
2. There will only be one bidding period and it will be at least 48 hours in duration. A deadline date/time will be given.
3. To apply for a shift block, a bid must be submitted by e-mail to the Call Center manager within the bidding period. No late bids will be accepted.
4. If a TSR bids on a new block and is ultimately awarded that block, their old block will become available. So, for any TSRs who would like a different block, even if that block is currently filled, he or she should indicate their preference so that if their desired block becomes available in the bidding process, they will be considered for it.
5. A TSR's current schedule block will not change unless he or she bids on another block. In other words, TSRs who are happy in their existing schedule block do not have to do anything during the bidding process: TSRs who do not bid will not, under any circumstances, be changed to another block. In doing nothing, a TSR's block is absolutely secure.
6. TSRs should not consider their bid officially accepted until he or she receives notice from the Call Center manger that it has been received.

7. If two or more TSRs bid on the same block, the block will be awarded based on seniority.
8. If there is still an open block after the bidding deadline has passed, we will look outside the company for a new employee to fill that block.
9. In accepting a new shift block, a TSR will be ineligible to bid on another shift block for a period of three months.

Filming an Interview

Here is a working procedure that we created in a matter of just a few minutes as we began to create marketing elements for our new Work the System Academy product. I add this rough-hewn draft to show that it is not necessary to be an experienced professional in a given endeavor in order to produce a procedure that will be entirely useful.

Three Cameras: Basic Setup

1. At the site, allow at least one hour for setting up.
2. Camera 2 has host audio. Camera 3 has guest audio.
3. Use two light umbrellas: one between camera 1 and camera 2, and the other between camera 1 and camera 3.

4. Cameras are to be set up out of harm's way so they can be easily monitored from behind.
5. Host framing (camera 2): vertical second button down/slight space overhead, with horizontal spacing at 60 percent left/40 percent right. Can be framed to shoot slightly upward.
6. Guest framing (camera 3): vertical second button down/slight space overhead, with horizontal spacing at 60 percent right/40 percent left. Can be framed to shoot slightly downward.
7. Camera 3 option: include back shoulder of host.
8. Carefully gauge backdrop so there is no vertical line converging with the host's or guest's heads. Is anything else distracting in the background?
9. Do the cameras have fresh batteries (transceiver and receiver for each camera)? It is the director's job to make sure all batteries are fresh. The major danger is losing audio.
10. Do a sound check.
11. All cameras should be connected to AC power, if available.
12. All cameras operate unattended. Do *not* adjust zoom. Do *not* touch. Do *not* walk in front of running cameras.
13. The guest and host should remain in the same position in their chairs for the duration of the interview.
14. The guest and host should not slump back in their chairs. They should stay upright or slightly forward. (A fish-eye lens makes whatever is closer look bigger.)
15. Turn *all* mobile phones off (if there are any landlines, their ringers should also be turned off).
16. All three people must start the cameras at the same time.
17. Use 1-2-3 countdown to simultaneously start cameras.
18. Each operator must confirm that camera startup was successful.
19. The director steps between the host and guest and does a single hand clap to sync the audio.
20. The host and guest must not speak (make sounds of agreement, laughing, etc.) while the other is talking.

21. In an informal setting, the production people are not to drink alcohol. (Perhaps it is OK for the guest.)
22. The production people are not to do anything that interrupts the flow of the host/guest dialog. They should keep their movements and chatter to a minimum; each should sit down, relax, and quietly monitor their own camera.

Summary Overview of Working Procedures, from the Employee Handbook:

Overview to Centratel staff: *We base Centratel's mechanical functioning on written working procedures. With hundreds of human and mechanical operating processes in action at any one time, keeping Centratel organized in any other way would be impossible. Working procedures guide everything from an emergency relay for a TAS account, to how we deposit payments in the bank, to job descriptions for staff members. Our comprehensive Employee Handbook is, in itself, a working procedure.*

Strict adherence to our written procedures is critical, but we counterbalance this strictness with our eagerness to make instant adjustments should the environment change or if one of us comes up with a better idea. Whatever your position with Centratel, if you have a suggestion for making things better, pass it on! If it's good, we'll change the written procedure and implement it immediately!

Exact yet easy-to-modify procedures provide a huge degree of freedom to the individual staff member because the guidelines eliminate guesswork. Answers and instructions are right there.

APPENDIX D

Implementation of the WTS Method in Your Business, Certification

Work the System Enterprises (www.wtsenterprises.com)

WORK THE SYSTEM Enterprises transforms companies and business owners' personal lives, using the WTS Method as the framework. To take the next step toward a business that depends (far) less on your direct 24/7 execution, and (much) more on scalable systems and processes, go to www.wtsenterprises.com. We offer coaching, consulting, live events, certifications, masterminds, and so much more, created specifically for business owners who are ready to make the leap.

And understand that you're not alone on your journey to becoming an efficient, growing business. One-on-one, we've revitalized over a thousand businesses just like yours. (See Appendix E for Case Studies.)

So, if you're ready to graduate from being the hardest-working employee in your business to being the leader of a thriving enterprise that functions perfectly without your every-minute presence, reach us at www.wtsenterprises.com.

—Josh Fonger

APPENDIX E

Sixteen Case Studies: From Chaos to Control

By Josh Fonger

THESE ARE REAL-LIFE case studies. The presentation of each follows the same format: First, an overview of the business owner's business and life before implementing the WTS Method. Second, a description of the transformation. Third, life after implementation.

Industry: Private Medical
Location: Texas, USA

From "In-the-Head" to "Managed Systems"

I own and operate a physical therapy center. When I first learned about *Work the System* I was working fifty-plus hours a week, between treating patients and managing day-to-day operations. My wife was pregnant with our third child and I needed help. I had read *E-Myth,* so I was familiar with systems thinking, but had not developed protocols within my practice. Then something horrible happened that forced my hand: my office manager gave her two weeks' notice. She had been with me from the beginning (in 2006) and had all of the business workings in her head. We scrambled to get as much of her knowledge down on paper as we could. It was a frantic two weeks.

I decided at that moment that we would learn more about building and maintaining systems in our practice so I wouldn't have to go through that pain again. I heard about WTS on a podcast, read the book, and then went through the WTS training program. Now we have our systems documented, which makes training current and new staff easier. And it serves as a great reference for tasks that are not performed on a regular basis. We review the systems on a regular basis to make sure they are up-to-date and continue to be the most efficient way of doing things.

By documenting our processes, our overall volume of business has increased along with our revenue. It is easier to delegate tasks and ensure that the job is getting completed as planned, with minimal supervision.

Now that we have our systems documented and the staff trained, I can take time off from the practice without worry. I am able to spend more time with my family with less stress about how the business is running when I am gone. The WTS Method is the missing link that has allowed me the opportunity to work less in my practice and more on the business while having my income go up.

Industry: Mental Health
Location: California, USA

From Complexity to Simple Efficiency

I am the CEO of a children's mental health nonprofit organization in Orange County, California. As a licensed psychologist, I developed an interest in adverse childhood experiences and the mental health problems they can cause, which led me to WTS. While we were operating as a team, there was ambiguity when it came to following consistent processes. For instance, there was one point where we had fifteen different templates for timesheets. Another low point was when we were using a highly inefficient audit tool that involved paper slips and multiple departmental checks. That was when I realized that things needed to change dramatically.

I first came across WTS when the book was recommended to me by a member of an entrepreneurial group I belong to. When I read the book, it was like a light bulb had turned on in my head. The point that really resonated with me was that businesses that are process-driven are sustainable and scalable. That was when we started systematically documenting all our processes and policies. Then I connected with Josh and found that we could actually have someone affiliated with WTS come and help us with the documentation on a project basis, which was ideal! For every system, we reminded ourselves of the Strategic Objective of the business. That helped us build the roadmap and make our systems much simpler and more precise.

Today, we have processes—working procedures—in place that allow new employees to learn the ropes and execute their tasks immediately after they join. Everything is documented, and we have our Strategic Objective and Operating Principles to guide us. Plus, we have a knowledge-based software system so that the principle of continuous quality improvement is built right in. We can now serve our clients better and interact properly with our funders—because the systems we have in place drive more efficient outcomes. In the last five years, we've grown enormously as an organization—and it's thanks to the terrific team behind WTS.

Industry: Online Training
Location: Tasmania, Australia

Dividing Family and Work Time

In 2003, my work took me to Mexico where I started teaching English and loved it. The internet was still growing back then, and I decided to use it to market a little book I had written on learning Spanish. Today, I have a team of people that use a curriculum I've designed to teach Spanish all over the world. I've always enjoyed trying new things, but it got to a point where I was spending long hours at work and doing tasks that I didn't enjoy. At one point, I recall reading a bedtime story to my daughter and then immediately turning to my laptop to send out emails. That was when I realized that home and business were becoming too intertwined. Something had to change.

I first heard about WTS through an online interview with Sam that I found. I joined the WTS training program and then had private sessions with Josh. With his help, I was able to put systems in place that freed me from doing things repeatedly and allowed me to delegate tasks to people who could do them faster and better. The basic principle I followed was that if I had to do anything twice, further duplication could be avoided by creating a system. This approach helped me recover my freedom.

Today, we're a team of five and we've built up scalable systems that have made us much more efficient. I don't even need to manage the systems anymore—I've hired a systems person for that. The things I do now for my business are mostly creative, always adding something new to what we offer. I also have more friends now and can spend more time with my two young children. There's a clear divide between work and parenting, which is how it should be. I'm extremely grateful to Josh for the vision he shared with me and the direction he gave us.

Industry: Property Management
Location: Illinois, USA

Going for It!

I have a property management business in Chicago. We've been doing well since we started in 2004 and there was never a year that we didn't make money. One problem we dealt with as a start-up was that we were always too late to hire. We would be six months behind, and then we would scramble to find someone. Also, we never really seized the opportunity for growth. We almost never ran financials or did budgets. It came to a point when in 2014 my partner and I asked ourselves whether we would rather fail trying to grow a "real business" or look back years later, regretting that we never tried at all and just played it small.

I first heard of WTS when someone in one of our local chambers recommended the book. I downloaded it and read it twice straight off the bat. I also downloaded the audiobook version later and loved it. Apart from the book, what I loved was the WTS podcast, where business owners talked honestly about the mistakes they had made and what they learned from them. Especially we learned the importance of building procedures. The book refers to creating processes that someone "off the street" can come in and immediately follow. WTS helped us learn this way of building procedures.

Today, we have a forty-strong team and our business has tripled in size. We're working on speeding things up now by bringing in people as needed.

My own role in the company has less to do with management and more to do with business development, which I love. My partner and I are both riding the dream with our company. As an entrepreneur, it's important to have a love for learning. That's something I've gotten really good at over the last few years, and it's what keeps us going. WTS helped us a lot in that regard.

Industry: Engineering
Location: New Zealand

Time Savings and Greater Capacity

I've been running my engineering business for seven years now. We do consulting work related to building (structure) science—we visit clients in different cities and analyze how energy and heat can be used more efficiently. I've always enjoyed solving problems, which is why we're a consulting firm. Initially, I was executing projects and also bringing new clients in, and after a while it started to be more than I could handle. It got to a point where I was unable to meet some of my commitments even after I'd told my clients that I would do the job for them within the time period they needed it. That was when I knew that things had to change.

I first came across the WTS Method through the book. It resonated with me, so I signed up for the WTS training with Josh. The first time I put together a process, it felt great. It was a small process—just turning a small task into a proposal for a client—but it ended up saving me over an hour for every proposal I wrote. I also ended up standardizing a lot of my proposals into templates, to save even more time. I'm working on a pricing process as well, one that someone else can take care of entirely without my intervention.

Today, I have a team of five people working remotely. We have detailed processes that we follow to keep things going smoothly. With our clients, too, we now have a comprehensive process to move from initial design to the final certification—like a life cycle for each client project. This is more convenient for the client, and more profitable for us. We're no longer falling behind on commitments, and we have enough people to help us now.

Industry: Pet Hotel
Location: Minnesota, USA

From Organic Dysfunction to Selling a Machine

I recently sold my high-end pet resort near Prior Lake, Minnesota. It was a business that I built from scratch. It offered luxury boarding and lodging facilities for dogs. Initially, our business processes were fairly "organic." It was the learn-as-you-go approach. I didn't have any managerial experience, so adding staff and managing employees became a challenge. Then around 2009–10, our business suffered a serious hit. I was in survival mode. I had to cash in my 401K, even borrow money from family members. That was when I realized that I was failing because of my approach—and that when it came to operating my business, organic wasn't the way to go.

It was soon after that I saw a video interview with Sam online and learned about the WTS book. I read the book, and then, in 2014, I signed up for the WTS training program and started looking at the strategic side of running my business. One of the changes I made was to involve my team members early on when I was building procedures. As the team expanded, we brought in more experienced managers and contractors who could use our procedures and add their own modifications. Another change we made was to have a schedule in place. We broke each day down into short time periods and laid out the process of how that day would go. This brought consistency into the business.

I was fortunate enough to be able to sell the business recently and transition into my next opportunity—becoming a certified Business Systems Professional under WTS, while also doing small business consulting. When we sold it, the pet resort had grown to around forty employees with about 1,500–1,700 active customers. What's more, while I had brought in a lot of systems and processes, we'd managed to keep some of that organic feel that we started with. By the time we sold the business, I wasn't involved in day-to-day processes anymore. The systems were doing all the work, which is what made us a success story.

Industry: Content Creation Agency
Location: Colorado, USA

Building an Asset That Lasts

I've been in the digital marketing space for over a decade now, primarily in SEO consulting. I started my company—my content production company—around six years ago with a friend, and one thing I noticed was how hard it is to provide standardized services to different clients across vertical markets, or even different clients in the same vertical market. On top of that, some clients would just stop paying and there wouldn't be enough cash reserves, which meant we would have to lay off people. My wife wasn't working at the time, and we had a young child to support; I was out of touch with most of my friends and family. It was a rough time. Ultimately, my friend and I were compelled to split the company and I started writing SEO-driven content on my own for marketing software companies.

I first came across an interview with Sam on a website over eight years ago, and I read the book a couple of times. It was in 2016 that I started the WTS program, and after I got on a call with Josh, I started thinking about how to scale the knowledge I had. I knew a lot about marketing software, and I wrote conversationally—now, I had to think about how to get contractors to write in the same style. My approach to creating new processes was, "How do I take something subjective—like writing style—and turn it into something more objective?" I broke down my writing process into different steps, like keyword research, introduction formats, and conclusion formats, and that translated into a lot of granular outlines and tutorial videos.

Today, we're a creative agency that produces a very specific kind of content, and we're up there with the best in our industry. We took the WTS Method and training and went from a startup to a seven-figure business. We have detailed processes and templates for every component of the pieces we write, from introduction to conclusion, which makes things much easier for our contractors and our editors. I'm no longer involved in everything, which is great. It's like building an asset—we're making small improvements every year, and over time that's what is making our business truly valuable.

Industry: Education
Location: Israel

Scaling Impact

I'm a karate teacher, and my business has a presence in multiple locations across Israel. I used to be a full-time special education teacher, apart from teaching karate twice a week, and a lot of my time went toward talking to the parents of my students about self-confidence. That's when I thought of integrating my self-confidence and my knowledge of karate into a process that would help kids aged seven to twelve years old learn martial arts and that also would teach social and life skills. My work life back then was hard, and there were many nights I couldn't sleep. My low point came when my daughter was born and I realized that I couldn't afford to have all of our household income depend on me, especially if I were sick and couldn't work. That was when I first thought of making a living where I wouldn't have to be involved daily.

I first came across WTS when I read about Sam on social media. I downloaded the book and listened to the audio version a few times over the course of a year. It took me another year before I joined the WTS training program and documented my business idea. In the process, I realized that the work I thought only I could do could actually be taught to other people who might even do it better than me. If I wanted the business to run without me, I would have to turn my creative work into a procedure. Which is what I did when designing my program.

Currently, seventy schools in Israel have incorporated my program into their educational system. Each school has a team of eight to twelve teachers who implement my program with the help of a teacher I hired as their guide. Some of my team members are people I've never met, but they're still doing a great job because they're following the procedures we've laid out. We've built a wonderful community of student-coaches that help kids cope with challenges and reach their highest potential. I'm extremely grateful to Sam and Josh for helping me reach a point where I'm working less and having a greater impact on my community at the same time.

Industry: Technology Sales and Installation
Location: Colorado, USA

From Stress to Confidence

Our business sells technology equipment to schools, government complexes, and commercial complexes. Initially, my brother and I handled everything, including all the equipment installment. But the business began growing and we had to hire temporary workers—workers who were not always reliable. I was also juggling on-site work and client interactions. I ended up experiencing a lot of stress and was even in and out of the hospital for a period. To top it off, my wife and I had just had our son. Things couldn't go on that way—I needed physical and mental help to handle all of it!

I first came across the WTS book online and enjoyed reading it. I didn't fully understand it, even when I signed up for the WTS training program. Then I started doing the one-on-one sessions with Josh and that was when things fell into place. I had created a few systems at first, but wasn't really "working" them. And then I figured out that I needed to focus on one thing at a time, things that would bring in business, which is what I did.

Today, I run a team of six employees. Things are good at home too—my son is now six. I still wouldn't say that I'm mega-successful, but we're for sure getting there. We're confident about what we do and the processes we have, and we're constantly looking ahead. WTS helped me be where I am today—more successful . . . and happier.

Industry: Website Development
Location: Illinois, USA

Scaling to Happiness

We help wellness entrepreneurs grow bigger, better, and more beloved brands. I've been designing websites since around 2005. I started this business with my best friend—a graphic designer—and incorporated it in 2014. Initially, we spent a lot of time spinning our wheels because we didn't know what to focus on. We were trying to provide everything to all of our clients—websites, social media, branding, email systems, and so on—and it wasn't financially sustainable. There were panicky moments when we weren't certain whether our clients would pay us that month. At one point, we were working for one week straight, eating our lunch at our desks and working through the weekend. That was when we realized that we couldn't be the only ones doing this—we had to figure out how to replicate what we were doing.

I connected initially with WTS because it was available in book form. I'm an avid reader, and I loved reading it. While I already have a lot of systems I use in my personal life, the book helped me see that I need to translate that into the workspace as well. I needed to create simple, logical systems that my team could easily use and replicate. The first thing I worked on was accounting and invoicing, on which I used to spend around sixteen to twenty hours a week. The moment I converted all of that into step-by-step processes, I saved myself fifteen hours a week and also realized that I could hire others to do those processes even faster.

Today, we have a team of eight, both full-time and contractors. I have clear guidelines and clear processes, so my team knows what to do for each task, down to a specific plugin or piece of code. We also have designers using these processes and they're perfectly in sync. This helps us work easily with remote teams now as well. WTS has helped us scale our business like never before, and we're all much happier for it.

Industry: Food and Beverage
Location: Ontario, Canada

Getting a Replacement

I've been running a custom bakery for fourteen years. Since I was little, I've always loved baking. Then, when my daughter turned one, I tried finding a fancier cake for her but couldn't. And there was no one around doing that, so I decided to learn and do it myself. One thing led to another and today, we operate a business out of downtown Brampton, Ontario, and I have a small team that works with me.

When you're building a team and you have more people coming on, you start thinking that you have to do everything and be there all the time. I felt like I had to watch over my employees to make sure things were happening the way I wanted them to happen. It started to get very stressful with two teenaged kids, as I was always at work.

I thought about selling the business, but my broker said it was maybe only worth a couple of thousand dollars. I asked myself, "Should I give up or should I keep going?"

That was when I first heard about *Work the System*. It was in January 2019 from a member of my accountability group. We're a group of ten or twelve women who meet for a couple of hours every week and help each other out with our goals. My friend shared how she had gone through the WTS Method already and how far her business had grown as a result. I was intrigued. I listened to the book twice while I was driving. A month later, I decided I needed to go in-depth.

The concept of having a "replacement" was a big turning point during my WTS training. I set that as one of my end-of-year goals, but accomplished it seven months early!

Today, we're in a really good place! Thanks to all the organization and systematization, we are making money and all collecting healthy paychecks. I used to work seven days a week. Now, I work maybe three days and I can take vacation with my family whenever I want. My kids see me a lot more, and they see the difference in me too. It's been one year since WTS—things have been nothing short of amazing!

Industry: Digital Marketing
Location: Oklahoma, USA

From Dread to Freedom

I operate a ten-year-old marketing agency that helps high-quality contractors thrive. I got into marketing the way most people do, by trying to help people. It's very rewarding to see my clients' businesses grow, and know I made an impact. Early on, it went so well that I began to hire one or two people because I couldn't do everything myself. That's also when the problems started.

I'd be so stressed out about the business that I'd get migraines. I was trying to do too much myself without really having the proper systems in place to delegate. The stress started bleeding over into every area of my life. Worst of all, I wasn't able to enjoy my personal life or time with my young family because I was so stressed out about the business. There was just this lingering sense of dread, of knowing there was a mountain of stuff that I could never conquer, and I didn't have a means or the time to deal with it. It was very discouraging.

My quality of life was suffering across the board and I just realized that the only path out was to be able to delegate. And in order to delegate, I had to be able to give other people clear outcomes, procedures, and paths to follow.

I initially read *Work the System* three times. I can't even remember how I came across it, but the "outside and slightly elevated" perspective really resonated. It made so much sense to me, that the world is just a collection of systems, and that you could go one layer deeper to tweak systems to produce better results. When you think about it, it's a simple cause-and-effect relationship.

The WTS training program went deep, providing the practical information I needed—like the tools and templates to actually make it happen. For example, I created a Procedure for Procedures. After this, I started telling people what we were doing, helping them understand why we were doing it, and then giving them processes to follow—kind of a picture of what success would look like.

This meant instead of having to micromanage everything myself, account managers could step in and do the job as well or even better than me. We're a marketing agency and we serve a host of clients over the country. But that client work needs to be done methodically instead of just allowing each account manager to do it their own way and hope that they're doing it right.

Now, I have complete flexibility over my time and schedule. I can be away for a couple of weeks, and nothing falls apart or comes crashing down. Everything just keeps humming along because I've got people who make smart decisions whether or not I am there.

Industry: Real Estate
Location: United Kingdom

Growing Three Companies with WTS Systems Management Strategies

I started my first real estate company seven years ago. I've opened two more since then. Life as an entrepreneur was extremely hectic, to the point where I'd wake up at 2:00 a.m. or 3:00 a.m. because I had a new idea to write down. There were times I would look around and see my colleagues and mentors look so calm and collected, and I would feel inferior. In addition, our business was plateauing. We were all working hard, but no matter what we tried or how many new staff members we brought on board, the money wasn't coming in. One of the hardest points for me was having to look at my team and think, "I can't manage you guys!" I used to think that my own passion and enthusiasm for the business would be enough to inspire the others, but I soon realized that it wasn't enough.

I first came across WTS when someone recommended the book to me. I don't read much, but I couldn't put this book down. Then I reached out to Sam and Josh, and they were immensely supportive about the systemization process and then hiring new people to take care of things. We started documenting everything, all the processes and objectives and key result areas, so that my team could just follow the process rather than relying on organic motivation alone. I started hiring more talented people than myself so that they could run the whole show instead of me.

Today, the business has grown three and a half times in size. I focus on running my third company, which deals with property acquisition, and I've hired people to run the other two. I'm also coaching mentees now in the same process of building systems so that they can grow their own property businesses like I did. Life for me is now pure freedom—I can now look for opportunities to make a real difference in my community, not just to make more money. As an entrepreneur, I'd say it's very important to play to your strengths and hire great people to take care of the rest.

Industry: Music Publishing
Location: California, USA

Workweek Down by 50 Percent

I've been in the music publishing business for twenty-five years. I own a company in LA that signs and develops popular songwriters and artists. Some of the artists I've signed are world class, famous personalities. I am like an angel investor in the music world. As a publisher, I give artists and songwriters seed money and help nurture them. If their music is successful, we get paid royalties whenever that music is played (i.e., in the mall, in an advertisement, when it gets streamed, etc.). I have twenty active songwriters, eight content writers, and three legal people whom I manage.

Before I read *Work the System*, my business was full of chaos, fire killing, and endless work. I was working eighty to one hundred hours a week trying to do it all. My typical day would start early in the morning dealing with the latest emergency with my team in New York. Then around 6:00 p.m. I'd work with my tech team in India. And around 11:00 p.m. it was time for calls with London before finally "calling it a day" around 2:00 a.m. Lather. Rinse. Repeat. Day after day. Week after week. It was exhausting and not fun at all.

Then one day, I was at a business mastermind group when someone suggested I read *Work the System*. As I read Sam's story about what his business was like before his systems transformation, I could totally relate. I realized I was too enmeshed within the day-to-day operations and I did not have an "outside and slightly elevated perspective." I "got it," and I made the commitment to re-engineer my business systems so I could take control of my life again!

One of the first working procedures I documented was on how to get our blog posts published. I wrote down each step—everything from how to choose which writer gets assigned the piece all the way to the proofreading. It was twenty-five steps in all. Then I delegated this to a project manager. Now something that used to consume hours of my time each week takes only ten minutes.

After applying the WTS principles to my business, my work is fun again. We had our first seven-figure year in over ten years in business. Plus, my workweek has been reduced by 30 percent (soon to be 50 percent!). I'm literally working less and making more. My team is happier, we're better at what we do now, and I'm more excited about the future than ever before! And now I'm the guy who recommends *Work the System* to every business owner I know.

Industry: Software as a Service (SaaS)
Location: Utah, USA

Giving New Life to an Old Business

I am a second-generation business owner in a small town selling software to business owners across the US. Before my "WTS Transformation," I was working literally every day. When a long-time customer wanted to complain, they talked to me. When we needed to hire a new salesperson, it was up to me. Every new initiative and project in the company—you guessed it—landed on me. Even though I had sixteen employees and dozens of remote contractors involved in the business, I could not delegate anything involving HR, growth, or innovation to them. I was stuck in the business each day, fighting fires while our costs were going up and our sales were flatlined. I wanted to sell the business to finally catch my breath, but knew that my business without me would not be worth much.

Even though I have had bad experiences with consultants in the past, I reached a crisis point where I really needed some help. I contacted WTS and had them physically work with me and the team to engineer a new future. Finally getting clarity for myself and the team opened up a whole new world of opportunities—opportunities I was missing due to dealing with the day-to-day. We developed a laser-focused Strategic Objective, user-friendly principles for decision-making, and developed actionable working procedures so we could consistently scale. My team now has direction and doesn't need to run everything past me. They are finally fully equipped to get their work done. They actually enjoyed making the business more efficient, which I didn't expect, and knew that this change was a long time coming.

Now, after only a few months of working with WTS, I finally have my life back! My wife already has two tropical cruises booked on the calendar and my kids see me with a smile again. When I have an HR issue, I know someone will take care of it . . . correctly! Same with customer issues. I even have a rock-star assistant now driving my special projects forward to keep us #1 in our space. When I first thought about making the changes the WTS consultant recommended, it gave me a stomachache. I didn't think they understood that a twenty-year business doesn't do well with change. But now, after looking at my financials, I see that my 5 percent growth projections were too small as we are growing at 20 percent. Simply put, when you get out of the way of your business and let the systems do the work, life gets better.

Industry: Public Relations
Location: Michigan, USA

Training in Two Weeks, Not Six Months

Our digital PR business is all about introducing inspiring thought leaders to millions of people with the help of podcast interviews. My experience working at nuclear power plants taught me that everything can be systemized. Back in 2014, I hypothesized that we could use podcast interviews just like guest blogs to gain trust. We beta tested it in 2015, and then my company was born. Today, we're a team of eighteen working with over one hundred clients. We've worked with authors, consultants, speakers, coaches, and brands to get them placed on targeted podcast interviews right in front of the end customer.

The first thing we realized that had to change was the effort we were putting in. We have an amazing team, but they were all putting in superhuman efforts and putting themselves on the line every day. Another problem was that it would often take six months for someone new to understand the system and start delivering value, which was too long. It got to a point where I felt like everything was on my shoulders. I would look around at my team and ask myself, "Why can't I find people who do it as well as me?"

And that had an impact on my personal life as well. I used to joke that I worked for an SOB—one who made me wake up at 4:00 a.m. and work weekends and cancel my vacations. Then, I looked in the mirror and realized that SOB was me! I had become a slave to the business, rather than the business serving me. That's when I realized this wasn't the life I wanted.

I first heard about *Work the System* on social media. I downloaded and printed the book and put it in a three-ring binder. And what struck me was that these guys were doing for business what Hyman Rickover did for nuclear power—creating a system and making it reproducible.

Today, I'm a lot more attuned to the importance of systems. We follow a more scalable approach, where we all look at problems as challenges to solve as a team. Earlier, it was about success in our service. Now, after WTS, it's about success in our systems. And we have amazing, dedicated people working our systems. Plus, new people who come on can learn all about our business in two weeks rather than six months, thanks to those systems.

APPENDIX F

Centratel's Procedure for Procedures

IT IS CRITICAL that each document shares the same format and tone.

Following is our master Procedure for Procedures, which contains precise instructions for creating a . . . working procedure. (See document at end of this appendix.) This is the "Mother of All Procedures," the master template for creating the hundreds of working procedures that are necessary for our operation.

Don't be discouraged by the length and complexity of it, and don't get bogged down in our technical parameters. Of all the procedures at Centratel, it's one of the longest and most intricate. Simply consider its essence and then create your own preferred format (or feel free to copy this one).

PROCEDURE FOR PROCEDURES

Updated 3/3/2020

Centratel's method of operation for all departments is based entirely on written procedures. There are too many simultaneous operating systems, both human and mechanical, to keep things together in any other way. Documented procedures are the bedrock of the company, guiding everything from emergency relay for a TAS account to how we deposit payments in the bank, to job descriptions for staff members, to the most fundamental direction of the company (the Strategic Objective). At the same time, these guidelines allow a huge degree of freedom to the individual. Centratel's functioning is based on "freedom and responsibility within a highly developed system of systems."

Specifics:

- Is there a recurring problem or task? Then a procedure is necessary or, if there is already a procedure, and there is a problem, modify the procedure to eliminate the problem or to streamline the task.
- When creating a procedure, get feedback from those people affected.
- *Procedures can be changed.* It's a matter of company policy that if a procedure can be improved by modification, addition, deletion, or outright elimination, it will be done quickly and without hesitation: "We operate within a strict framework, but that framework can be adjusted instantly." However, it is mandatory that the relevant department head be advised of any changes before they are made and, in fact, this person must be involved with the revision and must give final approval to the changes.
- *Recommendations should be made by using the Track Changes feature in Word. The date under the title and date in the footer should reflect the day the updates were actually made.*
- All procedures are posted on the Procedures drive.
- Upon posting, each affected staff member will thoroughly review the newly posted procedure. Questions and suggestions should be directed back to the person who created or updated the procedure.
- The new procedure will be followed exactly. If there is a problem, we must change the procedure, not work around it!
- Changes in a procedure should be immediately emailed to affected staff. Show the recent modification in blue type, to be removed later.

Design:

- Use template on P: drive entitled "Procedures Template" and in the Template folder.
- Create the procedure with an "off the street" simplicity. Be simple, concise, and thorough.
- Remember the overall goal: "Freedom and responsibility within a highly refined system."
- How much information should be included?
  - » *For narrative procedures*: Add as much information as possible, but do it in a way so that the information is easily found (use alphabetical listings, logical subheadings, numbering and bullet formats, simple and concise sentence structure, etc.).
  - » *For charts and graph procedures*: Design to be simple, concise, and quick to read. Often it will be necessary to leave out information in order to make it more readable. Limit the typefaces and sizes, special formats, etc.
- Start with the title, in the Heading 1 style (Verdana bold size 12).
- Follow the title with the date, in the Procedure Date style (Verdana regular 10).
- For subheadings, use the Heading 2 style (Verdana bold size 10); and if further subdivision is needed within those subheadings, use the Heading 3 style (Verdana italics size 10).
- For the body text, use the Normal style (Verdana regular size 10).
- For any bullets or numbering, use the default bullets and numbering styles.
- Procedures are addressed at the bottom of the last page in this way:

    1. Select View, Headers and Footers.
    2. Click in footer.
    3. 1st line: Choose Insert AutoText - "Filename and Path."
    4. 2nd line: Choose Insert AutoText "Created By." Add your

name. You may have to do this manually, depending on what computer you are using and how it is set up.

5. 3rd line: Choose Insert AutoText "created on."
6. Enter the date.

- Use italics and bold sparingly.
- Use the 1-2-3-step format when applicable.
- Use bullets or numbers when applicable.
- If there is a relay involved, use numbering and the same acronyms and methodology used in TAS relays.
- Do not assume anything, especially if you are creating a technical 1-2-3 procedure. Every step must be obvious and logical. Do not assume anything. Do not assume the user of the procedure will be knowledgeable or can read your mind: remember the "off the street" requirement.
- General layout: After the title, start the procedure with a concise narrative that provides a quick overall description of the what, why, how, who, and when of the procedure. This is followed, if applicable to the particular procedure, with bulleted or numbered instructions.
- Never title a procedure "Procedure for . . . " The title must be concise yet descriptive and make sense to an "off the street" staff member. The title must be logical so if there is a need to find the subject, it can be quickly found. Start the title with the subject and then a description defining what the procedure is meant to do (use this procedure title as an example).
- Critical: test the procedure before release! Use an "off the street" subject. This is a staff member who is not necessarily involved with the subject.

APPENDIX G

Centratel's Communication System

At Centratel, following the tenets of our Strategic Objective and General Operating Principles documents, we employ the latest communications technology. It's an interesting paradox: the simple effectiveness of our internal communications hinges on highly complex yet readily available technologies.

Right at the beginning of our transformation, we developed a working procedure for communication for use among ourselves, and for communicating with the outside world. Because it's simple and easy and fast, our people communicate a lot. Remember that a high quantity of communication leads to a high quality of communication.

With some exceptions, every Centratel staff member uses the same basic protocol. There is no confusion. This procedure has evolved with the technical and even social changes that have occurred in the last few years. Here it is.

INTERNAL COMMUNICATIONS: PROCEDURE AND FUNDAMENTALS

The tools of active communications:

1. Voice Mail (VM)
2. Email (EM)
3. Emailed voice mail (EVM)
4. Instant Messenger (IM)

5. Text messaging (TM)
6. One-on-one via phone
7. One-on-one in-person
8. Hard copy memo/procedure

What form of communication should I use?

1. Routine, not time sensitive: VM, EM, EVM
2. Time sensitive: IM, TM, one-on-one via phone or in-person
3. "Getting all my thoughts in order" detailed explanations: VM, EM, EVM
4. Personal and sensitive issues: one-on-one in person or via phone
5. Documentation is necessary: EM or hard copy memo/procedure
6. Information is complex/detailed: EM, hard copy memo/procedure, one-on-one via phone
7. Procedures: Soft copy on procedures drive and hard copy

Point-of-Sale

Point-of-sale communications means, most of all, that when someone asks a question, the response is *right now*. For instance, avoid saving a message for a future response. If you must delay your reply, immediately take the time to answer the message sender to say you will get back with a detailed answer later (and be sure to provide an approximate time he or she can expect your response). Understand this approach is especially applicable to email: the most basic rule is to keep your inbox near-empty by dealing with the issue *now*, via the point-of-sale mandate. With all of us playing this game all day long, things move astonishingly fast. Always remember that it's your job to get the wheels spinning NOW and to keep them spinning at maximum speed.

My Personal Inbox and Task List

In early 2014, I developed a dirt-simple personal organizational system in which my task list is incorporated into my Gmail inbox. For me, the simple beauty is *that my incoming emails, my delegated tasks, and my personal tasks are all in one place*, to be accessed from my laptop, smartphone, or desktop. To delegate a task, I compose it in an email and send it to the recipient, cc'ing myself. For personal tasks, I send the email to myself with the task title noted in the subject window. For tasking myself or others, or to double-check that a task was actually completed, I send myself messages to be delivered back to me at a future date.

It really is that simple. Emails and tasks are in the same place, thus avoiding the trap of a separate task list being shuffled to the back of the bus, only to be occasionally checked. I work hard to keep my inbox at less than twenty messages and tasks. This is my protocol for email. Use it or choose your own, which might include an outside task list and calendar.

Giving (Delivering) a Message via Any Medium

Consider quantity before quality. Centratel's definition of quality communication emphasizes high quantity. But note that the quantity aspect has more to do with frequency than with volume of content. If there is lots of communication, quality will evolve.

If in doubt about whether to communicate or not, you should communicate.

Rambling dispatches that contain more information than necessary, or messages that keep repeating the same detail, are a waste of two people's time. The voice-mail medium is particularly susceptible to fatiguing, inefficient messages. But then, sometimes a voice-mail message is faster and more meaningful than an email message. Sometimes a thirty-second voice mail will deliver the same message as a fifteen-minute email. Whatever the communication protocol, remember this when sending a message: "A great message is a concise message."

Not many people go a layer deeper to think about the mechanics, much less the quality of their communications. At Centratel, since our entire purpose is to provide the very best communication services, we *have* to be good at it! Much of the reason we are "the highest-quality telephone answering service in the United States" is because we unceasingly refine and improve the communication services we sell as well as our own internal communications. We think about communications all the time. It is a primary system that we relentlessly analyze and refine.

We have many communication tools. At any given time, is the best protocol being used? Before leaving a message for someone, what preparation is necessary for the message to be complete, clear, and concise? While leaving the message, is too much being said, or too little? Are you rambling? Using "um," "I mean," and "like" too often?

An effective training process is to record and review conversations with callers and clients. For most of us, there is incongruity between how we think we sound and how we actually sound. Recording our own conversations for self-analysis promotes conciseness, and points out flaws that would otherwise go unnoticed. Here are 90 percent of annoying verbal flaws (I list them in my own personal order of vexation):

1. Interrupting, or stepping on the end of the other person's sentences (obviously not listening)
2. Up-talking ("Valley girl")
3. Repeatedly adding "like"
4. Verbal fry (curiously, a mostly female anomaly)
5. Repeatedly saying "um" and "ah"
6. Beginning sentences with "so"
7. Repeatedly clearing one's throat

As of this writing, here's a great recap to most of the above:
https://www.businessinsider.com/bad-speech-habits-2014-8

APPENDIX H

Business Documentation Software[9]

BDS EXACTLY CONFORMS to the Work the System Method. It's an intuitive platform designed to make it easy for you to create, tweak, store, and distribute your three primary documents (especially including your working procedures).

With the included Quick-start guide you'll be up and running in minutes.

BDS is simple to use. There's no fluff or excess. It's about "bottom-up," point-of-sale, and constant refinement. Developed and hosted on the Cloud, it is accessible from anywhere at any time.

BDS ensures that your documents are available for use only after they've been thoroughly reviewed and approved per your management chain of command. This guarantees that your people are following the most accurate and up-to-date policies and procedures.

BDS's architecture is engineered so anyone within a department can recommend a system-improvement to a procedure by simply and privately submitting the idea to the department head or administrator.

Automatically via email notification, newly published documents, document changes, requests, questions, etc. are delivered to your preselected staff. No need to constantly check in to see what's new and what's changed. An important feature is the administrator's ability to insure confidentiality of documents between people and departments.

Subscription to the platform is month to month.

For a comprehensive overview, go to
www.businessdocumentationsoftware.com.

---

9 Note from Sam Carpenter: In 2018, I gifted ownership of this platform to my long-term developers, Emanuel Gug and Marcello Scacchetti. I receive no ongoing compensation for sales, and I am not involved with the internal affairs of the operation, except as an advisor.

APPENDIX I

Other Offerings

AUDIO, KINDLE, AND TEXT VERSIONS OF THIS BOOK

Text versions of this 4th edition are available via Kindle, or for free download in PDF format at www.workthesystem.com. Find the audio version on www.audible.com. For the hardcover version, go to Amazon or your favorite local or online bookseller.

SPEAKING ENGAGEMENTS

Sam and/or Josh Fonger will occasionally travel for presentations and workshops. Call 1-800-664-8351 or email at info@workthesystem.com.

PATHWAY ONE

Pathway One is an end-to-end, full-scale online marketing service designed to optimize online leads and sales for small- to medium-sized businesses: www.pathwayone.com.

APPENDIX J

Kashmir Family Aid

Just after the October 8, 2005, earthquake that devastated great swaths of Azad Jammu and Kashmir (AJK) and the northwest frontier province of Pakistan, I traveled alone to Muzaffarabad, the capital city of AJK, the epicenter of the quake. Local Kashmiris housed me as I assisted where I could. Not restricted to a guarded encampment, I was perhaps the only Westerner to roam freely through the region, unattached to an official NGO or the US military. I wrote newspaper articles and took photos in order to publicize the plight of the millions who were homeless, and I gave away cash.

The dazed survivors wandered the tent camps and streets wondering what to do next with their lives. It was devastation, with eighty thousand dead—a disproportionate number of whom were children who had been trapped in schools when the quake struck. Nearly every family I met had lost one or more close family members.

I came home and shortly thereafter created Kashmir Family Aid, a 501c3 nonprofit. Its narrow purpose is to provide assistance to the schoolchildren of the region. I had been to Pakistan several times on business before the earthquake, and I have returned many times since.

Note that Bend, Oregon, and Muzaffarabad, AJK, have become official sister cities.

I have an on-the-ground manager in Muzaffarabad who has been assisting me for the last fifteen years.

Please visit the Kashmir Family Aid website (www.kashmirfamily.org) and view the slide presentations and photos. You will find some of my newspaper articles there too. Will you consider helping us? A school with two hundred students and eight teachers can be totally supported for less than US $500 (tax-deductible) per month, but any donation goes a long way. Thank you.

—Sam Carpenter

APPENDIX K

Copyright Infringement

DESPITE MY FEELINGS that the first printing of the book needed more work, others saw the value of my writing, copying and (subsequently) profiting from it (with the help of offshore copywriters). So, between 2012 and 2016, I fought to preserve and protect my intellectual property in the book. First, I defended against a suspect declaratory judgment action filed in the U.S. District Court for the Southern District of Florida (1:14-CV-21838-UU) and appealed to the 11th Circuit of the U.S. Court of Appeals (14-13776 and 14-14283), with both Courts ruling in my favor. Simultaneously, I filed and prosecuted my own copyright infringement case against Schefren Publishing, LLC in the U.S. District Court of Oregon (6:14-CV-01395-TC), which was resolved in late 2015 with the entry of a stipulated judgment that specifically confirmed Schefren's copyright infringement by copying and publishing material from my book without my permission or attribution.

DISCLAIMER

(Continued from the copyright page)

Further, although the publisher and author have used their best efforts in preparing this book, they make no representations or warranties with respect to the accuracy or completeness of the contents, and specifically disclaim any implied warranties of merchantability or fitness for a particular purpose. There are no warranties which extend beyond the descriptions contained in these paragraphs. The advice and strategies contained herein may not apply or be suitable for your situation. You should consult with a professional where appropriate. The accuracy and completeness of the information provided herein and the opinions stated herein are not guaranteed or warranted to produce any particular results, and the advice and strategies contained herein are not suitable for every individual. By providing information or links to other companies or websites, the publisher and the author do not guarantee, approve or endorse the information or products available at any linked websites or mentioned companies, or persons, nor does a link indicate any endorsement by the publisher or author. This publication is designed to provide information with regard to the subject matter covered, and is offered or sold with the understanding that neither the publisher nor the author is engaged in rendering legal, accounting, or other professional services. If legal advice or other expert assistance is required, the services of a competent professional should be sought. Neither the publisher or the author shall be liable for any loss or loss of profit or any other commercial damages, including but not limited to special, incidental, consequential, or other damages.

INDEX

NOTE: At the end of most chapters is an illustration, a short true story that reflects the Work the System methodology. You will find a list of these stories here under the entry "illustrations." Each chapter also contains sidebars, which will be found under the main entry, "sidebars."

A

B

C

G

H

I

J

K

L

M

N

O

P

Q

R

S

T

Y

Z

ABOUT THE AUTHOR

SAM FOUNDED CENTRATEL in Bend, Oregon, in 1984. With a background in engineering, construction management, publishing, and journalism, and residing in Bend, Oregon, and Stearns, Kentucky, his outside interests include mountaineering, hiking, skiing, cycling, writing, reading, and traveling. His book, *Work the System: The Simple Mechanics of Making More and Working Less*, was first published in 2008 (see www.workthesystem.com). His second book, *The Systems Mindset: Managing the Machinery of Your Life* (see www.thesystemsmindset.com), was published in 2016. He is founder (in 2006) and director of Kashmir Family Aid. Sam is married to Diana Bybee Carpenter.